MICHELANGELO
ON AND OFF THE SISTINE CEILING

MICHELANGELO
ON AND OFF THE SISTINE CEILING

Selected Essays by CREIGHTON GILBERT

GEORGE BRAZILLER   NEW YORK

First published in the United States in 1994 by George Braziller, Inc.
The following texts © 1994 by Creighton Gilbert: "Preface," "The Proportion of Women," and "The Ancestors." "Michelangelo: An Introduction" © 1967 by McGraw Hill, Inc., assigned 1987 to Creighton Gilbert. All other texts, see Acknowledgments page, which constitutes an extension of this copyright page.

All photographs, unless otherwise noted, are reproduced courtesy of Alinari / Art Resource.

GEORGE BRAZILLER, INC.
60 Madison Avenue
New York, New York 10010

Library of Congress Cataloging-in-Publication Data:

Gilbert, Creighton.
      Michelangelo: on and off the Sistine ceiling / Creighton Gilbert.
            p.   cm.
      Includes bibliographical references.
      ISBN 0-8076-1338-x
      1. Michelangelo Buonarroti, 1475-1564—Criticism and
interpretation.   2. Michelangelo Buonarroti, 1475-1564—Friends and
associates.   3. Sistine Chapel (Vatican Palace, Vatican City).
      I. Title.
      ND623.B9G52   1994   93-41240
      759.5—dc20   CIP

Frontispiece: Michelangelo, *Pietà,* ca. 1550-55, marble, 7'5" high, Cathedral, Florence

Design by Abby Goldstein, New York
Books printed and bound in the United States.

First edition

CONTENTS

ACKNOWLEDGMENTS

The author and publisher wish to extend their sincere thanks to all those listed below who graciously granted their permission for the reproduction of the material contained in this volume on Michelangelo:

Art Bulletin, vol. 62, March 1980, "Titian and the Reversed Cartoons of Michelangelo," pp. 36-52. (Original title: "The Earliest Mining of the Sistine Ceiling, from 1511"). Reprinted by permission of the College Art Association, Inc.

Art History, vol. 3, 1980, "On the Absolute Dates of the Parts of the Sistine Ceiling," pp. 158-81. Reprinted by permission of the Association of Art Historians.

"All the World's a Stage . . . " Art and Pageantry in the Renaissance and Baroque, Papers in Art History from the Pennsylvania State University, vol. 6, 1990, "A New Sight in 1500: The Colossal," pp. 396-415. Reprinted by permission of the Pennsylvania State University, University Park.

Michelangelo Drawings, Studies in the History of Art 33, Center for Advanced Studies in the Visual Arts, Symposium Papers XVII, Washington, D.C., 1992, "Un viso quasiche di furia," pp. 213-25. Reprinted by permission of the Center for Advanced Study in the Visual Arts, National Gallery of Art.

The Burlington Magazine, vol. 103, 1961, "Tintoretto and Michelangelo's 'St Damian,'" pp. 16-20. Reprinted by permission of *The Burlington Magazine*.

Arte Veneta, vol. 15, 1961, "A 'New' Work by Sebastiano del Piombo and an Offer by Michelangelo," pp. 38-42. Reprinted by permission of *Arte Veneta*.

to
my fellow students
then and ever since
Esther Gordon Dotson
Stanley Meltzoff
Bob Parks

PREFACE

The first plan of this book was just about half its present length: a set of four essays on some aspects of the Sistine ceiling. Two had been printed about 1980 in professional journals, a venue suitable for incidental reasons. One was part of a study of Titian, of which it formed a large digression. I argued that Titian admired a technical trick of Michelangelo's, but since that trick had never been discussed, a pause to present it was needed. The second article was contributed to a group of essays honoring Peter Murray, a distinguished colleague.

When the two other studies on aspects of the ceiling took form, it seemed sensible to present them together. If valid, all four should interact and be more effective together. However, several publishers found no interest in a book of four learned essays, half of them old, even when they approached me about the kind of book I might be expected to do. So I am especially indebted to George Braziller and Adrienne Baxter, who liked the concept and wisely suggested enlarging it to include four more studies on other Michelangelo works. These have a somewhat looser fit, but all involve his interrelations in various ways with other artists—sharing an approach, being helpful, and just once in the ordinary way of being copied. Since Michelangelo is usually viewed as a loner, such factors have been little explored.

The first plan had a title that involved a gentle pun, *On Michelangelo's Ceiling*. When it grew, the book casually began to be referred to by its present title, almost as a nickname, and if the pun is lost, that is a small matter. The obvious missing piece was an overview of the artist to give context to these fairly concentrated, even microscopic, inspections of certain details. This is not needed by readers of professional journals, but they are the exception. The usefulness of general surveys of an artist like Michelangelo is obvious, and they are produced steadily. I have, on

9

request, produced several, written somewhat differently for different functions, one to go with a coffee-table-book equivalent, a second as an encyclopedia entry on a large scale, another for a short popular encyclopedia, still another for a book of biographical essays. But I have also turned down four or five other invitations to write them, chiefly for still other encyclopedias, since I would rather look into new questions than repeat myself. Happily, one of these existing introductions was available to be included here, to orient the reader of the specific essays.

Specialists on Michelangelo, like those on other subjects studied by relatively many scholars, argue and revise each other, as they should. Two of the six essays reprinted here have been the theme of later comment and doubt, which it is proper to note here. The others seem to have found endorsement.

The drawing of St. Damian was first discussed by David Rosand, who considers it to be not by Tintoretto but by Palma il Giovane, a lesser artist whom he had studied closely. This does not convince me, in good part because the technique is different, in its use of chalks, from any by Palma with which it is compared. However, as noted by Graham Smith, this does not affect the relationship to the lost Michelangelo, the "principal contribution" of my article. Smith then confirms that by citing a second drawing.[1]

The study of the chronology of the ceiling attracted the most detailed comment and proposals for refutation. That was natural, since the chronology of an artist's work has traditionally been one of the main concerns of Renaissance art historians. My article indeed opted for one of the two ways of seeing the chronology of the ceiling that had been supported before, proposing to give more evidence for it. It immediately evoked a response from Paul Joannides, who kindly said that the sustained effort and attention to detail in my essay, among other things, made my conclusions "seem impregnable." He dissents by observing that I did not deal with "visual qualities" that point the other way.[2]

The idea of my article was that the work was done in two stages related to different heights of the vault and scaffoldings, an upper one notably including the nine scenes and prophets and a lower one notably including the lunettes. The opposite theory is that there was one sequence from one end of the room to the other, involving both groups of images at once. Joannides's first and evidently chief objection to my view is that my findings assign, as he rightly says, "twenty months painting" to the top area and "two-thirds that time for the design and execution" of the lower. This he finds "difficult to credit" since the upper area has complex narratives with many difficult poses and the lower is less complex, and "could hardly have made the same physical or intellectual demands."

The objection may involve the opinion that not enough time is assigned the upper area, or that the lower is assigned too much, or simply that the proportion is wrong. At the time he wrote, little was known about the technique of execution of the ceiling, notably the number of days' work involved. However, the best comparison, Michelangelo's *Last Judgment* in the same chapel, has long been known to have occupied 450 net days of work, about the same twenty months after allowing for Sundays off, during which the artist painted 391 very complicated figures;[3] since this is a much larger number than in the vault, the twenty months also assigned to the latter do not seem hard to believe, after all. That leaves only the objection that he would, in my scenario, have worked too slowly on the lower level. Although the writer duly records that the time suggested for the upper level is for the painting only, and for the lower also includes the preceding design, his stress seems to be on the simple contrast of numbers and poses of figures painted in the two places. In the *Last Judgment* the whole process took five years, of which four-fifths preceded the painting; such factors must be allowed to vary a great deal from case to case. The study of the lunettes in this book suggests that they did, contrary to Joannides, make more intellectual demands than the narratives above, not on account of difficult poses (the one sort of demand that seems to be considered by him) but because they offer imagery far more innovative in relation to the tradition of their theme than do the narratives. The latter seem to have welcomed the opportunity to recycle the compositions of Ghiberti, among others. Joannides also subtracts from the elements belonging to the lower level the putti with the name plates, though they are there, as indeed he says. For him, nevertheless, they must have been painted concurrently with the prophets above them. The reason he gives for this suggestion, the fact that the ones first produced are in pairs of reversed designs and the later ones different, does not seem to have a logical connection with his conclusion, but a better one might be that they are part of the same framed images with the prophets above. However, the well-studied case of Giotto's Peruzzi Chapel shows that the Florentine craft tradition of murals allowed for painting upper and lower halves of a framed scene at two different times, from upper and lower scaffoldings, even if it cut a body in two, and the case of these putti is less a problem.[4]

More in general, Joannides here rejects the evidence offered simply because it does not match the average or familiar situation, without giving any evidence on the specific case. When the information suggests that something out of the ordinary happened, however, that is no reason to negate it.

The rest of Joannides's comments reflect the classic tradition of connoisseurship, which has served well in usual cases. This approach proposes not only to assemble the work of artists by adding to those known through documents and the like others found to resemble them visually, but, more to the point here, to form an artist's chronology by adding to those with dates those others that most resemble them, or even simply to bracket works together when neither has a date. Here the matter arises of the Sistine spandrels, which are in between the narratives and the lunettes, and on the upper level with the former. Joannides rightly says I did not discuss which part of the work I believe included them, as I indeed did not, having no evidence, and makes this an obstacle to my views. If they belong to the lower, later, part in my scenario, he writes, then there would have been a physical difficulty to reach up from the lower scaffolding, which indeed is a plausible point. However, if they belong to the upper level with the narratives, then, he says, the artist had, at the earlier stage, when painting them, already produced a work very close in "style and mood" to the lunettes below, so that there is no stylistic reason to assign the lunettes to a later date. That would also be true. To be sure, Dotson, as discussed below in this book, disagrees about the closeness in mood of the spandrels and lunettes. I am closer here to Joannides's view, but his argument shows only that nothing in style

12

would exclude the painting of the lower lunettes at the same time. He offers no basis for saying that they actually were painted at the time nor any counter arguments to the non-stylistic reasons against that.

The connoisseurship of visual similarity of works, assigning them to the same date, is handy, but it has rightly been much criticized for treating artists as always proceding in a linear sequence, never jumping around as in real life. It is based, moreover, on factors similar to handwriting, in particular those that are produced without a special intention or even attention being given by the artist, like the ears cited by Morelli. It can work rather well in such cases, but less well when we are dealing with the more conscious qualities that connect these spandrels and lunettes, their sharing of the same kind of thematic representation, the passive families, as against the mobile heroes of the central narratives. That is a matter less of Morellian style than of what Poussin later was to call "mode." Thus, when we think of Michelangelo coming to the lunettes a year later, it can hardly be "difficult to credit" that he purposefully picked up the "mode" of the thematically related spandrels he had done in the preceding campaign. At any rate Joannides, aside from the postulate that a Morellian average formula applies, has not actually offered anything to the contrary.[5]

Joannides's other main point has to do with the complications of reconstructing the scaffolding, which he rightly suggests presents difficulties, but where again he does not bring up any particular point that would rule out my theory. I am gratified with the attention to the scaffolding in the recent literature, since it never seems to have been a theme of enquiry earlier. The cleaning process in the 1980s naturally encouraged further thinking about it, though previous such campaigns did not. A rejection of my ideas about its form was the total theme of an article by Frederick Hartt, published in the same journal in which mine appeared, like Joannides's, but several times the length of his. A further discussion has also been published by Mancinelli.[6]

The factors calling for attention in such a reconstruction are now much more fully before us. The holes in the wall found under the lunettes doubtless served, as has been noted in recent writings, to hold beams, and these would be *sorgozzoni,* corresponding to the dictionary

13

meaning of that word, more probably than they would be beams projecting from a free scaffolding as I had proposed. They would reasonably belong to the second, lower, scaffolding I proposed, and this as other developments actually have not produced any materials contradicting the basic schema of two periods of work. Perhaps the most remarkable finding of all in the recent cleaning has been the discovery that the lunettes were produced in a completely different technical method from the narratives above, abandoning the use of paper cartoons. It is possible that, working in a single procedure from entrance to altar, Michelangelo kept switching between these two techniques, though it would seem rather odd, and is certainly not dictated by the circumstances. (Nothing similar appears in other fresco cycles.) The shift in technique would seem more plausibly to be related to a later campaign, but this implication remains to be discussed.

Hartt's essay proposed "devastating objections" to my ideas about the scaffolding, but they seem less strong when, in his very first point, he finds my statement "true," and objects only that it refers to a less frequent usage than one he cites. The following objections simply urge that the procedure I offered would have been laborious, with vivid language that may seem to invoke hyperbole; we are first told that my scheme would call for "continuous, noisy and expensive planking" (no other objection on this matter is raised); next that it would have involved "strong vibrations," "shaking brushes, pots, paints"; next that the working area would have been so limited (though I had not claimed a specific area) as to make it hard to find room for materials or for "unrolling, cutting, assembling and otherwise deploying the immense cartoons." (Today, it is believed that Michelangelo's use of cartoons was limited, even on the vault, and there is no reason to suppose they were large rather than a series of sheets, conditioned by standard paper sizes). The next difficulty is simply described as a "formidable procedure, wasting many hours," and the last, "most dubious of all," is the one direct negation, saying that it is wrong to call a wooden tower firmer when weighted on top." A contrary expert view is offered, but this turns out in detail to refer less to the actual top than, "especially," to cantilevered extensions, which does not negate what I claimed.

Hartt was less fortunate in his own alternative views. Picking up my remark that a single scaffolding covering the whole vault at once had been usually presumed, disregarding its blocking of light, he explicitly approves it, saying that the light would not be a difficult problem. He proposes oil lamps and tallow candles to paint by. Other vaults were painted from such platforms, he states, first citing the naves of the upper and lower churches at San Francisco in Assisi. Yet no one, I believe, has asserted that such platforms filled a whole nave at once; rather, they are presumed to have filled one bay at a time, leaving the ends open, in fact like the partial platform I proposed. Platforms for smaller chapels would get similar light from the open end. I believe that all writers now assume the partial platform for the Sistine Chapel that I proposed, in one form or another.

As positive support for his case Hartt offers two items in detail. One is a passage from the diary of the pope's master of ceremonies about the opening of the Sistine Chapel for worship. He says it "describes" the "very scaffolding whose existence has already been postulated by somewhat more tangential evidence." He gives this "wonderful text" in English, with the Latin in a footnote, from which I cite some of the words: "Today for the first time our chapel [*Capella*], now that the painting has finished [*pingi finita*] was opened [*aperta*], since for three or four years a roof or vault [*tectum sive fornix*] was [*fuit*] always its [*eius*] concealment [*tecta*], covering the same [*ipsam*] completely from the rays of the sun [*ex solari*]." The scaffolding is presumably "described" in the words "a roof or vault was its concealment, covering the same," a fairly odd way to name it. "Its" and "the same" evidently modify "the painting," but only in English, where Hartt has supplied that noun; the Latin simply said the chapel was now "finished being painted." "Its" and the feminine "same" actually modify the noun next to the former, the vault. The noun "concealment" will not do for *tecta,* which again is not a noun (except as a plural, "roofs," which would take a different verb, *fuerunt,* "were," and in any case is not what Hartt means). *Tecta* is in sequence with *finita* and *aperta* as modifiers of the subject *capella:* "The chapel, having finished being painted, was opened, since its vault had been *tecta*" (either, literally, "covered," past participle of *tego,* or, figuratively, "concealed," in complement with "opened"). Nothing here says what kind of

15

thing, scaffolding or other, had concealed it. We are only told it had been fully covered "from the floor" *ex solari*. (Hartt's rendering "rays of the sun" uses the only meaning of this word in smaller dictionaries, the adjective "of the sun," and he supplies his own noun.)[7] The diary tells us nothing supprising, since it was known from other sources that Michelangelo had screened off his working area, and that was traditional; earlier stories offer anecdotes of artists not letting curious patrons see them at work. One such tale helpfully specifies that "as is the habit of painters," an artist wished to be totally enclosed in *asse* (boards) or *stuoie* (woven cloth sheeting or reeds).[8] To remove this was, indeed, "unveiling." Hartt calls that term "misleading" for the Sistine, even though he does partly endorse another scholar's idea that a "protective canvas" had been "stretched across the chapel under" the working area. It indeed seems likely that this is what was removed. If there had been a large scaffolding to remove, that would have been more striking to the diarist, one would think, than what he does report, so the text seems to weigh against that idea. In any case, whatever the scaffolding was like, we are not told there.

Nor are we told by a Michelangelo drawing Hartt calls "especially eloquent" support for his view. He believes it shows the "scaffolding he proposed to use for the lunettes." I would have liked to agree, since that would require that there was a separate scaffolding on this lower lunette level, a contradiction with Hartt's general view that he seems not to articulate. The drawing, however, shows a nine-step staircase, where the situation beside the lunettes would call at most for four. A very different reading of this drawing by Thode, the only detailed one, not mentioned by Hartt, seems right to me.[9] Mancinelli similarly argues that this drawing shows scaffolding, but thinks of a different one, crossing the whole vault, as some sort of scaffolding surely did. Both views seem blocked by an insuperable difficulty in that the support under the structure shown is an arch form, while all agree that the scaffold was wooden. All known scaffoldings are built of straight boards, which may be stepped or inclined if needed; a curved one would require costly carving and seems bizarre.

The specific form of the scaffolding certainly calls for further investigation. That is what makes such debates interesting, as is everything connected with Michelangelo.

16

ͻ

tic

corre

an artis

vious line

record urgi

that such allu

del quattrocento ν.

6. F. Hartt, "The E
5:1982, 273–286; F. Ν.
117:1983, 362–367.

7. Solarium in classical La
with meanings of architectu
Latinitatis Lexicon Minus, 1976,
chief room is called the solar.

8. F. Sacchetti, *Il Trecentonovelle*, 19
by a Florentine about a Florentine ar
that usage had changed by Michelange

9. H. Thode, *Michelangelo, Kritische Untersu*

POSTSCRIPT

While this book was in preparation, the most frequent question I have been asked was about the recent cleaning of the ceiling, and whether and how I might address it. The same circumstances that have put it in the forefront of attention have also produced a great deal of comment on it already, to which I have no significant points to offer. In any case it may be time now to revert to those matters that made us feel interested in that cleaning in the first place, this artist's breadth of expression.

NOTES TO THE PREFACE

1. D. Rosand, "Palma il Giovane as Draughtsman," *Master Drawings*, 1972, 154; G. Smith, "Tintoretto and Michelangelo's St. Damian," *Burlington Magazine*, 1981, 614.

2. P. Joannides, "On the Chronology of the Sistine Chapel Ceiling," *Art History*, 4:1981, 250–253.

3. D. Redig de Campos and B. Biagetti, *Il Giudizio universale di Michelangelo*, 1944, 1:105.

4. L. Tintori and E. Borsook, *Giotto: The Peruzzi Chapel*, 1965, 15, cf. diagrams 7a and 7b. The joins in the plaster, reflecting the sequence of scaffoldings from upper to lower, occur "across the middle of each scene." The Peruzzi project was not produced with the usual small patches of each day's work in fresco; it was painted dry. However, it would not be logical to speculate that only in such dry work could such breaks in a scene based on the position of a scaffolding be acceptable procedure. It would evidently remain allowable in other cases of paintings whose scale called for two levels of scaffolding.

5. Joannides's fifth and longest comment, not addressed here, also argues a "stylistic" line from one end of the chapel to the other, quite correctly, and assumes that it corresponds to a chronological line. It does not consider, however, that a year later an artist might find it right to refer to earlier work, thus perhaps replicating the previous line, when a second part of the same project is involved. A fifteenth-century record urging a crew of painters in a chapel to make their works look alike suggests that such allusions would match the aesthetic of the era. (Cf. C. Gilbert, ed., *L'arte del quattrocento nelle testimonianze coeve*, 1988, 147.)

6. F. Hartt, "The Evidence for the Scaffolding of the Sistine Ceiling, *Art History*, 5:1982, 273–286; F. Mancinelli, "The Technique of Michelangelo as a Painter," *Apollo*, 117:1983, 362–367.

7. Solarium in classical Latin is a rare word for terrace. In Late Latin it is common, with meanings of architectural spaces from attic to pavement. (J. Niermeyer, *Mediae Latinitatis Lexicon Minus*, 1976, s.v.) Visitors to English castles may recall that the chief room is called the solar.

8. F. Sacchetti, *Il Trecentonovelle*, 1946, 418. This may have been written in the 1380s by a Florentine about a Florentine artist working elsewhere. One might speculate that usage had changed by Michelangelo's time, but there seems no basis for that.

9. H. Thode, *Michelangelo, Kritische Untersuchungen*, 3:1913, 90–91; cf. 1:1908, 248.

MICHELANGELO: AN INTRODUCTION

To many people today, Michelangelo is the greatest sculptor who has ever lived; to some, the greatest artist. The pages that follow do not attempt to prove this, or to explain it, but only to arrange the chief facts and analyze the special characteristics of the chief works in a way that will assist the reader in using his own eyes.

THE ENVIRONMENT. What Michelangelo's own eyes first saw was Florence in the 1480s. A proud and energetic city, and an independent state, Florence had been a leader in international commerce and politics for two hundred years. Its social structure was dominated by great families, much like clans, which established banking houses with branches and correspondents from England to Syria, developed wool and silk manufacturing companies, and shared the honors and responsibilities of a frequently elected government. The city exploited its recent growth and its absence of a feudal past to emphasize its status as a republic. It was never a democracy, but held voting power mainly in the guilds, which were not unions but associations of executives and shop owners. The great families were also civic boosters, and supported ambitious projects for public buildings and churches. These were superbly successful because Florence also developed a continuing studio tradition of talented artists. The painters, sculptors, and architects of Florence were a specialty product, boasted about and utilized at home and sought after everywhere else.

In the fourteenth century civic commercial republics existed all over Italy, but by the fifteenth they were receding. The smaller were conquered by the larger, and most of the larger were conquered by tyrants, who set up hereditary dynasties. Hence, Florence seemed like an island of representative liberty, and rather traditional. This requires emphasis, since we often tend to imagine history as a general development from feudal monarchs to nineteenth-century parliaments; but to fifteenth-century men it seemed the opposite. The Florentines reacted to their relative isolation by becoming more self-conscious and self-assertive about their free city and its ethical superiority; the statues of David the giant killer, which were frequently carved at this time, symbolize it. The irony is that Florence was a republic only superficially after 1434, when it was taken over and ruled by the Medici, a family whose talent for government is illustrated by their refusal to accept either title or office. This change seems to have been preceded by commercial decline. The population remained static at about 40,000, the other families declined into branch managers of the Medici banks or futile opponents, and the wool trade became evidently less interesting than real estate. The third Medici, Lorenzo, ruled from 1469 to 1492. No banker like his grandfather, who founded the family power, he was a talented diplomat and poet, and also an art collector—but chiefly of Roman antiquities, contrary to the popular tradition that he was a great supporter of living artists. His nickname in history, *"il Magnifico,"* is often supposed to be a personal tribute, but actually was a customary term of the period, a semiformal designation for "lord." In the 1470s his rule was shaky, but he grew enormously popular in the 1480s after surviving a conspiracy and warding off with dashing diplomacy an invasion by the king of Naples. He designed free pageants and maintained a group of writers in his villas, securing money from his banking cousins.

Michelangelo's background is typical of Florentine society. His great-grandfather had been a successful banker, his grandfather an unsuccessful one. His father felt too well bred for trade, and lived in shabby gentility on a small income from land and intermittent government jobs. He was agent in the hill village of Caprese when his second son, Michelangelo, was born on March 6, 1475, but was back in town a few months later. The sons were sent to school, but in 1488 Michelangelo was apprenticed to a painter. An apprentice usually started at eleven; he was late because of his schooling, which reflects his family's mild pretensions. Yet it does not seem that the family really put obstacles in his way.

Renaissance painting in 1488 was in full career, not revolutionary but very active. Florence was still the single greatest source of talent among European cities, both in painters and sculptors. A new development of the age of Lorenzo was that the city considered its artists as its chief claim to fame. The newer examples of an established type of writing dealing with the "Lives of Leading Citizens" now treated mainly artists. The architect Brunelleschi, who had died in 1446, now became the first artist in history to be the subject of a full-scale biography, while a young architect (Giuliano da San Gallo) completing one of Brunelleschi's building designs fought to keep the original plans unaltered, perhaps an unprecedented idea. If these acknowledgments boast of the past and seem a little decadent, another change seems even more so. In the 1480s the two leading Florentine artists, the painter-sculptors Pollaiuolo and Verrocchio, left for Rome and Venice, where they received larger commissions than any available at home; and simultaneously the most brilliant younger talent, Leonardo da Vinci, also left for Milan, where he stayed twenty years. Never before had such a vote, as it were, been cast against the city. A new pattern was emerging, in which Michelangelo was to be one of the great instances; Florence remained for a time the chief source of good artists, but they were drawn away to work elsewhere, leaving behind a "second team."

The leading artists remaining in Florence in the 1480s were the sculptor-architect Benedetto da Maiano, the architect Giuliano da San Gallo (later active in Rome), and the painters Ghirlandaio and Botticelli. The first two are known today only to specialists, but the second two can be called a "second team" only by comparison with Leonardo, their equal in age. Yet their retrospective, withdrawn, and even archaic qualities are intrinsic, and belong to this period. If their works are often referred to as especially typical of the Renaissance, that is probably because their traditional aspects make them fit the general trend more conveniently than earlier, more exploratory works do. The same applies to Benedetto da Maiano's masterpiece, Palazzo Strozzi, often cited as the classic town mansion of the century. Botticelli's archaistic line, humanistic subject matter, conventional space, and (in his late work) mannered religiosity had little interest for younger artists, none outside

Florence and none for Michelangelo. Ghirlandaio's faithful presentation of bourgeois life, the family portrait and civic group, differs from earlier painting by being more external, but reproduces its space and form unthinkingly. He appealed to middlebrow taste and to Michelangelo's father, and it was to this successful master that the son was apprenticed.

EARLY WORKS. The apprenticeship was scheduled for three years, but was cut short, apparently after only one. The explanation that Michelangelo was too brilliant for his master derives from his own reminiscences sixty years later, taken down by his pupil Condivi, and cannot be taken at full value. But he was certainly persuaded by a friend and fellow apprentice to change to sculpture, drawn by a very unusual attraction. He obtained permission to frequent Lorenzo *il Magnifico*'s collection of ancient Roman sculpture, which was set up in a garden and had a kind of curator, a sculptor called Bertoldo, respected mainly because he once had been an assistant to the great Donatello. Lorenzo gave access to bright boys, apparently as a sort of cultural largesse; and Michelangelo was installed in his mansion and at his dinner table—again according to his own memory in old age. But it does seem to be a fact, and is a remarkable exception to the social norm of apprenticeship education and workshop life. Was the garden also an art school? Did Michelangelo also absorb the neo-Platonic ideology of the writers in Lorenzo's court? These further possibilities, often mentioned, seem uncertain. The closest he definitely came to the latter interest was when the poet Poliziano read him a Latin poem which he adopted, rather loosely, as the source for the theme of his first sculpture when he was about sixteen; and the poem is notably a direct narrative rather than a symbolic allegory. The sculpture, the *Battle of the Centaurs* (fig. 1), is a high relief in marble and shows naturally enough a close knowledge of ancient Roman reliefs on sarcophagi, swarming with a net of figures. It also marks his concern with solid forms and vigorous action and the power which is their joint product, an equally natural token of admiration for Donatello.

In 1492 Lorenzo de' Medici died, and his unskillful son Piero was toppled from power in 1494. Michelangelo fled into exile, showing a

22

Figure 1: *Battle of the Centaurs*, 1492, marble relief, 33 x 35", Casa Buonarroti, Florence

hypersensitivity to political dangers that led him to the same step more than once in later life. In Bologna he obtained a small commission for three marble figures needed to complete a set on the monumental tomb of St. Dominic. Much like the individual figures in the *Centaurs*, they have in their small scale a hard force and insistent presence, in marked contrast with the current preference for thin shapes and surface emphasis. Returning home, he found Florence dominated by the extraordinary monk Savonarola, who had already had a role in expelling the Medici. A passionate antisecular revivalist, preaching the imminent doom of the decadent city, he has captured the imagination of later centuries; but the idea that Michelangelo felt his influence seems to be based on very little evidence, having its chief support in the attraction of linking two such personalities. Actually, Michelangelo was in half-secret contact with the remaining Medici, and on their advice left for Rome to find better patrons. Before leaving he carved a Cupid, and soon afterward a Bacchus, both highly non-Savonarolan images! The *Bacchus* (fig. 2), carved on order of a Roman banker for his garden of ancient Roman marbles, is his first big statue that survives, and is different in important ways from all the later ones. To evoke the drunken god, slightly staggering or beginning to dance, Michelangelo experiments with asymmetry, emphasizing the twisting motion in the process, with only a slight precedent in Roman statues of Bacchus. Though drunken, he is also a god; and though in casual movement, the statue is also massive. These concerns seem to blend in the torso, soft, fleshy, and effete, but smoothly stretched and taut rather than flabby. The spiral effect constantly invites the eye to look around the cylindrical form for the completion of a partial effect, until it returns to its starting point, never fulfilled. This is the only statue by Michelangelo in which the front view is not complete and dominating; all the others resemble reliefs to the extent that they were evidently designed to be placed in front of walls.

In 1498, vouched for by the same banker, Michelangelo obtained from a French cardinal the commission for the over-life-size *Pietà* (fig. 3). Like the *Bacchus,* its polished surface of hard marble suggests yielding softness, but in major ways it is very different and reveals some of Michelangelo's basic qualities for the first time. The two figures,

24

Figure 2: *Bacchus*, 1467,
6'8" high, with base,
Bargello museum,
Florence

Figure 3: *Pietà*, 1499, marble, 5'8" high, Vatican, Rome

although in contrasting horizontal and vertical positions, and contrasted in textures of cloth and skin, are strongly united in one blocky pyramid. The thickness and the broad simplicity of surface that mark this cubic form suggest great internal density. Hardness and plainness work, however, at the expense of feeling. The features are idealized, the faces bland; the Christ type is closely derived from Verrocchio's face of Christ in his monumental bronze group of *Christ and Thomas*, a key Florentine work of the 1470s. In modern terms, Michelangelo's choice is formalist rather than expressionist, and the pathos which a spectator may feel derives from previous associations with the subject, reinforced by the artist's contribution of a sense of weighty significance. Michelangelo at twenty-three commanded more power and grandeur than any other sculptor alive, and had superseded the ornamental and naturalistic preferences of his close predecessors, but he remains entirely within the Florentine tradition of balanced, simplified, rounded form. The same is true of the *David* (fig. 4).

When Michelangelo left Rome to come back to Florence a second time, he found that the city was subsiding from the intensity of the Savonarolan years, after the pope had caused the monk to be burned as a heretic. Unwilling to restore the Medici, the citizens thought to restore the republic to the form last known in 1434. The new government, which was to last about fourteen years, inevitably had a retrospective and artificial air. It is not surprising that it made much of monumental art in public places, reviving a pattern that had been spectacularly successful in the early fifteenth century—with major works of Donatello, Ghiberti, and Nanni di Banco—but had given way in the Medici period to small sculpture for rich private interiors.

The *David* was commissioned in 1501 for the cathedral, but when finished was set up in front of the city hall, where certainly its republican symbolism was more pointed. The easy transfer from church to state context reflects the fact that the church's building and adornment were organized by a guild committee, interchangeable with the city council. Thirteen feet tall, ironically given the giant size suitable to Goliath, *David* is as plain, solid, powerful, and unexpressionist as the *Pietà*. The fact that both have been among Michelangelo's most popular works in

27

Figure 4: *David*, 1501-1504, marble, 13'5" high, Academy, Florence

Figure 5: *Madonna and Child*, 1502, 32" x 33", Bargello Museum, Florence

modern times is a subject for the psychology of mass culture. Possibly it is an example of the phenomenon that in other cases has given special acceptance to the juvenile works of a great artist, such as the "blue period" of Picasso, which though articulate and professional would not have become famous without the glory reflected back from his later, more individual achievements. What perhaps happens is that a part of the public, informed that an artist is great, sincerely wants to admire him but finds his work peculiar and difficult; the more conservative youthful works are then gratefully discovered and become the object of sincere and respectable love. In the case of the *David*, and recently the *Pietà* too, this response is given still more assistance by the impressive size of the figure and its conspicuous availability without requiring a visit to a museum.

Before finishing the *David* in 1504, Michelangelo had designed a second smaller statue of the same subject in bronze, which has been lost but is known from a preliminary drawing. It shows a startling change in approach. The same change is apparent among a group of several small Madonnas of the same years, done for private patrons. The *Bruges Madonna* (a small work for a church) was very traditional, even archaic in its iconlike, motionless verticality. The same was true of the circular marble relief now in the Bargello Museum in Florence, where Mary's masklike face rests on a solid, angular body (fig. 5). In sharp contrast, a second circular marble relief of the same subject, the Holy Family, now in London, is based on a design of intertwining curves in three dimensions, from the turban on Mary's turning head to the Child stepping over her knee and the bird beating its wings in the hand of the boy John. The abrupt change between the two Madonna reliefs and two *David* figures can be pinpointed to 1502, without a gradual transition. The earlier set also includes the *Bruges Madonna*, while the later set includes the *St. Matthew* (a record of another project for large public sculpture, never carried beyond this one unfinished work, fig. 6), the round Madonna painted for the Doni family, and, largest of all, the project for the *Battle of Cascina*. This first big mural planned by Michelangelo also provides the clue to what triggered the change. It was part of a government project for murals in the remodeled city council chamber, along with

29

Figure 6: *St. Matthew*, 1505, marble, 8'10", Academy, Florence

another painting planned by Leonardo da Vinci. Leonardo returned home in 1500 to find himself famous, was given a studio, and became a public person visited by crowds. In his studio he worked on his *St. Anne, Virgin and Child,* an organic mound of twining bodies which exemplifies his lifelong concern with living processes and continuums of movement and work, from human muscles to ocean waves. His city council mural was to show a cavalry fight, with leaping horses and rising dust, while Michelangelo's showed athletic nudes jumping from a swim in a river as the enemy approached. Both subjects, Florentine military victories, were also intended to show off the special brilliance of the two most illustrious Florentine painters. Like all the other young Florentine artists, the twenty-seven-year-old Michelangelo was clearly fascinated by the vitality and expressiveness of the fifty-year-old Leonardo, whose long absence had caused him to skip the natural moment of influencing a younger generation until he had developed his own work to an overwhelming climax. The young Florentines had seen nothing like it, except the work Leonardo had himself left from his youth. Michelangelo's greatness emerges in the fact that, absorbing Leonardo's fluid action and growth, he loses nothing of his massive simplicity. From this moment, creating figures as vibrantly alive as they are densely solid, he is the mature Michelangelo that we know.

This critical turning point has partly been obscured by the loss of the larger works of these years, known only in fragments, drawings, or copies. These losses often have a single cause, Michelangelo's new tendency to plan on a grand scale and at the same time to be constantly enticed by new proposals, so that much was never finished in spite of his inexhaustible hard work. This first happened to a plan for fifteen statues for the cardinal of Siena. Now both the *Battle of Cascina* and the set for which the *Matthew* was begun were set aside forever, in 1505, in favor of the tomb of Julius II, a gigantic scheme not finished after forty years.

POPE JULIUS AND THE SISTINE CEILING. Julius II was certainly the most Michelangelesque of patrons. Elected pope in 1503, he decided in 1505 to tear down St. Peter's, a very large building of immense symbolic importance, in order to build a still larger one. The present St.

31

Peter's emerged after a hundred years, after many stops and starts. While the pope was leading his own armies against rebellious towns of the Papal States, he was raising money for his new church by selling more indulgences, with an effect on Martin Luther and on the history of Europe that seems ironically appropriate for this vehement pontiff. Almost at once he thought of placing his own tomb in the new church, with some forty large marble sculptures by Michelangelo. (It was three years later that his good taste or magnetism to artists led him to take on the little-known, twenty-five-year-old Raphael, who at once started painting for him his great series of frescoed rooms.) Michelangelo responded with enthusiasm, but the pope's was less enduring. After the artist had spent months in the Carrara marble quarries, and watched one of the barges carrying his blocks sink in the Tiber, he was told that Julius had decided "not to spend another copper on stones." Michelangelo's reaction was to flee from the city, back to Florence. The pope exerted some political pressure and Michelangelo had to come before him, as he later recalled it, "with a rope around his neck," only to be set to a new project, a colossal bronze of Julius himself to be set in the center of Bologna. (A few years later the citizens, in a revolt, melted it down.) Then in 1508 Julius shifted Michelangelo again to a scarcely less huge project, the ceiling of the Sistine Chapel (figs. 7, 7b). Michelangelo was annoyed, since he was a sculptor primarily. Did the architect of St. Peter's, the great Bramante, intrigue for this shift so as to get a larger share of the available funds for his own work? Michelangelo was disturbed enough to think so. It was annoying for a second reason: ceilings in churches and chapels are minor compared to the walls, which in this instance had been frescoed thirty years before by Botticelli, Ghirlandaio, and other distinguished painters. Ceilings normally showed no scenes, but only single figures or ornament, a natural distinction we automatically make today when we buy wallpaper. To make his task more important, at least, Michelangelo got permission to paint scenes on the ceiling as well as single figures. Of course they are awkward to see, but the power and success of the work was so great that for centuries this unreasonable scheme of painting scenes on the ceiling was followed in other buildings without special thought. He had to paint awkwardly, too, standing on the scaffolding with his head thrown back on his shoulders (not lying down, as is sometimes said).

Michelangelo divided up the area with a very original framing system in order to organize the large scenes, the large single figures retained from the first proposals, and a host of smaller representations. The nine scenes of the Book of Genesis—three of the Creation of the World (fig. 7a), three of Adam and Eve, and three of Noah—are an inevitable choice, because scenes of Moses had been painted on the walls, and the natural narrative sequence is downward. The twelve large figures are prophets and sibyls—sibyls being women appearing in various pagan mythologies, such as the Delphic Oracle, who were now interpreted as having made prophesies similar to those of the Old Testament prophets. Michelangelo started painting at the end of his narrative, with the Noah stories, and the adjacent prophets and sibyls, then moving with both scenes and figures toward the other end. It is surprisingly little noticed that the first seven prophets and sibyls were painted in one size and the last five in a larger size. All fit nicely into their painted frames, and the inconspicuousness of the change in size is a token of the subtlety of the frames. The change itself has a good aesthetic reason, which is that the scenes first painted, of Noah and Eve, contain quite a few figures, while those painted later, of God creating the world and man, contain only one or two, and they are therefore larger. The change also tells us that Michelangelo was able to revise his arrangements after he had started work. The point where the scale of the figures changes is also a point where, it seems, he took a rest of several months. Through the whole four-year period we can see him constantly evolving his style and approach. Four phases can be readily distinguished, which for clarity may be labeled *a, b,* (rest), *a prime, b prime.*

In the first figures and scenes Michelangelo actually retreats to ways of working that resemble his earlier approach, abandoned about 1502. Psychologically this is natural; familiar old ways would have given him reassurance, faced with an immense task against his will and in the wrong medium. But confidence appears to have grown quickly; and indeed ideas and forms may evolve more rapidly in sections of a large project than in an equal amount of work on smaller separate ones, because

33

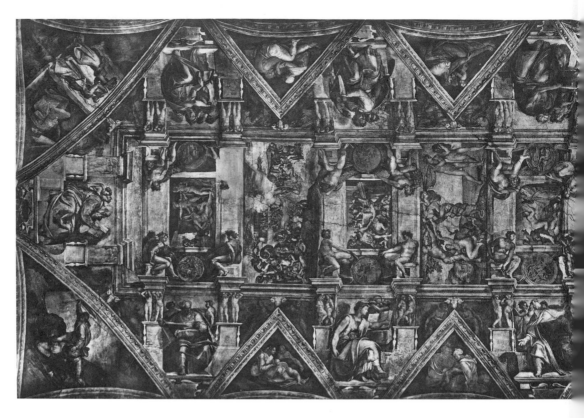

Figure 7: *Ceiling of Sistine Chapel*, 1508-1512, fresco, 131 x 44', Vatican

Figure 7a: *The Creation of Man*, 1508, fresco, Sistine Ceiling, Vatican

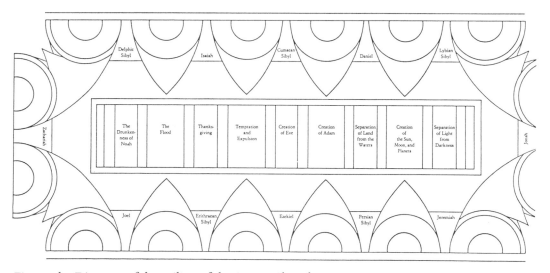

Figure 7b: Diagram of the ceiling of the Sistine Chapel

of the feeling that things that occur to the artist when it is just too late to make a change can be quickly applied to the following sections, each a revised edition of the last. Here the first rather classic and static forms shift to a very original statement of power and stress, mobility and involution, in phase *b*. After the "rest," this evolution does not by any means continue from the point where it had left off. Instead, it again starts out with clear and quiet forms and moves to complex and active ones. There is even a kind of "retreat" again when the first new prophets actually reuse poses from the first phase. But in more significant ways there is no repetition. The immobile figures of *a prime* (fig. 8) are unlike those of *a* in that they have learned expressive richness from *b*; and likewise the sweeps of movement in *b prime* are far more internalized and make less of their impact through physical energy than the figures of *b*. In short, in the four discernible stages, *a, b, a prime, b prime*, Michelangelo moves twice from the quiet to the active, but the second time around he does so on a subtler level.

As soon as the ceiling was finished, Michelangelo seized the opportunity to resume work on the pope's tomb. In about two years he carved the *Moses* (fig. 9) and two *Slaves* now in the Louvre (fig. 10a; fig. 5, p. 156). They are naturally very similar to the prophets and the attendant athletes on the ceiling. The *Slaves* were intended for the lower story of the tomb, and some sixteen of them would have been placed in pairs that flanked female figures of triumph. They share some of the structural or caryatid quality of the Sistine athletes, but their symbolic point is not clear. Early reports make them either provinces conquered by the pope or the liberal arts reduced to slavery by his death. In either case, the expressive quality of a figure whose struggle is subsiding offers a more complex tone than a simple conflict: the defeat of the figures is explicit. The internalized focus of their bodily strain also recalls *Jonah*, the last prophet painted on the ceiling, perhaps more than any of the athletes.

THE MEDICI YEARS, 1516–1534. Pope Julius's death in 1513 did not stimulate work on his tomb but rather, leaving his family's position in crisis, after a short period of pressures and counterpressures tended to impede it. So did the election of his successor, Leo X, son of Lorenzo

Figure 8: *The Persian Sibyl*, 1510-1511, fresco, Sistine Chapel, Vatican

Figure 9: *Moses*, 1513, marble, 7' 8" high, San Pietro in Vincoli, Rome

Figure 10b: *Atlas Slave*, 1513-1516, marble, 10' 5" high, Galleria dell'Accademia, Florence

ESCLAVE.

Figure 10a: *Dying Slave*, 1513-16, marble, 8' 6" high, Louvre, Paris

dc' Medici. With the new power base in Rome, the Medici had just regained control of Florence too, so that Michelangelo's two habitual cities were one as to patronage. Leo certainly wanted him for his own projects, both because he was a cultivated connoisseur and because he was concerned to reassert the somewhat battered dignity of his family with the aid of the most famous living creator of imposing monuments. Michelangelo protested that he had to finish Julius's tomb, but this may have been only a half-hearted objection, since he was certainly fascinated by the grand plan to cover the bare front of San Lorenzo, the old Medici parish church in Florence, with a marble facade giving space for many big sculptures. He worked on this project for about four years, mainly in marble quarries in and near Carrara, but the time was a waste since the project was canceled. Midway through his work on it, he suddenly had to move from the Carrara quarries to those at nearby Pietrasanta, which happened to be in the territory controlled by Florence and the Medici. The Pietrasanta quarries were undeveloped, and so Michelangelo had to begin by designing a road on which his marble carts would make the run from the quarry sites he chose down to the sea. He was annoyed at this new and typical delay, and yet seems also to have enjoyed solving this large-scale engineering problem. In a similarly ambiguous way, he was first glad to leave the tricky Carrarese, but later sighed that he had ever left them.

At the same time Michelangelo probably did quietly give a little time on the side to the Julius tomb, carving four more slaves which he did not nearly finish, although today they are among his most famous works (fig. 10b). Although he unquestionably meant to produce completed figures, the nineteenth and twentieth centuries find them just right as they are. This is not merely because of our sensory approval of sketchy textures and records of spontaneity; the stone blocks seem to express the theme, the power against which the slaves hopelessly struggle. There is clearly a problem of art theory here: how can we call Michelangelo a great artist, and yet admire so much a work whose visual quality is an accident, contrary to his intent? Perhaps the answer is in a third intermediate concept, recorded in Michelangelo's remarkable poems. One of their metaphors, used several times as a token of

Figure 11a: *Tomb of Giuliano de' Medici*, 1524-34, marble, The Medici Chapel, San Lorenzo, Florence

Figure 11b: *Tomb of Lorenzo de' Medici*, 1524-1534, marble, The Medici Chapel, San Lorenzo, Florence

various kinds of failure, is an unfinished statue abandoned because the artist could not realize his vision. The carving remains in "the husk that is raw and hard and coarse." Thus he considers such works failures, as was traditional; but, as a new idea, he is vividly articulate about them as a distinct phenomenon. This would seem to earn him the unique position he has, between artists whose unfinished works are merely discards and artists today who use the unfinished as an expressive idea.

The canceling of the San Lorenzo project merely made way for a new one for the same patrons in the same church. Two young scions of the Medici had died, and their burial stimulated the building of a special chapel. The Medici Chapel took most of Michelangelo's attention for fourteen years, and is the most nearly complete of his big sculptural projects. Leo and his cousin Cardinal de' Medici, who succeeded as Pope Clement VII after a short intervening reign, were more permissive than any previous patrons of Michelangelo's.

The chapel had first to be built, and its interior walls show the growth of Michelangelo's architectural interests first seen in the painted frames of the Sistine Ceiling. A lively relief in many planes frames the sculptures and interlocks with them. The white marble wall areas are separated by gray stone strips. Outside the areas with sculpture, niches develop fantastic anticlassical forms, and windows above are trapezoidal. Cornices are interrupted, capitals are smaller than their pilasters but support huge pediments, and heavy blocks emerge from narrow clamping recesses. Such caprice, possible because the artist was not a craftsman with solid training, is certainly meant to be noticed, and to evoke a sense of the maker's and the forms' freedom of organic action in balance with the geometric gravitation of the structure. The two seated Medici are elegant in their antiquarian armor (both were generals of the papal army) and suggest by their higher position that they pin down the diagonal figures below which might otherwise slide away (figs. 11a, 11b). The very original sarcophagus caps leave the four statues of *Day, Night, Dawn,* and *Twilight* (also a novel choice) resting on arcs of a circle. According to some notes that Michelangelo jotted down, the symbolism seems to be that time moves on, *Day* and *Night* apparently circling, and leads to death; and then that the dukes' death cuts off all light on earth. The two

43

Figure 12: *Dawn*, detail from *Tomb of Lorenzo de' Medici*, 1526-1531, marble, 6'8" long, The Medici Chapel, San Lorenzo, Florence

Figure 13: *Night*, detail from *Tomb of Giuliano de' Medici*, 1524-1531, marble, 6'4" long, The Medici Chapel, San Lorenzo, Florence

forces, the circle-borne figures and the dukes placed over them, seem to match these conceits, which have a startling tone of courtly adulation, reminding us of Louis XIV heralded as the beneficent sun god. Yet they seem consistent with the fancy-dress uniforms and the aristocratically thin and graceful bodies of the dukes, and the similar forms of the Madonna on the third wall to whom they both turn.

The female figure of *Dawn* is extraordinary (fig. 12). She seems to push herself up with her foot against a bellows or cloud form, and the keenness of the pressure seems reflected in her knit brows and tossed head. By contrast, the beautiful *Night*, even in her complex pose, seems an image of large-boned grace and simple elegance (fig. 13). In the male figures, the suggestion of sensitive meditation in *Twilight* seems correspondingly subtler than the physically emphatic mass of *Day*. *Day* and *Night*, which thus seem less evolved, were carved on flat bases and lie on their backs; *Dawn* and *Twilight,* lying on their sides, have curved bases, and so seem to have been designed later, when the details of the circular tombs had been settled.

Michelangelo's new courtliness, soon noticeable in his letters, reflects a great social change toward absolutism. The Emperor Charles V sealed his control of the Italian cities with the sack of Rome in 1527 and his coronation by the defeated Clement VII in 1530; he then graciously made the Medici official dukes of Florence. Simultaneously, he and other rulers began to appear in their portraits nonrealistically, frozen into impersonality with allegories of their status. Something of this appears too in Michelangelo's *Victory*, one last figure carved about 1530 for the Julius tomb, the last time he tried to give that project his real attention (fig. 14). A thin youth with a remote look stands in an implausible but gentle spiral, one knee holding down the stocky, bearded figure of the defeated. More than any other work of Michelangelo's, this has logically been linked to the interest in neo-Platonism illustrated, at the same date, by his poems to Tommaso Cavalieri, which express his devotion to the real or imagined accomplishments of this young Roman aristocrat. Their philosophical or moral concepts involve the self-suppression of the rebellious body through awareness of a beauty which, with aspiration, constantly becomes less tangible and more spiritual,

45

Figure 14: *The Victory*, 1532-1534, marble, 8'7" high, Palazzo Vecchio, Florence

until at last the soul dominates both morally and aesthetically and leads to immortality.

The highly personal and refined qualities apparent here are visible also in the most important architectural work that Michelangelo had yet produced, the library built in the convent next to San Lorenzo to contain the books left by Leo X. The entrance hall with its staircase is famous today as the most brilliant example of Mannerism in architecture, bizarre and witty, reversing conventions and what seem natural and reasonable ways of constructing (fig. 15). Columns are sunk into walls instead of standing in front of them, and rest on flimsy brackets halfway up a wall instead of on the floor; corners are probed instead of being sealed. Michelangelo took into consideration the basically irregular relation to space of a man on a staircase, and the proportional extreme between height and breadth in the stairwell space, as his points of departure for the expressive details with which he manipulated the wall surfaces.

The most violent military event during Michelangelo's lifetime was the sack of Rome in 1527, in which the Medici Pope Clement VII collapsed, remaining in his castle for six months after the sack and a refugee in a nearby small town for a year after that. Since Clement was also the ruler of Florence and the client for Michelangelo's buildings and sculpture, these works were left in suspense. The city of Florence took advantage of the Medici weakness to create once again a republic—the last—which lasted two years in a state of siege. Michelangelo worked as director of fortifications, and designed towers for artillery of the most ingenious originality. Yet later he fled to Venice and hoped to go to the French court. He returned and was pardoned; and then, when the city fell, was also pardoned by Pope Clement and resumed his work for him, bringing the chapel and the library near completion in the next four years.

Many scholars for the last hundred years have debated about Michelangelo's patriotism, trying to find among these obscure details proof that he was a lover of freedom. Actually, these concepts derive from nineteenth-century liberalism and are not applicable here—a fact hard for us to conceive. What Michelangelo did love was his city, and his changing responses according to what might be to its advantage are similar to those of his great fellow Florentine Machiavelli. Machiavelli,

47

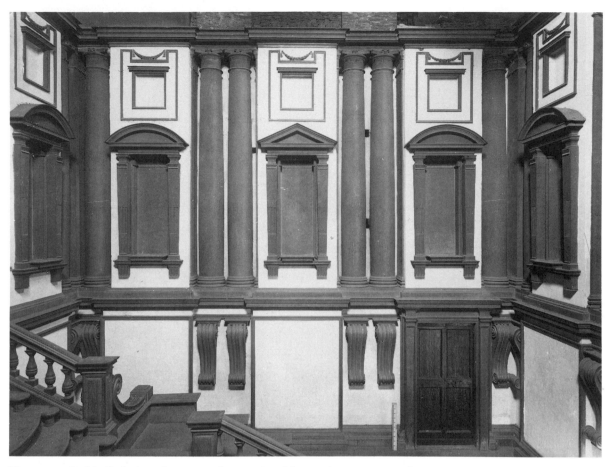

Figure 15: *Stairhall*, designed ca. 1523, Laurentian Library, San Lorenzo, Florence

Figure 16: View of the Sistine Chapel with *The Last Judgment*, height of room 68', Vatican

also active in these years, worked for a democratic government but cultivated the young Medici princelings too.

THE LAST ROMAN YEARS. In 1534 Michelangelo left Florence for the last time, leaving the court of the Medici dukes to stay quietly in Rome for thirty years. He came to a papal court where the innovating forces were the reform movements of the new religious orders and the Council of Trent. Through his friend the Marchioness Vittoria Colonna, the devout widow and close associate of reforming cardinals, Michelangelo soon became linked to the leading edge of this trend. The change shows before long in his poems, and is spectacularly quick in his painting. Paintings occupied most of his time in the decade 1535–1545. First the *Last Judgment* (fig. 16) and then the two frescoes of the Pauline Chapel develop a drastically plain and direct style, with squarish rather than supple figures, almost as if the conquering and defeated figures of the recent *Victory* had changed places. The figures may show complex and difficult actions, but the complexity is clear rather than tricky. The one large-scale sculpture begun in these late years, the *Pietà* worked on "for his own pleasure" about 1550–1555, shows a similar approach (fig. 17). The square torso of Christ, with spindly limbs, sinks down as a dead weight, while the old man above tries to pull him up and the two women at the sides strain against the downward pressure that shears against them. The weight of the marble is charged with pain, a slow and massive fatality of grief, that is deeply expressive and yet uses direct, ordinary presentation rather than being subtly interiorized, like *Jeremiah*, or intricately driven, like *Dawn*. Michelangelo abandoned the work in impatient dissatisfaction; now in Florence Cathedral, it shows the attempts of a young sculptor to finish the figures, especially the Magdalene.

In the first of these Roman decades Michelangelo also worked off some obligations. He did most of the carving on two middle-sized statues, *Rachel* and *Leah*, which with the Moses were installed on the reduced tomb finally provided for Pope Julius II. They show the mild piety of other late works and are also highly polished, unlike any other late works, for the simple reason that they were finished and placed. The

Figure 17: *Pietà*, ca. 1550-55, marble, 7'5" high, Cathedral, Florence

result is that to us they seem so dull that most people refuse to accept them as works of Michelangelo, which they are. He also carved a bust of Brutus, the assassin of Julius Caesar, for a humanistic friend's lavish patron—all three being Florentine republicans in exile. When he became ill, and was old and alone, another exile who was a rich banker took him in, and was rewarded by what must be the most impressive present ever made by an artist, the two *Slaves* now in the Louvre, which had become unusable in the smaller revised tomb of Julius. Yet later, frightened and hopeful that he could return to Florence, Michelangelo denied the republican link and courted the duke. His gifts had started in the 1530s, with a statue made for a ducal councilor to make up for his involvement in a republican revolt, and with drawings of neo-Platonic allegories for Tommaso Cavalieri. These and the Crucifixion drawings now given to Vittoria Colonna were perhaps the first drawings in history ever made as finished works of art, meant to be seen outside the studio.

After 1545, when he was seventy, Michelangelo lived alone with an elderly servant, fending off celebrity hunters, anxious about a sensible marriage for his nephew and heir, and wearing a candle in his cap while he chipped at marble all night. He made no more paintings or sculpture except for two pieces made for himself and not finished. His work was now in poetry and architecture, his two non-manual media. The poetry is his finest—religious, quiet, personal, and unhappy. The architecture, apart from the completion of Palazzo Farnese for the pope (fig. 18), is devoted to large and public plans. It centers around St. Peter's, where in 1547 Michelangelo became chief architect without fee. He worked there steadily for the rest of his life, rescuing an abandoned torso and establishing the essentials of its present form. There his older relief style grows impressively more evocative of structure in three dimensions (fig. 19). The same is true of his project for the square on the Capitoline, the ancient symbolic center of the city, a pioneer concept in city planning; the actual building there was done after his death. Colossal pillars, as in St. Peter's, here alternate with openings on the ground floor and thus evoke skeleton construction (fig. 20). Above, the openings are replaced by contrasting curtain walls, held up by normal-size columns tiny in contrast with the pillars beside them, and rhythmic accents silhouetted

Figure 18: *Palazzo Farnese*, after 1546, Rome

Figure 20: *Palazzo dei Conservatori*, designed 1538, Piazza del Campidoglio, Rome

Figure 19: *St. Peter's Basilica*, after 1547, Rome

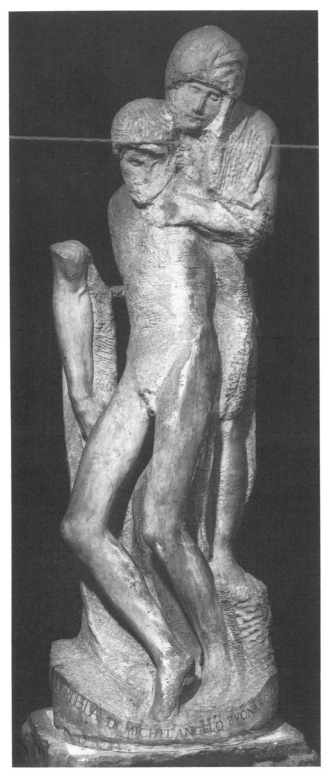

Figure 21: *Rondanini Pietà*, 1552-1564, marble, 6'4" high, Castello Sforzesco, Milan

on the roof repeat the pillars; thus the building richly blends dynamic display and a sense of engineering logic. The latest projects, the unbuilt church for the Florentine community in Rome and the city gate later reworked, the Porta Pia, move beyond that stage to reduce the high-relief effect of the surface, developing a pure structural and spatial architecture whose walls have a thin, papery, dematerialized effect.

This last, most remote and abstract, most ethereal and resolved style is probably more accessible for us in the Rondanini *Pietà*, the last sculpture (fig. 21). Worked on by fits and starts for years, from the abandonment of the previous *Pietà* to the week of Michelangelo's death in 1564, it seems to show three distinct projects. In the last the two figures are whittled down almost to Brancusian living form, yet retain their specific religious statement. As Mary holds Christ, they make two parentheses, (((, except that Christ has slipped lower. Our feeling for the roughly textured, and our romantic response to the unexpressed, may make us respond intensely to this scratched ghost for the wrong reasons; but when it is seen in relation to Michelangelo's entire span it is also able to induce a response that enhances even one step further our understanding of his scope.

PART ONE

ON THE SISTINE CEILING

Figures 1a-b: Michelangelo, putti on the throne of the Prophet Joel, fresco, Sistine Ceiling, Vatican

THE PROPORTION OF WOMEN

It is natural that the smaller sets of figures on the Sistine ceiling are little noticed. One set of very small ones comprises the putti seen on the sides of the prophets' and sibyls' thrones; each of the twelve seers has a pair of putti on the left and another pair on the right side of the throne, forty-eight putti in all. They turn out, in a quick survey, not to be mentioned at all in most of the more thoughtful recent studies of the ceiling, those by Kuhn, Von Einem, Liebert, and Hibbard. One sample pair, or none, is commonly offered in picture books.

It may seem striking that any part of this ceiling is obscure, since it is perhaps the most famous work of art in the world. Yet so are several other parts; in so vast a quantity of figures, attention naturally focuses on a few, commonly on the largest, most active, and most varied. The putti seem very repetitious, and that helps to make them seem "merely decorative" (as another thoughtful recent writer said in his sole allusion to them).[1] Some earlier writers, however, did consider them, notably those very thorough scholars Thode and Tolnay in the early twentieth century.[2] Condivi mentioned them in the artist's lifetime, though Vasari did not; Condivi, as often, may have been implying here a criticism of Vasari's inadequacy. Perhaps the most impressive and very early token of recognition is the fact that the only known drawing copied from the ceiling by Raphael is of one of the pairs of putti. This has been interpreted as showing how thorough he was, but may mean that in this earliest time the putti were of interest.[3]

The ceiling makes its various sets of images very distinct from each other. The major sets—prophets and sibyls, nudes above them, central stories in a row, and ancestors of Christ—and minor ones, too, all differ in size, color, and shape, while each set is uniform. As a result, we are keyed to look from one prophet or sibyl to the next, almost unaware of jumping across parts of other sets that lie between. In particular, each such unit is enclosed in a strong and distinctive frame, excluding neighbors that belong to other sets and signaling the way to spot its mates with identical frames. The set of putti are at the same time part of the distinctive frames of the set of prophets and sibyls. Thus units are tautly tied to each other in a web, every set being spread out over the whole ceiling, in a structure as complex as it is clear, letting us follow in smooth confidence.

All the frames are made to seem three-dimensional, like window frames projecting from a wall; each set of frames projects to a different degree, still another clue about which set of figures it encloses. The putti are among those projecting the most, exceeded only by the prophets and sibyls. Those, however, being very large, also project further back, making the putti very prominent on this criterion. Yet there is more to make them inconspicuous, besides their small scale. The other equally small figures, who are the nearby putti holding the name plates, and the only ones still smaller, who are the ones in the round gold medallions, are colorful, in flesh-color or gold, while ours are gray, to let us read them as carved in the stone of the thrones. The gold medallions also have highly varied narrative action, while our putti are simply variants on one type.

Their stoniness, to be sure, suggests a special interest of the artist in them, since they alone on the ceiling allude to his favored medium of marble sculpture. They would be produced by first making a drawing on paper, transferable to the final version we see with a simplicity unavailable in any other set. That may, on the other hand, imply a wish to take care of them rapidly, and hence slight attention. It has always been noticed that only twelve drawings were needed to produce the twenty-four pairs. Michelangelo could use each of them directly and then a second time after flipping it over. The back of each drawing generated a mirror image, the basis of the second painted pair, and the two pairs occupy the two sides of the throne symmetrically (figs. 1a-b). The same system was used in other sets, notably the nearby bronze-colored nudes in triangular frames. In the case of our pairs, observers agree that one of each two analogous pairs is livelier and more strongly modelled. It is presumably the one made from the direct drawing; the flipped one can be less convincing, partly because right-handed gestures become left-handed with no further adjustment. Assistants, it is reasonably thought, did the mechanical job of painting the second pairs. As to the first, it is debated whether the master did them or they, too, were mechanically produced from the drawings.

The mirror-image formula enhances the impression of a decorative scheme like carved furniture. The putti seem to move in patterns like dance steps—the dance-like poses may have been chosen with this in mind. All of this may seem to reduce their significance on the ceiling even more. Altogether, it seems that, among the many factors that could add to or subtract attention from them, the latter have prevailed.

A surprise awaits when we look closely. In each pair one is male and one female, most unusual in Renaissance imagery. To be sure, this factor is not explicit in all twelve drawings. Six show both infants' genitalia clearly, three show those of only one (two the male, one the female), and three conceal both in the turning movements. Yet writers have reasonably agreed that in the latter the system does not change from the one used in all checkable cases. Thode, who discussed the putti in most detail, claimed that in the last three he could still say which was the male and which the female figure, the one being aggressive and the other reacting. He did call both figures of one pair male and those of a second pair both female, but later writers silently dropped these variants; Tolnay thus concluded that the pairs "always couple a boy and a girl."[4] All the pairs, varying in energy, are interactive; sometimes one copycats the other's movements or pushes the other away.

Italian Renaissance art is famous for putti, especially in the century up to the Sistine, but they are almost never female. Why that is so would call for its own investigation of social presumptions, though they may seem obvious. The Italian word *putto,* then as now, is an ordinary colloquial term for a little boy. In English it is art historians' jargon for a boy in Italian art, often naked, and no corresponding term *(putta)* for a girl exists in this case. Writers on Michelangelo never seem to have asked why the putta appears here or whether she exists elsewhere.

Two other instances have turned up, by the usual art historical procedure of keeping watch over a long time. Both combine a single putto and putta, and both are on carved chimney pieces of the 1460s. One,

Figure 2: Desiderio da Settignano, putta, marble fireplace, Victoria and Albert Museum, London

Figure 3:
Putti on fireplace, marble,
Palazzo Ducale, Urbino

from the workshop of the Florentine sculptor Desiderio da Settignano, is in the Victoria and Albert Museum in London. The lintel, as well described in the museum's catalogue, has at the center a coat of arms, that of the Boni family, in a wreath, held up by two male putti. Unusually, they differ, in that the one on the left is naked but the other "wears a thin vest," through which, however, the genitalia are plain. Further out toward the ends the lintel has two busts, "(left) a young man and (right) a young woman," and at the extreme ends "(left) a winged girl" (fig. 2) and "(right) a boy." Amusingly, the cataloguer, who used the word putto before, now drops it, though these children fully match the type; no doubt he did so because there was no way without awkwardness to refer to the female as a putta.[5]

The other chimney piece is in the Ducal Palace at Urbino, in the room called the Sala di Iole after this object. The side posts comprise full-length nudes inscribed with the names of Hercules and his wife Iole, and the lintel has a Bacchic scene, with male putti as usual. Further above, a putto and a putta hold up a coat of arms (fig. 3). The two chimney pieces share the odd detail that the putta is on the same side as the male adult, and vice versa. The Florentine one has been supposed to have been made for a marriage, but even if that is not so, the pairing of putto and putta obviously echoes the adult couple. Whether common or not, the formula seems elementary enough to be easily absorbed in the culture in which Michelangelo a generation later would be learning sculpture. Yet the putta remains very rare, present only for a specific reason.[6]

Some kind of context for Michelangelo's putti in pairs seems to have been sought only by Tolnay. A not very convincing suggestion he offers as a source is a carved classical group of Cupid and Psyche kissing; they are about thirteen, not the five or so that Thode reasonably suggested for our pairs, who are not *amorini,* as Tolnay calls them. He is better in arguing their involvement with the stone. This echoes Condivi's term for them, *termini,* those who hold up the lintels, as the two in the Florentine chimney piece do. Condivi may have been using Michelangelo's words, as he often did. Yet this does not explain them.

Since they are virtually invisible from the floor, some sixty feet below, and the sex entirely so, they hardly can have conveyed didactic

63

messages to viewers or been meant to. The chimney pieces offer an obvious clue; our pairs, too, echo the nearby pairs of adults, the alternating prophets and sibyls, Persica, Jeremiah, and so on. This simple finding allows a new observation about the artist's working thoughts; in planning the larger set of figures, the fact of their being of the two sexes was a conscious concern.

We may view the prophets and sibyls either as a set on the ceiling, with a common scale and frame system, or as two interweaving subsets. Along the two sides of the chapel, we see in one case two sibyls alternating between three prophets, and on the other side the reverse. Hence each figure has neighbors of the opposite sex on both sides and across the way, but one of the same sex diagonally opposite. Quite differently, both ends have a male figure, Zachariah over the entrance and Jonah over the altar. They, however, do not compose a visual pair, since one can never see both at once. Their ties instead are to their neighbors, nearest if only on a diagonal, on each side; in each case one neighbor is also male, repeating the type of diagonal tie noted, while the other is female, repeating the type of adjacent neighboring noted, since we are inclined to treat all the figures in a steady series even when we have to turn a corner.

The Sistine sibyls, more famous by far than any others, have hence wrongly been supposed to be typical of sibyl imagery. Thus the excellent scholar Arthur Hind said that "grouping of the semi-mythical sibyls with the Hebrew prophets on nearly equal terms was of course a custom familiar in all forms of art before and during the Renaissance." When he goes into more detail, he more correctly suggests, as does Tolnay, that sibyls usually had lower status than prophets.[7] This would be the case when the two groups appeared together, but the more common circumstance showed the sibyls either entirely alone or as a distinct but lesser set in a complex monument. The way they interact with prophets has not been addressed in the large sibyl literature, which has dealt in partial and scattered ways with the wide and puzzling variants.

It is plain why sibyls interested Michelangelo's culture. It was fascinated with non-Christian religions and naturally found those of the classical world ready for exploration. Usually, however, the goal was to show that only Christianity was valid, the indications to that effect by pagans serving to reinforce the point. The austere archbishop of Florence around 1450, Antonino, remarked on the "witness to be had from the gentiles about the faith" with sibyls as his best examples, but at once cautioned that their value was limited.[8] In 1474 the very different Florentine Marsilio Ficino, in his treatise on the Christian religion, surveyed the sibyls in two chapters.

The Delphic oracle, with her links to Oedipus and Socrates, is the only sibyl remembered today. Many women prophets were described by ancient authors in scattered ways, usually in close connection with a place. Pausanias collected several in his guide to Greece.[9] Roman writers systematized the information. Their sayings were collected in Greek verse in one work, the *Oracula Sibillina,* generally without assigning them to a particular sibyl. The Roman Varro listed ten sibyls, naming his sources in older writers, whose works like his are lost. This passage, however, was quoted by the early Christian writer Lactantius, whose book, *Divine Institutions,* fixed the list of ten for the Middle Ages and the Renaissance, even as to its order, with the Persian first and the Tiburtine last (from the town of Tibur near Rome, now Tivoli). Lactantius also quoted from the *Oracula* over forty of the sayings. Since the whole text of the *Oracula* had a small circulation, the sibylline prophecies known later were almost only those Lactantius had quoted. They also were the ones that tended to fit Christianity best. He again noted that, except for the Erythraean sibyl, few could be identified as authors of particular sayings. His aim may be viewed as complementary to that of the Renaissance humanists. Just as they hoped to win favor for classical culture by showing that it could prophesy Christ, so he used the same materials to win favor for Christianity in a still pagan culture.

His account won its greatest fame when St Augustine quoted from it in a chapter of the *City of God,* a great work over the centuries. He repeated some ten of the quotations, mainly about the Passion of Christ and one longer one by Erythraea about the Last Judgment. He then went on to quote the Hebrew prophets similarly in seven chapters, a typical ratio.[10]

The set of ten sibyls seems to have been noticed in the Middle Ages only in encyclopedias of general knowledge, from Isidore of Seville to

Vincent of Beauvais. These authors wished to expand history beyond the Judaeo-Christian frame, and found the sibyls convenient since they were reported by Lactantius to have lived in varied eras. In this period more interest did focus on three individual sibyls. The Erythraean retained her important link to the Last Judgment, since a prophecy of it had the fascination of still referring to the future. This is most conspicuous in the great thirteenth-century hymn "Dies Irae"—which was still being set to music again in the nineteenth—whose first verse appeals to the "witness of David and the sibyl." The Cumaean sibyl, from a town near Naples, gained immortality from two references to her by Virgil, the Middle Ages' most admired poet (as Dante makes clear). He had made her Aeneas' guide to the underworld, where he learned about the future of Rome, and, even more powerfully, had invoked her in one of his short eclogues, prophesying greatness for a new baby, which the Middle Ages made a reference to Christ. Finally, a medieval tale about Emperor Augustus told how he received a prophecy that one greater than he would be born, Christ. In its earlier forms the prophetess is anonymous, and sometimes she was called Erythraea, but by 1300 she had firmly been identified as the Tiburtine sibyl, presumably because among the ten only she lived near Rome.[11]

That last story and Virgil's eclogue both centered on Christ's birth, just as Augustine had on the passion. More Nativity prophecies soon emerged, most remarkably in a paragraph-long section of a work called the *Vaticinium Erythraeae,* the *Prophecy of Erythraea,* written in the 1250s and soon attributed to the strange contemporary prophet Joachim de Fiore, whose complex foretellings of the end of the world had much effect.[12] The *Vaticinium* also included an allusion to the Augustus story, and its phrases about that naturally were soon treated as a saying by Tiburtina. A phrase from the *Vaticinium* is carved on a scroll that the monumental figure of Erythraea holds on the facade of Siena Cathedral, carved by Giovanni Pisano about 1280. She is in a set mainly of Hebrew prophets, but it also includes one Hebrew prophetess, Miriam, and Plato and Aristotle, thereby evoking very early the idea of Christ being foretold by women, by pagans, and in this case by a pagan

66

woman. In a second set of large statues, two sibyls, Erythraea and Tiburtina, join six Hebrew prophets on the bell tower of Florence Cathedral, carved around 1340 by Andrea Pisano; Erythraea's scroll shows another phrase from the *Vaticinium*.

Giovanni Pisano also produced the first sets of sibyls in the visual arts, aside from one or two illustrated manuscripts of universal histories. These are on both of his great pulpits, and their fierce expressiveness and mobile stress make them, as all agree, Michelangelo's most powerful predecessors. The first, of 1301 in Pistoia, is a hexagon, the second, of 1310 in Pisa, an octagon; they respectively show six and eight sibyls fitted at the corners, a suggestion that the particular number was not a concern. St. Augustine, citing Varro but not his list of ten, had simply said there were "many" sibyls, and may have been the authority here. Giovanni as a youth had assisted his father, Nicola, on a pulpit in the Cathedral of Siena, an octagon, and in his own pulpits followed its thematic choices in most respects. On the corners Nicola had shown eight virtues, the canonical seven plus Humility, a virtue that could be added when needed. As the virtues could not be cut down to six, Giovanni had to find a different theme for the corners of his hexagon. The solution of sibyls may have come from his own earlier Erythraea figure, whose appearance is similar to the female allegories of virtue, and been retained as a success when later he did his octagonal pulpit.

The pulpits are like the Sistine ceiling in comprising many subsets at different degrees of projection forward (as in other ways) and suggest how particularly suitable to sculpture this method is. The sibyls, twisting their heads upward, gaze at narratives of Christ's life, which are the chief subset of the work. These show events of the Nativity, the Crucifixion, and the Last Judgment; sibyls had become associated with all these. Besides the emergence of the *Vaticinium* with its Nativity references and the "Dies Irae" on the Last Judgment, another popular work of the time, *The Golden Legend,* had recently cited as a prophecy of the Crucifixion a phrase from the *Oracula Sibillina* that Lactantius had not quoted, perhaps a unique case.[13]

Boccaccio in his book on famous women of around 1350, while noting that the sibyls were said to be ten, gave accounts of just two, the

67

Figure 4: Lorenzo Ghiberti, doors, bronze gilt, Baptistry of San Giovanni, Florence

familiar Erythraea and Cumaea. His account of the former echoes the *Vaticinium,* and that of the latter combines Virgil with a story not involving prophecy, taken from a classical historian. (When the king of Rome would not pay her price for her nine prophetic books, she burned three and offered the rest for the same price; he again refused. After she burned three more, he did pay the same amount for the three still left.) Two sibyls seem to appear again on Ghiberti's Doors of Paradise in the Florentine Baptistery of 1424–1444. The frames around the ten narratives show fifteen male and five female figures, and Vasari called the latter sibyls (fig. 4). Two, however, are Hebrew heroines, Miriam again, with her tambourine, and Judith, with the head of Holofernes and her sword. Two others, though, seem to be the same individually famous sibyls earlier carved across the street by Andrea Pisano, Erythraea and Tiburtina. To combine Miriam and a sibyl with Hebrew prophets—as most of the male figures here are—recalls the formula of Giovanni Pisano at the Cathedral of Siena, a city where Ghiberti spent some time.[14] Erythraea alone was included around 1445 by Fra Angelico in the frame of his huge Crucifixion at San Marco in Florence, with many prophets; her scroll shows the saying assigned to her by Angelico's close associate, Archbishop Antonino.[15]

Larger series, however, became more frequent at this time and soon dominant. They perhaps first appear in mystery plays about Augustus and the Tiburtine sibyl, such as one performed in 1385 but not new then in all likelihood, followed by a sequence of prophecies by twelve sibyls, also about the Nativity. These have the traditional ten names plus Agrippa and Europa.[16] This introduces a type that would share attention with the previous ten-sibyl set, as Dotson showed.[17] The twelve always focus on the Nativity, while the ten may, like Augustine, focus on the Passion or, like Lactantius, spread through the life of Christ more generally. The mystery play introduces a set of sayings about the Nativity for the twelve that remained the usual ones.[18]

The reason for adding Agrippa and Europa is not that new classical reports had been found; these two names and others had already existed as extra or alternate names for some of the ten. Thus what happened was, rather, a wish to expand the set to twelve. What caused that is not

69

known, but a plausible explanation is again related to Joachim of Fiore, the prophet with whom the *Vaticinium* had been associated, which had provided new sayings for Erythraea and Tiburtina also about the Nativity. Joachim dealt in the mysticism of numbers and liked to expand the twelve apostles to other sets of twelve.[19] In any case, the twelve were supplied with Nativity sayings that came, besides the *Vaticinium,* from Virgil (for Cumaea) but otherwise were evidently new, along with the newly named sibyls.[20]

The twelve were first painted, as far as is known, around 1430 in Rome, in the palace of Cardinal Orsini, as part of a larger project. Secular art of this period tends more often than the religious to be lost, and the themes harder to imagine from descriptions, giving too much weight to our impression that most of the art was religious. Orsini's project may have been the most imposing early Renaissance monument of painting in Rome. A visiting Florentine merchant, Giovanni Rucellai, best known as Leon Battista Alberti's greatest architectural patron, first recorded it on a visit in 1450, and the writer Filarete alluded to it soon after. Rucellai's diary of his Roman visit, along with pilgrimage churches and ancient ruins, mentions just this one contemporary work. Vasari confusingly mentions it twice, partly contradicting himself, but lets us know that it involved a series of famous men by Masolino. Unconnected at first with this, an illuminated manuscript was published in 1912 showing some three hundred famous men and women from Adam to around 1400, with inscriptions, the largest illustrated world chronicle known. (It includes ten prophets and two sibyls, Erythraea and a variant on Samia.) The manuscript was attributed to Paolo Uccello and others until it was, in 1966, proved to be a copy of the Orsini room, by the discovery of a manuscript list giving the same three hundred names and inscriptions under a title referring to the "Sala Theatri" in the cardinal's house.[21]

Again separately from this, a letter has long been known from the leading humanist Poggio Bracciolini to his colleague Roberto Valturio, a leading figure at the court of Urbino. It mentions several topics, which recently have allowed it to be dated 1454.[22] Poggio goes on to say: "I now have no time to investigate what you ask me about sibyls, but I will help with advice. Cardinal Orsini, who died in the time of Pope Eugene (i.e.,

between 1431 and 1447; our cardinal died in 1438) had all the sibyls painted with great diligence, with inscriptions, in the Sala Paramenti of his
house, so you may write to Rome to get a learned man to note the names
and epigrams and send it to you. You will find nothing more exquisite."
This letter was rightly linked in 1936 to a text, surviving in several copies,
headed with the title "Sibyls as described in Rome in the room of
Cardinal Orsini, with their prophecies," and two verses, reading: "Here
are the sibyls, not all of one age, who told of the future God of the Virgin
mother." It was understood that this text was the result of the report that
Poggio had suggested be made. Unfortunately, with an overlooked exception, it was not realized that his correspondent, "Roberto
Ariminensi," was Valturio, nor was the date of the letter known, nor was
the first sentence cited indicating that Roberto had requested information on sibyls. As a result, it was not taken into account that the list
Valturio obtained has a relation to an event of that year in Rimini involving a second grand series of sibyls. This will be explored below.

The Orsini list,[23] apart from some oddities, names the twelve sibyls
we have noted, attached to their prophecies of the Nativity, and also
names the ancient lost authors whom Lactantius had cited as authorities on them. (This shows direct use of Lactantius, since Augustine had
not repeated that detail.) The twelve sibyls then reappear through the
century in several specific contexts. One of them is in popular art, in
mystery plays in various cities and a related set of prints in Florence.
Here the sibyls are usually matched with prophets, usually more numerous than they, who also foretell the Nativity. In a Bologna play there
are sixteen prophets.[24] In the best known one, in Florence, echoed closely in the prints, there are thirty figures in groups of three; the first nine
groups comprise two prophets and a sibyl, while the tenth is of three
prophets only. (This last prophet, who replaces an expected sibyl to
break the rhythm, is Zachariah; we cannot but recall that in the Sistine,
too, Zachariah, as the last figure over the altar, breaks the even weight-
ing of prophets and sibyls.) The nine sibyls here have some original
names—Sofonia, Michea, Osea—obviously borrowed from those of
prophets not being used on the occasion (Zephaniah, Micah, Hosea),
suggesting a semiliterate context.[25] A very long play in Piedmont, at

71

Revello, in contrast balances six prophets and six sibyls (including the new Europa) in alternation.[26]

The other main context of sibyls with Nativity sayings is in partial sets, often only four, especially in Nativity chapels, where they fill the four triangular spaces of a Gothic cross vault. First, the Sassetti Chapel of 1485 at S. Trinita in Florence, painted by Ghirlandaio, with a Nativity altarpiece, has been shown in a classic study by Fritz Saxl to involve strong references to the classical pagan world.[27] The sibyls of course underline that. Outside, over the entrance arch, we first see in a very large scene Tiburtina informing Augustus of the Nativity, with a large view of the architectural monuments of Rome between them. Inside, on the four triangular vault surfaces, Cumaea comes first next to the entrance and thus to Tiburtina. Her scroll does not simply quote Virgil but, uniquely, credits him, so that only one word from the quotation itself follows: "Teste Virgil Magnus." Opposite, above the altar, the other most important position, is Erythraea; thus the three traditional individually important sibyls dominate. No others seem to have been found interesting; one of the two slots remaining, at the sides, went to the obscure Agrippa. Evidently she again is meant to refer to Rome, since the city view mentioned makes the most prominent building the Pantheon, whose lintel bore the name of its builder, Agrippa, then as it does now. Choice was then entirely exhausted, it seems, for the final sibyl is shown holding her scroll so that no words show. This design, denying her an identity even to those who were familiar with the sayings, cannot be an accident.[28]

Michelangelo, who apprenticed with Ghirlandaio in 1488, of course knew this work, as well as the vault the Florentine Filippino Lippi, then probably the city's leading painter, did in the 1490s in Rome for a chapel in S. Maria Sopra Minerva, where the altarpiece is of the Annunciation. Above it is the Cumaean sibyl with the Virgil text, and opposite her over the entrance is the Tiburtine, the other sibyl linked to Rome. There are no others so linked. The two sibyls in the side spaces are the Delphic and the Hellespontic. They have in common that they are the two from Greece, and perhaps a geographic choice was made referring to the other region that humanists associated with classical antiquity.

One painter at the time in Rome, Pinturicchio, made sibyls almost a specialty, with one larger set to be cited later and two more chapel vaults. A chapel produced for a major churchman in the small town of Spello, with narratives of the infancy of Christ, combines the standard Erythraea and Tiburtina with Europa and Samia, for no reason that is obvious today. In 1507, in Rome, in the choir of S. Maria del Popolo, he painted a complex scheme of three interwoven sets, each of four figures: evangelists, doctors of the church, and sibyls. Eryhthraea, Cumaea (under her variant name, Cimmeria), Delphica, and Persica are all inscribed. The names are needed, since Delphica has the saying that is regularly Agrippa's in the twelve-sibyl tradition of Nativity sayings, and Cimmeria is given one of Erythraea's, who has another of her own. The one given to Cimmeria does not come from the usual twelve-sibyl set at all, but is from the other tradition of sayings from Lactantius, the prophecy of the Last Judgment, and its text is amended to say "Dei Filius" instead of "Rex." The aim or aims of all this editing remain to be explained.

During the later fifteenth century the ten-sibyl tradition with texts from Lactantius flourished, too, in another cluster of contexts. It more commonly shows the full series rather than a shortened set of four or the like, and is rarely in popular art, but rather in special commissions to major artists. These are not found in Rome. This begins in 1454 in Rimini, when the city ruler, Sigismondo Malatesta, was employing the Florentine sculptor Agostino di Duccio for many projects in his Church of San Francesco.[29] This building by Leon Battista Alberti is better known as the Malatesta Temple, and the tone of its ornament was such as to make Pope Pius II, the ruler's enemy, denounce its "pagan tales and profane images." One of Agostino's series even shows the muses. The sibyls are carved in relief on the two entrance piers of a chapel, on the three sides of each pier facing out to the church, across to the other pier, and in to the chapel altar, on two levels, adding up to twelve reliefs in all on the two piers. As Freund observed, the Rimini humanist's request in 1454 for ideas on sibyls is plainly intended to help with ideas for this project. The oddity is that he did not use the report he got. The Orsini list showed twelve sibyls, and there were just twelve spaces here for carvings, but they are filled with two prophets and ten sibyls instead. They

73

are anonymous (except for Tiburtina, shown with burning books), but their scrolls have in most cases prophecies from Lactantius, retaining his point that the sayings are not to be assigned to individual sibyls. The twelve-sibyl scheme was thus rejected, quite possibly because Lactantius had the authority of antiquity. There were twelve panels to be filled with reliefs—there is no simple way to arrange five panels in a pattern on a pier—so the remaining two were used for other figures, the choice naturally falling on prophets. They got the two positions ranking highest, in the upper tier facing in to the altar, one on each pier, the major prophet Isaiah on the right, the minor one Micah on the left. Hierarchy is also clear in the remaining placements; the rest of the right pier goes to five sibyls with texts quoted by Augustine on the Passion; the one text still left from that source goes to the top sibyl adjacent to Micah on the other pier, facing across. The remaining upper spot, facing out on the left pier, shows a text by Lactantius that Augustine had not quoted, and the three below have no texts, all the appropriate ones evidently having been considered used up. The planner, as noted, had consulted Lactantius directly, and that writer had many more sibyl sayings, but not about the Passion.

In 1465 Lactantius' book became the second book printed in Italy (after one by Cicero), a choice perhaps less odd to us in view of the interest seen here. He uniquely matched the era's interest in classical treatment of Christianity, and had already been so used in the Orsini lists and by Antonino. Ficino in 1476 quoted him liberally in his book on Christianity.

The prophets here are the first to be part of a single set with more than a few sibyls (as in Michelangelo). Though fewer, the prophets have the rank, as if leading a chorus, and are possible to name, while the sibyls are not. Their scrolls are about the Nativity, which calls for another enquiry.

In 1455 another humanist, Porcelio, visited Rimini, and addressed a long flattering poem to the ruler, including praise of the temple. The two lines on the sibyls read: "Then you see two sibyls, not all of the same age, who told of the future God of the Virgin mother"—exactly those noted at the head of the Orsini list. In Porcelio they are in the midst of a long series of such lines in the same meter—preceded by two on the tomb with an elephant, two on the zodiac, two on the muses[30]—while they stand alone in the list. From that we see that Porcelio's text is earlier, and they were quoted from it on the list, even though Porcelio wrote after the sculpture was done and the list is a year earlier. The evident explanation is that our manuscripts of the list do not preserve the original form, but include additions after it arrived in Valturio's hands in Urbino, indeed others besides this one. They also include, as the title in fact specifies, other sibylline sayings from Cologne, puzzling when regarded as part of the original compiled to describe the Orsini room, but a natural part of Valturio's procedure in assembling options. No doubt he got material from more than one correspondent.

This reconstruction helps to clarify the oddest element in the lists as we have them, that they include prophets. They do so despite the fact that the title, which promises information on the sibyls in the room as well as those from Cologne, mentions no prophets, though they are more fully reported in what follows than the Cologne sibyls. Thirteen prophet names interweave with the twelve sibyls, but in two cases the same prophet is repeated—making it again unlikely, if still not impossible, that they record actual paintings in the Orsini house. Valturio, who as we saw needed prophets to fill two places in his program, evidently penciled in ideas next to each sibyl to find the most suitable ones; this hypothesis is confirmed in that the two he did choose, Micah and Isaiah, are the same two who occur twice in the lists, each accompanied in one case by the same quotation carried on his scroll in Rimini. What is odd is that all thirteen prophet texts foretell the Nativity, thus matching not the Lactantius scheme but the twelve-sibyl one in the Orsini room. Then too, Porcelio described the Rimini series as all about the Nativity, even though it is the theme only of the two prophets, not the sibyls. Evidently Valturio, while preferring Lactantius, was also convinced by the Orsini model that the theme to be prophesied should be the incarnation.

The edited Orsini lists, with the interweaving prophets, circulating in a number of manuscripts, provided a model for planning matched equal sets of prophets and sibyls, even though no such imagery had been produced. Soon it did appear, as in Michelangelo. It is found in one of the mystery plays, even if with capricious variety in prophets. It most notably finds a following in the odd little book issued in 1481 by the Dominican Filippo Barbieri. He was concerned whether the pagans had or had not prophesied Christ, assigning a debate on the matter to Sts. Jerome and Augustine. The book appeared in two versions on the same day,[31] of which one included along with the sibyls and their Nativity texts, the obvious choice, twelve parallel texts about the Nativity from Hebrew prophets, not the same selection as in the Orsini manuscripts. The prophets did not pertain to his topic, however, and disappear from two later editions. He too presented one of his prophets twice, indicating that they are here to correlate, through their sayings, with the twelve sibyls who are the real focus. The book has also interested art historians as the first ever printed in Italy illustrated with new woodcuts, i.e., not with reused German blocks. It was also supposed by Mâle, until the Orsini list was published in 1936, to have inaugurated the twelve-sibyl formula with Nativity texts, and thus to have had much influence. Yet it is not generally noted that it used only two blocks for pictures of ten of the sibyls, using separate ones only for the traditional Erythraea and Tiburtina, the latter in a scene with Augustus. The repeated other ones clash with his verbal accounts of the sibyls' appearance, and new woodcuts were made for a later edition.

He may well have influenced the partial sets of sibyls from the set of twelve by Ghirlandaio and Filippino Lippi. Of special interest is Pinturicchio's full set of 1494 in the Vatican, done for Pope Alexander VI's Borgia apartments. It is the only painted set of all twelve after the original Orsini one, and the only one accompanied by twelve prophets, as in the edited Orsini description and one of Barbieri's two early editions. Yet again the choice of prophets is different. It shares with the Orsini room also, and only with it, the set of twelve sibyls and their Nativity sayings in a room not focused on the Nativity, but a reception room in a prelate's palace. It had another separate stimulus to the form it took, which is not generally noted, the adjacent Borgia room, also by Pinturicchio and also pairing twelve prophets, this time with the twelve apostles.[32] In this second room the theme is the apostles' creed, and it was traditional to show them with scrolls, each taking a verse, and joined with suitable prophets. Both rooms are constructed with twelve lunettes, also doubtless constraining the results.

The other type, with ten sibyls and Lactantius texts, also flourished after the Rimini series. The sibyl literature has omitted the next

instance, which consists of two panels at Christ Church, Oxford, painted about 1475 in the style of Botticelli, rightly admired for their forceful
drawing and expressiveness; since they differ from Botticelli's own specific style, they have been assigned sometimes to him in part and sometimes to his most notable pupil, the young Filippino Lippi, then
eighteen.[22] The sibyls are named, and the five on the first panel are
unique in matching exactly Michelangelo's five. The text, elegantly inscribed in one continuous paragraph under the figures, marks a fresh
choice from Lactantius, also unique, all about the Last Judgment.[34] The
traditional connection with the "Dies Irae" naturally validated an ex-
trapolation to other similar sayings. Yet the person who arranged this
evidently combined the usual religious devotion and classical interests
with a higher intensity of philology. Altogether it suggests a humanist
who could not afford an expensive artist but could find youthful talent
in a shop. That matches the Medici circle, where at this date Botticelli
was already a figure and Ficino was quoting much from Lactantius in
his book on Christianity.

The most monumental sibyls of all are those of 1481–1482 in the
Cathedral of Siena, a major part of its unique pavement in inlaid marble.
Each aisle is completely filled with a row of five sibyls, forty meters long,
equal to the length of the Sistine Chapel (where sibyls do not fill the whole
length). In 1501 Michelangelo was working in one of these aisles on his
Piccolomini altar, a moment in his career often overlooked. This is the
one case in which it is certain that an earlier set of sibyls was well known
to him. They have more Renaissance grandeur than Ghirlandaio's or
Filippino's. Later Michelangelo famously asserted that painting is inferi-
or to sculpture, and painting is better the closer to sculpture it comes.[35]
These two-dimensional drawings made of marble are an unexpectedly literal realization of such a prescription. The Sienese masters who designed
them, such as Urbano da Cortona and Federighi, reflecting Donatello, or
Matteo di Giovanni and Neroccio, reflecting Verrocchio, had cast aside
the older Sienese tradition for modern Florentine sculptural modes.
Their classical poise and *contraposto* exploit sculptural weight and balance
more than any other Sienese work of the time, but the oddity of their
medium has tended to exclude them from the history books.

Figure 5: *Erythraean sibyl*, marble inlay floor, Siena Cathedral

Figure 6: Perugino, *sibyls and prophets*, fresco, Collegio del Cambio, Perugia

Each figure is accompanied by two elaborate inscriptions.[36] One gives her name and Lactantius' citation of the older authority about her. The other gives a saying, in seven cases one of the Lactantius texts, as one would expect in a series of ten. The others are, for Cumaea, lines from Virgil's eclogue, and for Tiburtina, the usual phrase from the *Vaticinium*—in both cases texts that had been co-opted by the twelve-sibyl system—while one sibyl, Erythraea, actually uses one of the Nativity sayings invented for that system (fig. 5). Again the three most famous sibyls get special treatment, in the first two cases evidently because these sayings had also become tightly linked to them and almost inevitable. Erythraea is not assigned either of her famous texts, the Lactantius one about the Last Judgment or that from the *Vaticinium,* but these were too long for the marble inlay if used in full, and that may be why a shift to the other source was adopted.

Of the seven sayings from Lactantius, four are the standard ones from Augustine, exhausting his citations about the Passion. The fifth is the same one that in Rimini had been taken directly from Lactantius, and the sixth is one of the short texts on the Last Judgment that had recently been adopted on the Botticelli panel. The seventh seems to be novel, an all-purpose line: "Know him as your God who is the son of God." The re-use of all the others, albeit from various intermediate sources, suggests an active exchange of Lactantius materials going on at the time. The effect of blending the basic Lactantius group of Passion sayings with three about the Nativity and still others is to assemble prophecies of Christ's whole career, even including the Last Judgment, in the way that was suggested above as possible in Giovanni Pisano's sets, where the sibyls gaze at a narrative also of that career. The slight, if distinct, involvement with the modern emphasis on the Nativity sayings, more associated with the twelve-sibyl set, is given a distinct spin in that two of the three such cases choose texts borrowed from original classical sources, and one reinforces that direct appeal to classical origins with visual details; Cumaea is given the attribute of her burning books, as in Rimini, and her leafy branch, the golden bough with which she guided Aeneas in Hades. In 1488 an eleventh panel was added in the nave, with a unique image of Hermes Trismegistus. Lactantius had treated him also as a pagan prophet of

79

Christ, and Ficino had recently translated his works. He is shown hand-ing a book to two onlookers, one male and one female, and his inscrip-tion, calling him a contemporary of Moses, reinforces a visual likeness to images of Moses giving the tables of the law to the people.

Four of the artists were commissioned in September 1481 and paid in July 1482. They were thus evidently not affected by Barbieri's book, published in December 1481, nor by the focus on Nativity sayings of the twelve-sibyl set. Rather, both the pavement and Barbieri share a gener-al concern with sibyls, and the limited attention to the twelve in Siena may indicate circulation of the Orsini list in manuscript. A special ele-ment in the series is that, like Michelangelo, it does not arrange the sibyls in the standard sequence from Persica on, but seems random.

Perugino's monumental set of sibyls of 1500 at the Collegio del Cambio in Perugia again assigns a special role to the three traditionally chief ones and uses varied texts from Lactantius. The Collegio was a courtroom for mercantile disputes, and in part follows the tradition for such places, established by Slepian,[37] in which justice is exemplified by classical heroes and shown through allegories. Here one of the three painted walls presents just such classical heroes, while a second shows the unusual pairing of the Nativity and Transfiguration of Christ. That balance of the classical and the Christian on two walls seems summed up in the only fresco on the third wall, with six prophets on one side and six sibyls on the other (fig. 6).

The sibyls form two rows of three, with the three famous ones standing in front, and behind them Persica, Libica, and Delphica—num-bers one, two, and three in the sequence first set up by Varro and used ever since. They are seen only in part behind the front row, and their scrolls show only a word or two of their inscriptions, adding to the im-pression that their individual identities are not important; again we have a choral group. All six sayings from Lactantius are a new choice. The three in front, reading from left to right, make up a single saying, quot-ed in bloc shortly before by Antonino.[38] Since he had also, in the same passage, quoted more familiar lines, the selection is evidently purpose-ful. Antonino characterized this group as accurately foretelling Christ's miracles, such as curing the sick and feeding the hungry.

The six prophets on the other side likewise form two rows of three, making distinct points. Those behind are Isaiah, Daniel, and Jeremiah, three of the four major prophets (omitting Ezekiel), those who could represent prophets in general when no specific one was required; two of them also have scrolls on which one word or none shows. Isaiah does show his verse about the Virgin who conceives, doubtless the most famous of all prophecies of Christ and thus inevitable. These figures seem to be a chorus like the three background sibyls. Moses, David, and Solomon, in front of them, are prophets only in a broad sense, more specifically rulers and lawgivers, authors of books of doctrine and law (the Torah, Psalms, and Proverbs). They thus are suitable to the room and analogous to the classical judges and lawgivers in the other frescoes. The two trios of Hebrew prophets and lawgivers also relate to the scene of the Transfiguration, showing Christ between Moses, the lawgiver, and Elijah, the prophet. The link in turn between that scene and the Nativity may reflect the formula, first articulated at the Council of Nicaea, that those two events proclaimed Christ both as son of God and as ruler. The Transfiguration by itself is sometimes viewed as a prophecy of Christ's role as judge at the end of the world, again suitable to the room.[39] It must be admitted that among these cross-references, the sibyls, and their focus on Christ's miracles, are not neatly accounted for.

Perugino's balance of six prophets and six sibyls is closer than any other grouping we have seen to Michelangelo's of seven and five, or five and five on the side walls; all five of Michelangelo's sibyls appear among Perugino's six. The only other painted set with such balance was Pinturicchio's in the Borgia apartments, with twelve and twelve. That one was certainly known to Perugino, whose ceiling is also like Pinturicchio's, in presenting planets through classical gods. However, the specifics of Perugino's figures are very unlike Pinturicchio's. Pinturicchio did not show the three lawgivers, and the three major prophets he shows are paired in two cases with sibyls absent from Perugino's set; his scrolls, as expected in a set of twelve, are about the Nativity, as Perugino's conspicuously are not. Perugino's message thus seems very different, yet it is likely that he found some visual stimulus for his layout in the earlier scheme.

81

What did all of these earlier formulations mean for Michelangelo? Some of their interests seem absent in him, such as any special concern with the three traditionally famous sibyls or connections with ancient Rome; his omission of Tiburtina would exclude those. Other factors consistent in the earlier series seem likely to have been meaningful for him. They all focus their prophecies on Christ, whether specializing in the Nativity, the Passion, the miracles, or the Last Judgment (respectively in the sets of twelve, the Lactantius tradition as in Rimini, Perugino, and Botticelli) or whether avoiding such specialities in favor of a complete range (as in Siena and quite possibly in Giovanni Pisano). In every series all the sibyls share the same message like a chorus, or like a scholar's footnote in which he builds up authority for his own conclusion. The fact that they do not make different points is conspicuous in the speeches of the mystery plays. Even when they survey all of Christ's mission, as in Siena, several sibyls make each point. This is most consistent with Lactantius, for whom the prophecies are not linked to specific sibyls.

In the sets of twelve, each sibyl is assigned a particular saying, yet they all praise the Nativity. Dotson, whose study of the two traditions is most thorough, concluded that in the twelve-sibyl type, "with one exception to be discussed below, each sibyl always has the same text in images," that exception apparently being the frequent substitution, in the case of Erythraea, of her longer *Vaticinium* passage, also about the Nativity. However, in the details Dotson then presents, the standard formula, that of the Orsini lists, is varied in five of the sets discussed by her most in detail, involving six of the twelve sibyls. Only Pinturicchio seems to be entirely faithful, in two of his three sets.[40] Nevertheless, her conclusion is surely right as to general effect.

Dotson also concludes that the set of twelve is the dominant one in this period; she writes, "A few Renaissance representations of sibyls are accompanied by texts . . . apparently (from) Lactantius . . . but most, . . . in fifteenth and early sixteenth century art, both in Italy and northern Europe, are supplied with the Orsini oracles." That is quite true as stated, but it can be much qualified. The Orsini texts do dominate the mystery plays, since they are about the Nativity or the related story of

Augustus; passion plays seem not to include sibyls. As noted, the "popular art" preference for this type also includes the Florentine prints. It may also dominate in northern Europe, notably in illuminated manuscripts, an area less studied since Mâle. In Italian painting and sculpture, however, the twelve-set's importance is diminished in that it is most often seen in an abbreviated form, especially in the fours of chapel vaults.

A survey of the fuller sets—unsurprisingly less numerous—whether independent works or coequal subsets in larger monuments, would comprise the lost Orsini room by Masolino, the Rimini sculptures, the Botticellian panels, the Siena pavement, the Borgia apartment, and the Perugino frescoes, with a possible predecessor in the Giovanni Pisano pulpits. These also have in common that they are inventive works by prominent artists and are not in contexts of the Nativity. Of these just two, the Orsini room itself and its successor by Pinturicchio, use the Orsini list. As noted, the Siena scries uses it in minor part, just as conversely the chapel vaults with four sibyls sometimes use the Lactantius texts in minor part.

The importance of all this is that it bears on what message Michelangelo's sibyls send. If the Orsini set of twelve was indeed dominant, then it would be likely that Michelangelo was using it too. That tradition (and not the other) tends to give each particular sibyl one saying that remains hers, and one could then treat Michelangelo's sibyls as saying knowable and distinguishable things. This is Dotson's main proposal. However, the fact that all the sayings simply present the Nativity introduces a difficulty, for the individuality of different sibyls, established in this way, is very limited, and can only be enhanced by paying attention, as Dotson proposes, to "their other prophecies," that is, the parts of their sayings that allude to other matters, different in each case. This idea suggests that Michelangelo was not only focusing on their secondary concerns but making the sibyls have a message unlike that of all previous sibyls in the sets of twelve, which was the Nativity. The first sibyl, Persica, may illustrate how Dotson would do this. Her saying, in the Orsini list, reads in full:

> Behold, O Beast, you will be trampled, and the lord will be given birth [*gignetur*] on the earth [*in orbem terrarum*] and the womb of

a Virgin will be the salvation of peoples, and his feet will be the
health of man.

As in the rest, the Nativity is certainly the main thrust. Dotson emphasizes the phrases about the beast and the theme of a glorious advent,
which are indeed different from what the other sibyls say. The beast is
the same, she suggests, as the one in Revelation 13:1, though he is not
trampled there, just the opposite. The link is the single word. Persica's
prophecy, through this, is held to be about the world ending. She is also
to be associated with her neighbor on the ceiling, the prophet Daniel,
who, in the one text of his that Augustine emphasized in the same part
of the City of God where he cites the sibyls, had prophesied Christ's
coming in glory; Dotson takes note that Daniel elsewhere prophesies
the end of the world. So Persica, who here is held to prophesy the "final
trial symbolized by the beast," goes on in the last part of her saying to
prophesy the "triumphant appearance of the Lord."[41] This interpretation depends on translating *gignetur* not as "being born," the literal
sense certainly meant by previous users of sibyl sayings, but figuratively as "brought forth" in glory. The end of the world does not, however,
appear on the Sistine ceiling, and Dotson explains that the nearby scene
of God creating the world is a prophecy of it. She offers similar readings
of all nine scenes, in which the future event correlated with each is held
to be the one the sibyls foretell in those phrases of their Nativity sayings
that differ among themselves.

This means that there is no longer a problem in the fact that the
sibyls lived later than the events in the nine scenes of Genesis. They
could, to be sure, prophesy in the ordinary ways events seen elsewhere
in the chapel, including their usual theme of Christ's accomplishments,
shown lower in the fifteenth-century cycle on the wall. Dotson, like
Tolnay and others, treats Michelangelo's part of the chapel as entirely
self-contained. Art history, which tends to use artists' styles as the starting point, may here dubiously confer a further separateness as to religious meaning on the part of the chapel imagery that is the product of
that style. We may look differently if we presume that a pious viewer
would tend to read the messages in terms of the whole chapel around
him. If the sibyls all prophesied the Nativity, in a way familiar at the

84

time, they could prophesy a fresco of the Nativity on the wall by Perugino. It is however, part of a set of eight scenes of Christ's life ending with the Resurrection; one might then be more inclined to see the sibyls, ranged all along the ceiling, prophesying the whole of that lower cycle. This would match what the sibyls certainly do in the Siena pavement, and would evidently meet the expectations of a moderately educated viewer. This formula seems to have nothing to bar it. However, if it is postulated that each sibyl named makes a distinct prophecy, then we must turn away from Lactantius (used in Siena) and take the distinctive Orsini materials, modulating them further to focus on what they say not about the Nativity.

The reading here preferred, that these sibyls like others are a chorus, reinforcing each other, rather than a series of varied soloists, might also be doubted on another basis, starting from Michelangelo's unique style. He makes his sibyls grandly different in type and pose, and it may be that these differences extend to their messages. (Dotson, however, does not correlate her suggested messages with the particular visual qualities of each sibyl.) The alternate reaction is that it simply was visually desirable to make the chorus members vary visually, rather than be uniform in a way suggested by their single message. Vasari, whose aesthetic reflects the culture of Michelangelo, praised the sibyls and prophets for their "varied attitudes, beauty of textiles, variety of dress, all in sum with miraculous invention and judgment, so that they seem divine to one who distinguishes their emotions."[42] Indeed, faced (if he was) with numerous figures all meaning the same thing, the artist would certainly be pressed to keep inventing new visual characteristics, as he did also in the nudes above and elsewhere.

When we ask why Michelangelo chose from the sibyls the particular five whose names he gives, we seem again to be led to the choral interpretation. The five are simply the first five on Lactantius' list, although that has not been obvious. As normally presented, the first five would be Persica, Libica, Delphica, Cimmeria, and Erythraea; Michelangelo has no Cimmeria, choosing instead Cumaea, who is seventh. However, Cumaea replaces Cimmeria as fourth not only in some Lactantius manuscripts, as noted by Migne and then by Dotson, but also in the first printed edition in 1465; this explains why the sequence also places her fourth in the Botticellian panels, which has been considered a puzzle.[43] It was observed above that the first three in order comprise Perugino's back row, surely chosen as a generic chorus. To take Michelangelo as intending separate messages, one would have to say that the messages he wanted matched by chance the first five names encountered.[44] The random order in which he arranges them also matches the Siena pavement and again suggests interchangeability.

Support for the view that the figures are all making their usual prophecies about Christ comes from the single case of one of the prophets, Jonah, on which all viewers have concurred as to the message meant. He foretells Christ's resurrection (one of the eight scenes on the wall below, at the opposite end of the room). The New Testament alludes to Jonah only once, when Christ remarks that "as Jonas was three days and three nights in the whale's belly, so shall the son of man be three days and three nights in the heart of the earth" (Matthew 12:40). Such rare cases when the New Testament actually picks up something from the Old were naturally the optimum cases for claiming that the latter was prophetic, and gave each such prophecy one unambiguous reference forward.

Michelangelo's imagery differs from the great majority of earlier sets of sibyls in the nearly equal balance with prophets in one set. Sibyls had appeared either by themselves or with lesser status than the accompanying prophets most of the time. The rare precedents for equality include one of the mystery plays (from Revello in Piedmont), Pinturicchio's Borgia room, and Perugino's fresco with six of each.[45] Those precedents in painting quite likely were known to Michelangelo and gave him general validation, but he does not match them in detail, choosing notably quite different prophets. Apart from the inevitable four major prophets, Michelangelo's three choices from among the twelve minor prophets, Jonah, Zachariah, and Joel, do not appear at all in Perugino's set, and only Zachariah, the one whose book was the longest, is in Pinturicchio's.

86   A likely clue to Michelangelo's message is this choice of the three minor prophets. As indicated, they were optional, unlike the major ones, and unusual, while unlike the sibyls they are unambiguously

attached to differing statements. In the case of Jonah it was seen that his prophetic message could be firmly identified as just one, the Resurrection. The major prophets, so called ever since Augustine because they wrote long books and appear in the biblical sequence before the others, made many prophecies, so one cannot be sure which is meant (while one can prove almost any hypothesis from among them). It is notable that Michelangelo placed his minor prophets at the extreme ends of the ceiling in two cases, Jonah and Zachariah, and that the third, Joel, is immediately next to Zachariah at the lesser end, near the entrance, while the major prophets are in the middle. This would seem intentional, suggesting lower status at the ends. (It is also at the ends that there are no sibyls and no scenes including women.)

Zachariah also made many prophecies, and so he may not be helpful either; his book is even a little longer than that of one major prophet, Daniel. A helpful check is provided by a work very popular in the fifteenth century, the *Biblia Pauperum.* It consists of woodcuts of forty incidents related to Christ's life and achievements, each supplied with four prophecies from the Old Testament. Ten of the incidents are shown to have been prophesied by Zachariah (as against only one by Jonah).[46] Such multivalency is a warning against taking a verse from a prophet's book as the intended message, a not uncommon procedure in the literature.

Jonah's single prophecy is isolated not only in the New Testament and the *Biblia,* but also in Augustine's survey of prophecies about Christ. Augustine sets him apart by remarking that he prophesied not in speaking but "in suffering." That may well match the way Michelangelo (and Ghiberti before him) shows only this prophet with no book or scroll but with an attribute of his story, the whale.

Joel is similarly univalent, with only one prophecy in Augustine and in the *Biblia Pauperum,* the same one that is his only text directly cited in the New Testament. Augustine underlines this uniqueness by saying of Joel "one of his I will not omit" (18:30). The passage is the only place in the Bible where the word "Joel" appears, outside his own book. One may then expect that a viewer in the Sistine Chapel, seeing the label "Joel," would recall that prophecy too, unless he recalled nothing. It is attached to him consistently on scrolls in images, such as the Orsini room of three hundred famous men and in two of Pinturicchio's Borgia apartments. Augustine quotes it at length:

> Your sons and daughters shall prophesy, and your old men shall dream dreams, and your young men see visions. Even upon the servants and the handmaids in those days will I pour my spirit. (Joel 2:28–29)

It is in Acts 2 that this passage is cited by St. Peter, when the disciples at Pentecost spoke in tongues and were jeered at by those who said "these men are full of new wine." Peter's defense was that they were fulfilling Joel's prophecy, and so Joel has become the prophet of Pentecost. However, no Pentecost scene is on the walls of the Sistine Chapel, and no scholar seems to have argued that this is what Michelangelo's Joel signifies.[47] Certainly when the text came in the nineteenth century to warrant a place in Bartlett's *Familiar Quotations* its link to Pentecost had long been discarded. That had not happened in the sixteenth, but in biblical commentary we can find its message extended; if Joel is univalent, his one text is not univocal. It has been found to be interesting because it is perhaps the main statement on the phenomenon of prophesying itself, as distinguished from specific prophesies. In the Sistine Chapel we are so concerned with all kinds of prophesying that this reason for the presence of Joel, the oddest of the choices, comes too naturally to be excluded.

The text fits the ceiling even more neatly because it speaks of both men and women as prophets, exactly what we see here to such a rare degree. That this analogy was not triggered by seeing Joel seems implausible. The text not only suggests the equality of men and women but, in its second sentence, that gentiles prophesy, also as seen in our series. This draws us away from Pentecost, where only men spoke. If this seems like extrapolating too much, it is nicely confirmed by a writer in 1509 who, ignoring Pentecost, instead made the verses the backing for another idea. Cornelius Agrippa tells us, in his book on the *Nobility and Superiority of the Female Sex*, that women are wrongfully suppressed from roles in civic life, as in lawsuits and administration. They are "even excluded from preaching the word of God, in contradiction to scripture where the Holy Ghost, through the mouth of Joel, promised them:

'Your daughters also will prophesy.' " He continues further upbraiding men for acting contrary to this divine command.[48] This author wrote his book in France but then passed the years 1511–1517 in northern Italy, where his main activity was to lecture on Plato's *Symposium* and on Hermes Trismegistus. He thus belongs to the culture derived from Ficino that also in good part formed Michelangelo.

When we consider the general planning of the ceiling, after the change from the original idea of twelve apostles (to be considered below), we find that the choice fell instead on prophets and sibyls—still twelve figures, but less usual ones. While wondering why that was, we may be helped by postulating as probable that this choice was antecedent to the selection of the particular prophets and sibyls; the reverse would be difficult. When we see that the sibyls are simply the first five on Lactantius' list, as printed, we may infer as more likely than not that single choices were not of concern; the choice of the four major prophets may be viewed as similarly ordinary, even automatic. The three minor prophets instead had to be selected from among the twelve the biblical books provide. Jonah, all agree, alludes to the Resurrection, thus supporting the impression that the general point is to prophesy Christ's career; Zachariah is available to prophesy many of its events, so that, even if we are unable to pick the right one, there is no awkward issue. Joel alone is problematic, a truly rare choice in the period, with one meaning that does not seem to fit. Hence when we find that he can also be understood as asserting prophesying, by men and women, the main activity of these very prophets and sibyls who had been newly chosen for this revised program, there seems no reason to reject this comfortable fit. It matches the even rarer choice of pairs of putti and putte on the thrones, in indicating what was being thought about.

If such concerns could be found in only one of the ceiling's sets of images, they would be dubious. The other major set with rare themes is composed of the four corners, the one place where such rarity coincides with complexity of composition and narrative. Though the themes of Esther saving the Jews and Moses with the brazen serpent are neither obscure nor rare, they have not been found to have appeared together earlier in one set, reinforcing each other as here. The other two

89

Figure 7: Michelangelo, *Death of Haman,* fresco, corner lunette, Sistine Ceiling, Vatican

Figure 8: Michelangelo, *Drunkenness of Noah*, fresco, Sistine Ceiling, Vatican

themes, at the other end of the ceiling, of David killing Goliath and Judith killing Holofernes, were quite famous Old Testament stories, and they had been actively associated with each other. That seems not to have happened in the visual arts in the Middle Ages, where images of David consistently show the mature king, but they were notably linked in fifteenth-century Florence. Most famously, Donatello's bronze David, often seen by the boy Michelangelo in the courtyard of the Medici palace, had a powerful match in the same artist's bronze Judith, given somewhat lesser status in the garden behind. Ghiberti's bronze Doors of Paradise show Judith in the frame next to the large scene of David killing Goliath, whose specific layout has rightly been called the closest precedent for Michelangelo's. Judith seems to be David's full equal in one less famous Florentine fresco, to be discussed.

The unusual layout of Michelangelo's scene of Judith, as I have suggested elsewhere,[49] survives from an earlier plan to show her in a lunette, where her action of going down a step would be convenient. The scheme in the David scene, where the villain appears front and center, reappears in the Esther scene and, in a modified way, in that of the brazen serpent. All agree that the four scenes make the same point of heroes of the Old Testament defeating evil enemies of the Jews and thus prophesying Christ's salvation of all men. In the Esther scene, the villain Haman still seems to throb while tied to a tree, whose branches make it the cross the Vulgate specified.[50] The three other main characters in the story, Esther, whose decisiveness defeated Haman, her counsellor and foster father, Mordecai, and King Ahasuerus, whom she persuaded to order the condemnation, occupy the three extreme corners of Michelangelo's triangular field, seeming to give visual form to Dante's account of "one crucified" and the other three, whom he names, "around him (fig. 7)." Esther, leaning forward intently, is the smallest. This motif, of the small background figure setting in motion the events that end in destroying the foreground villain, was appreciated by Raphael, who adopted it one year later in his large *Expulsion of Heliodorus,* again an enemy destroyed at the behest of the tiny priest seen far back.

The hero of the fourth scene, Moses, is not shown at all, though from Vasari on he has always been named in allusions to it. We know

91

the story not so much from the Old Testament account of the event (Numbers 21) as from Christ's citation of it (John 3: 14–15): "As Moses lifted up the serpent in the wilderness, even so must the Son of Man be lifted up, that whosoever believeth in Him should not perish, but have eternal life." This has always been taken as Christ's own prophecy of his salvific crucifixion, and as asserting that it in turn was prophesied in the case of the serpent. God, we are told in Numbers, had sent fiery serpents to punish the Jews in the desert for complaining about him. On their appeal against this to Moses, he is instructed by God to "make a fiery serpent and set it on a pole," after which those who look at it are cured of their bites. Christ's quotation requires us to treat the pole as a cross, easier for readers of the Latin Vulgate, which omits the words "on a pole." Despite that, commentators of course discussed the pole, and Michelangelo shows it. As Haman's tree, another quasi-crucifix, is in the center of that fresco, the pole is in this. The parallel has to overcome the paradox that the serpent on the pole, made of bronze, was salvific, the opposite of the real ones. That the evil fiery serpents become homeo-pathically good on the pole is easier to follow in the Hebrew, since the same word is used where we have first "fiery" and then "bronze" (i.e., produced by firing), so that, as with Haman, the impaling of evil brings good. The two scenes thus make a pair, if a new one, which in analogy to the prior pair of David and Judith again matches a male and a female hero. The case of the prophets and sibyls and their putti thus recurs.

The nine central scenes of Genesis had a weight of tradition making them least open to novelties, yet there is a powerful one at the center. Among the three subsets of three scenes each, the first, at the altar end near Jonah, is of course all male, where God creates the world in three phases. The third set of Noah is all male in only one of its three scenes, of the drunken Noah and his sons, at the furthest end near the entrance (fig. 8). The rarest subject of the nine is a family event, the sacrifice of thanksgiving after the flood, where Noah, his wife, his three sons, and three daughters-in-law all play busy roles, as if at a picnic (fig. 9). The par-ticipation of the women is not indicated in the text (Genesis 8:20), where the sacrifice is performed only by Noah and God thanks him and his sons only. The wives are mentioned nearby only when the eight people all exit

Figure 9: Michelangelo, *Sacrifice of Noah*, fresco, Sistine Ceiling, Vatican

Figure 10: Michelangelo, *The Temptation* (detail), fresco, Sistine Ceiling, Vatican

from the ark, in verse 18. Ghiberti in the Doors of Paradise included them in the sacrifice scene, as if reinforcing their nearby appearance in the scene of exit, yet they only watch the men sacrificing. Michelangelo promotes them to participants, giving them something like the priestly role Agrippa claimed for women on the basis of Joel's prophecy.

The scene of the flood makes them even more emphatic, especially in the foreground. Nearest us, a woman with a melancholy expression and very full breasts perhaps alludes to the absence of her child. That is suggested by the contrast with the nearby giant mother in charge of two infants; this single parent is the most emphasized of the very many people in the scene. Of several couples nearby, one comprises a man carrying a woman on his back, a second is an embracing pair, and furthest left a woman is helping a child while a man, barely visible at the frame, holds it steady. There is only one notable group of two men, the old one carrying his dead adult son. The two first women are in Michelangelo's oeuvre the most noticeably muscled, a point to be explored shortly.

The middle subset of three scenes of Adam and Eve has inevitable gender balance, and perhaps is the point of departure for all the other cases so far observed. One fresco is devoted to the creation of each of them, and they sin and are expelled together in the third. There is greater male emphasis only in that the frame of the *Creation of Adam* is larger, in the alternating system of the scenes. Novelty appears in the showing the two sinners. Most images naturally follow the account in Genesis 3, where the serpent tempts Eve, who eats the fruit, then "gave also to her husband," who eats it too. In the Doors of Paradise, a typical representation of the same four events (and only those) as in Michelangelo's three frescoes, Eve hands Adam the apple. Though Ghiberti is always noted as the closest model for Michelangelo's *Creation of Adam,* as to the interaction of figures, the sin is shown very differently. The other model most often cited for Michelangelo's *Temptation,* Jacopo della Quercia's marble relief, similarly shows the dialogue of Eve with the serpent while Adam is only an onlooker. In the Sistine Chapel, however, in what seems to be an unprecedented initiative, Adam reaches pressingly to get an apple from the tree. There is no way to see him getting one from Eve, or even learning about its delights from her, for she is just now receiving it in her hand. Thus Adam takes a new initiative in sin; when, for once, the male figure is given novel emphasis over the female, it is when he commits original sin (fig. 10).

The important role of Adam in the sin was of course understood, as evoked in the child's rhyme: "In Adam's fall, we sinned all." Yet it always was stipulated to follow Eve's. Part of what made Adam's sin important was that here, as seen before, the Old Testament was being read in terms of how it foretold the New. (This is not at all specific to the Sistine Chapel, but routine in the period.) The New Testament analogue was naturally Christ's Temptation, because Christ was the "second Adam" (1 Corinthians 15:45–47), but of course by contraries: "As in Adam all die, even so in Christ shall all be made alive" (verse 22, same chapter). That Christ had not succumbed to temptation thus did not diminish the analogy. A theologian, in mentioning the earlier case as analogous to Christ's, would properly specify that the serpent overcame Adam "through Eve,"[51] but such a popular text as the *Biblia Pauperum* cut this down to "the serpent overcame Adam." The accompanying woodcut simply shows both Adam and Eve standing with apples in hand, which evades the issue of referring Adam's sin back to Eve. One can read it as allowing for that, as in the Bible text, or concerned only with Adam as sinner, as the caption does. The latter reading provides a simpler link to the adjacent image of Christ tempted. The most famous earlier Florentine image of Adam and Eve sinning, Masolino's fresco in the Brancacci Chapel, also shows them each standing with an apple. In rare cases, Adam does act; he takes the apple directly from the snake in a panel of 1387 by the German Master Betram, somewhat as in Michelangelo, but Eve is eating and pointing out the snake to Adam, making her still the persuader.[52] In Michelangelo's scheme, we cannot blame Eve at all for what Adam does as he sins. One might perhaps do so by stipulating that the scene shows them in two moments, Adam's reaching gesture being later, and a basis for such a claim would be that the same fresco also shows the later Expulsion. No one, however, has ever interpreted the fresco in that way. Thus, to repeat, when Michelangelo for once innovates to make a male figure more vigorous than before, it is to show him as evil and to absolve the woman.

95

Although thinking of Adam's sin was evoked by the link to Christ's Temptation, Michelangelo is not focusing on foretelling the New Testament event. That incident is shown on the wall below in an odd miniature form, behind a different incident, and the bracketing on the ceiling of the Temptation and Expulsion from Eden also works away from such a standard allusion. Instead, the effect of exculpating Eve, which seems so unusual, is an idea that was discussed in Michelangelo's time in the same context that quoted Joel with a feminist spin. The case of Eve was far more important, for in mainstream theology her sin was the reason given first in misogynist claims for the subordination of women. A dialogue of 1516, "In Defense of the Female Sex," denies that Eve enticed Adam, just as Michelangelo does. It points out that both had free will, and Adam was the worse, because God had issued the prohibition on eating the fruit only to him. Hence Adam rightly got a greater punishment, extending from him to all humanity.[53] Agrippa had made the same point in 1509 in much more detail:

> Man, not woman, had been forbidden to eat the fruit. . . . God wanted her to be free from the start, so it was man, not woman, who sinned in eating, man, not woman, who brought in death, and we have all sinned in Adam, not Eve, and are charged with original sin not through the fault of our mother, a woman, but of our father, a man. . . . God did not punish the woman for eating, but having given man the occasion to eat, which she did from ignorance, tempted by the serpent. Man sinned in full knowledge, woman fell into error in ignorance and because she was abused. For it was she that the serpent tempted first, knowing she was the most excellent of creatures.

This text goes on, even more remarkably, to explain that Christ chose to be incarnated as a male out of humility, to expiate the first father's sin. All this, which in our culture may seem quaintly scholastic, for that era had the force that might, for instance, pertain to denying the class struggle or the Oedipus complex in a culture where these were orthodox postulates. Agrippa returns to the matter again to assert that we all have been subjected to sin and to death "in Adam, not in Eve."[54]

96

Michelangelo's unique image makes Eve the less intent on sinning of the two, as the text makes her sin the less. Still earlier, in quattrocento Italy, the issue of whose sin was the greater, Eve's or Adam's, had been argued between two humanists.[55]

Besides the nine Genesis stories and the four in the corners, just one other subset of Sistine frescoes involves groups of interactive figures. These are the ancestors of Christ, and here the role of women is even more prominent and more original. In short, the phenomenon pervades the whole. The series of the ancestors will be discussed in a separate chapter. Here, it need only be pointed out that the new role of the ancestresses has a simple explanation in its relation to the nearby subset of the Genesis stories. Adam and Eve had been shown together, but, more unusually, so had Noah and his wife, and Noah's sons with theirs. One of these couples, Shem and his wife, are already ancestors of Christ. The women in Noah's family are equal to their husbands, Noah and his wife sharing the position behind the altar of sacrifice. The role of the later ancestresses is simply a continuation.

Of the forty generations of ancestors in the eight spandrels and sixteen lunettes, the females have an equal role in all the spandrels and in fourteen of the sixteen lunettes. They lack that role in just those two lunettes to which more than two generations of ancestors are assigned, three in one case and four in the other, and thus are crowded and abbreviated, for reasons to be discussed in the next chapter. The abbreviation inevitably selects the men, whom the biblical text names, and there are only two women with the three men and only one with the four. This exceptional case has gone unnoticed since these lunettes are the only part of the Sistine complex that no longer exists, Michelangelo having destroyed them to make space for the *Last Judgment*. Though he did so for this reason, he may not have regretted as much the disappearance of these images where he had not followed his preferred procedure.[56] By contrast, the eight spandrels not only all include the ancestresses, but as they were executed one after the other they tended more and more to show women not equal but dominant, culminating in the two of the fifth bay; there the men appear only in shadows behind their wives' shoulders. The eight spandrels are in the center of the room, the same area where women also are prominent as sibyls and in the cases of Eve and Noah's family, as against the male-dominated ends.

The emphasis on women seems to increase from the top down. In the top area with the nine scenes they are important only in five; among the prophets and sibyls they account for five out of twelve and for half of the putti on the thrones; finally the ancestors show women equally, except in two lunettes and dominantly in all eight spandrels. The only all-male subsets on the ceiling are the very small circular medallions, the famous large nudes over the thrones, and the smaller similar pairs of decorative nudes in triangles.

All this emphasis cannot have occurred by accident, making it the more surprising that it seems never to have been spoken about. In this period such major roles for women were rare, but less rare than has been thought. Jordan has surveyed a very broad range of feminist writing in sixteenth-century Europe. She shows that two types of argument in favor of women's equality were dominant. The first was to show spiritual equality, and in this the case of Eve played a key role.[57] Erasmus was among many writers who discussed this topic, sometimes accepting it and sometimes much qualifying it. The second is about virility in women, arguing that every point that is usually cited in men to prove them superior also occurs in women. Some writers find that this is true only of exceptional women, while others widen it, for instance to include all widows (because of their economic independence) or to all women. It is also argued that if this is not widely realized, it is because men have written history.[58] Virility takes all kinds of forms. In the most famous discussion of the status of women in the period, Castiglione's *Courtier,* the debater supporting women says they can do everything men can, and illustrates this point not in the ways we might expect, but in speaking of rulers of states, generals—with Joan of Arc featured—and even women wrestlers, carrying the argument to the enemy by citing the few cases that would most often be viewed as really restricted to males.[59]

Michelangelo's sharing of just this view is shown in a poem of the 1540s to Vittoria Colonna, his great spititual guide, which begins: "A man, within a woman, no, a god, speaks through her mouth." Later in a letter that enclosed a copy he wrote of her: "Death took a great friend

Figure 11: Michelangelo, *Cumaean sibyl*, fresco, Sistine Ceiling, Vatican

from me," using the male form *amico*.[60] Her inspired speech is her spiritual leadership, the male identity her virility. The women in the ceiling show virility in the famous musculature, like Castiglione's wrestlers. It is most notable in the aged crone, the Cumaean sibyl (fig. 11). The most ingenuous visitor is struck by this emphasis. It derives first, in a technical sense, from the use of only male models in life drawing in this period, so that we also find female figures in the paintings of Andrea del Sarto and Raphael based on their drawings from the male model. The society did not approve of posing by women. Michelangelo differs in that the male qualities are still plain in the resulting paintings, but only selectively. On the ceiling, they are seen most vividly in the Cumaean and Libyan sibyls and in the mothers in the flood mentioned above, not at all in the ancestresses of Christ. These latter run a wide gamut of feminine effects from the bony housewife of Eliezer-Mathan to the sweetly turning, long-necked youthfulness of Akim-Eliud and the sharply observant coquette of Jacob-Joseph. Indeed only a minority of all the women shows male characteristics, but they have often been assigned by popular writers to Michelangelo's women in general. They are shown in those women who are presented as powerful, whether in prophecy or in coping with the deluge, and not in more ordinary figures. The phenomenon has also been linked often to another impression common in a wide public since it emerged in England in the late nineteenth century, that of Michelangelo as a homosexual. A check on the representation of women by artists of the same period who were involved in homosexual activities, Leonardo and Cellini, shows nothing like this, and there seems no basis for the theory.

What generated the special approach to the role of women on the ceiling? Our earliest information about how the project took form is in a letter by Michelangelo, in 1523, to a man who was helping him to deal with finances and clients in Rome. Going back to his early negotiations concerning the ceiling, he mentions how Pope Julius II had given him the ceiling to do, and that "the first design was of twelve apostles in the lunettes, and the rest ornament, in the usual way." Yet soon "it seemed to me that this would turn out a poor thing, and I told the pope," who "gave me a new commission that I should do as I wished," and this produced the final work.[61]

This report conflicts with conventional wisdom that in this era artists (although it is not suggested about poets) received detailed directions about their work from patrons, going beyond general titles often to details of symbolic messages. There is little actual basis for this formula, which has produced many iconographic and patronage studies. Better evidence suggests rather than patrons were much concerned about making a grand impression, something that could be achieved by elaboration or by securing an outstanding artist.[62] Such values in the culture are indeed suggested by the quoted report, in that the artist would be persuasive in seeking changes by claiming the old plan was poor, and that he would then go ahead. The accuracy of the story is supported by the existence of a Michelangelo drawing showing a scheme with apostles. Most writers indeed have accepted that this happened, but have then added that, if not instructed by the patron, Michelangelo probably, or for some "unquestionably," brought in a theologian to advise him. The basis for this conclusion is the other postulate that there is a complicated allusive message. This opinion is widespread, but the particular message has never been agreed on, leaving many competing theories. Each thus may be doubted, and none seems to have focused on explaining those elements in the imagery that depart from the usual, such as the part played by the women of Noah's family in the sacrifice.

A support for the presence of complex symbolism in the Sistine Chapel has been claimed in a text of 1510, alluding to the wall narratives in it. Quoted in English, it states that "the more erudite the paintings in a Cardinal's chapel" the better, as they stimulate imitation of the actions shown. The Sistine walls and also the chapel of Filippino Lippi, cited above for its sibyls, are the instances given. Not in a chapel, but in a "summer room," the same author recommends "riddles and fables" to "sharpen the intelligence." After quoting these phrases, Dotson summarizes that they call for "erudite and complex" paintings, and takes the Sistine as an example of such "stimulating complexity," though complexity was not mentioned.[63] "Erudition" was, but it is not notable in the cited chapel by Filippino, whose Annunciation and other scenes seem not to have been claimed to extend to levels of meaning beyond the plain ones. The

101

sentence before those quoted seems even less indicative in that way; it says images of Madonnas and lives of saints are those that "ought to be approved most." The instances given are saints working in a kitchen or in a garden, to inculcate humility, and no others. How such works could be called "erudite" is explained by referring back to the opening of this chapter, where the word *eruditio* occurred and was rendered by the recent English translator not as erudition but "lesson." Viewers are said to be drawn to paintings that benefit them through "lessons of history brought to life." Indeed simple "instruction" is the basic dictionary sense of the Latin *eruditio;* this is a case like many where the rich English language has several words with related meanings and assigns to one with a Latin root the grander aspect, using *eruditio* for erudition, although the original in Latin also embraced the humbler one. Transliteration is then deceptive. The text of 1510 urges, actually, an old formula, found in Thomas Aquinas and often recurring up to 1500, on the usefulness of religious art, emphasizing the stimulus it may offer to devotion and to following the example of saints.[64] As this text of 1510 was the only one offered to show complexity as a norm for paintings at the time, we may instead adopt it on further inspection to see the Sistine imagery more simply. (It asks that the "summer room" show pictures of "mathematical instruments" like hydraulic machines, maps, rare animals, and finally the "riddles and fables" mentioned. Visual riddles and fables appear in the drawings of Leonardo da Vinci, along with maps and machines, as pictograms or rebuses, like those on the puzzle pages of newspapers today.[65] This is the "brain sharpening" the text recommends.)

Studies of patrons' concerns have not taken advantage of what we do learn from Michelangelo's report, that the patron, the pope, wanted the twelve apostles. That was on the lines of an ordinary scheme for a vault with twelve sections. The pope was familiar with such a series in the Borgia apartments, where he had lived until 1507 and where Pinturicchio had shown the same figures with texts of the apostles' creed. That this was simple and not a special doctrinal statement seems confirmed by his willingness to let it go.

102

How Michelangelo proposed to make it all less poor is seen in what he did, which was to shift from single rows of figures to narratives. This

was the most honored kind of painting from the fifteenth to the nineteenth century, especially from artists' viewpoints. They were not often
shown on ceilings before this, though it goes too far to say that never happened. A conspicuous if distant precedent was the mosaic cycle in the
dome of the Baptistery of Florence, including stories of Adam and Eve.

This would add richness, but the replacement of the twelve apostles
by the equal number of prophets and sibyls did not. It seems reasonable
that the latter seemed more harmonious than apostles with the Genesis
stories, because they belonged also to that earlier era. Genesis stories, it
has commonly been agreed, were chosen here over others because of
the convention that time is shown from the top down, and so events had
to be selected earlier than those on the wall of Moses. But then why not
twelve prophets, an easier shift from the twelve apostles? That is, why
sibyls in alternation? If the nine central narratives were chosen first, and
the novel approach to the exculpation of Eve was involved in that, as it
seems it must have been, the sibyls and the pairs of putti of both sexes
would seem to follow.

A humanist or theological adviser may indeed have been involved,
solicited by the artist on these questions. He need not perhaps have been
a famous leader of thought, but someone the artist knew who had ideas
like Agrippa's. The ideas do not seem so complex as to require inventing a superstructure to account for what we see.

In the visual culture of Renaissance Florence there had been one famous Genesis cycle, on the Doors of Paradise by Ghiberti, still a tourist
attraction second to few. Vasari called it "the most beautiful work in the
world, ancient or modern." To be sure, it is almost antithetical in style
to Michelangelo in its curvilinear thinness and ornamental grace. Yet
Tolnay and others have repeatedly shown that Michelangelo used its
compositions whenever possible, in the stories of Adam and Eve, Noah,
and David. The narratives of Ghiberti have in their frames twenty single figures in five rows at the sides, in addition to Adam and Eve at the
top and Noah and his wife at the bottom. Of the twenty, five are female,
one in fact in every row with three men, which suggests intention. 103
Vasari called the female figures sibyls, and it seems that two of them are.
This would also have offered Michelangelo a comfortable model, on

Figure 12 a: *Judith, Miriam, Esther, and Ruth,* vault, Orsanmichele, Florence

Figure 12 b: *David, Moses, Joshua, and Judas Maccabeus,* vault, fresco, Orsanmichele, Florence

which he greatly expanded. The scheme for the doors provided by Leonardo Bruni included no women; they would thus belong to the later definitive plan, which Ghiberti wrote that he had made himself.

Florentine painting also provided a model for equal male and female images, in fact one that shows them on a large scale in frescoes in the vault of a famous church, yet today virtually overlooked and largely un-published, a startling phenomenon itself. That it continues to remain unnoticed while feminist studies develop is even more surprising; it may well have to do with the anonymity of the works, since the history of Florentine painting is strongly involved with known personalities.

The cycle is at Orsanmichele, most famous for the sculptures out-side by Donatello, Ghiberti, and others (figs. 12a, 12b). The church has the rare structural quality of forming two equal aisles, reflecting its prior secular use. This lent itself, one may suggest, to the segregation of male and female worshipers on the two equal sides; such segregation, as in Orthodox Jewish synagogues today, is known from various casual records.[66] Each aisle has three bays, and the one study of the frescoes has rightly noted that these are assigned in succession to persons of the era before the law, that is, before Moses, to those in the era of the law, and to those of the Christian era of grace.[67] In the first bay, the triangular section showing Adam is matched with one showing Eve, and similar-ly Noah, Abraham, and Jacob are matched with Noah's wife, Sarah, and Rachel. In the next bay the similar pairs are David and Judith, Moses and Miriam, Joshua and Esther, and Ruth with Judas Maccabeus. (This David and Judith may be the only precedent for Michelangelo's giving them equal emphasis, and it even occurs in a triangular fresco vault like his.) In the third bay not all the figures are identifiable—there is a very wide choice—beyond Christ, the Baptist, and the Virgin.[68]

These anonymous works of about 1400 were also part of Michelangelo's early casual culture. Thus even the imagery of equality among religious heroes was available. It may not have required a great deal of theological counsel after all.

1. J. Wilde, *Michelangelo, Six Lectures*, 1978, 56.

2. C. de Tolnay, *Michelangelo*, 2:1945, 168–169, gives a thorough survey of prior opinions.

3. F. Mancinelli et al., *Michelangelo e la Sistina*, 1990, 141–143. The author of the entry on this drawing, A. Nesselrath, rightly points out the puzzle of how Raphael would have been able to see the small figures so high up, debating between the floor and the scaffolding. Another possibility is that he saw the drawing, discussed below.

4. H. Thode, *Michelangelo: Kritische Untersuchungen*, 1:1908, 410–414. He called the two putti on Isaiah's throne both female. While the outline of the genital area of one is triangular and the other sacklike, the latter has no forms inside that outline, which explains Thode's deduction. The real reason for this emptiness is perhaps that the drawing used was done in an abbreviated way, as seen in other drawings associated with Michelangelo (e.g., those reproduced by L. Dussler, *Die Zeichnungen des Michelangelo*, 1959, figs. 120, 121). Thode calls the two on Libyca's throne both male. One is seen from the back, and his reason seems to be that they are seen wrestling, with equal energy. Such activity by females was not alien to Michelangelo's thinking, as discussed below. Tolnay, as above note 2, 69.

5. J. Pope-Hennessy, *Catalogue of Italian Sculpture in the Victoria and Albert Museum*, 1964, 1:135–138. See also M. Godby, "The Boni Chimney Piece," *De Arte* (published by the University of South Africa), 27:1982, 4–17.

6. If it is true that they are specially associated with chimney pieces, the reason might be that this is one of the few monumental forms of the era found in houses more than anywhere else, and hence perhaps evoking the balanced roles of the two sexes there.

7. A. Hind, *Early Italian Engraving*, 1938, 1:154.

8. Antoninus, *Summa Theologica*, Pars 4, Titulus 8, Cap. 1, Section 3, and again more briefly in Titulus 11, Cap. 4, Section 5.

9. An excellent survey of some nineteen scattered traditions is provided in the classical encyclopedia of Pauly-Wissowa, A. Rzach, "Sibyllen," 2nd series, 2:1923, 2074–2103.

10. Lactantius' work, *Divinarum Institutionum*, is most accessible in the edition of Migne, *Patrologia Latina*, 6:1844. He quotes sayings of the sibyls in his books 1, 2, 4, and 7, some forty-five in all; at their first appearance (Book 1, vi) he names them and the writers who reported them, as listed by Varro, and says that all of them left accessible sayings except Cumaea, whose books the Romans kept hidden, and observes that one cannot say which said what, except Erythraea. Augustine, *City of God*, Book 18, Chapter 23, quotes one long passage assigned to Erythraea and a group of short ones all from Lactantius' fourth book.

11. The best general account of the emergence of the sibyls is still that by E. Mâle,

L'art religieux de la fin du Moyen Age en France, 1922, 253–264, though it has been extended and amended in many particulars. Important changes were offered in the unfortunately brief and almost inaccessible thesis by L. Freund, *Studien zur Bildgeschichte in der neueren Kunst*, Hamburg, 1936.

12. The *Vaticinium* was published by O. Holder-Egger, "Italienische Prophetien des 13 Jahrhunderts, *Neues Archiv fur ältere deutsche Geschichtskunde*, 15:1880, 155–173. The Nativity prophecy is on p. 161. This text remained unknown to many later writers on sibyls, so that the later appearances of the sayings in it seemed puzzling, e.g. to E. Dotson, "An Augustinian Interpretation of Michelangelo's Sistine Ceiling," *Art Bulletin*, 61:1979, note 167, where it appears as "the Erythraean Letter."

13. *The Golden Legend* cites this brief saying about the wood of the cross in its chapter on the feast of the exaltation of the cross, reporting that it is attributed to "the sibyl" in the "Three-Part History." The latter is a medieval world chronicle by one Sozomenes. The saying appears on scrolls held by some later sibyls, and Mâle suggested that its authority was Sozomones. *The Golden Legend* seems more likely, since the *History* had relatively small circulation.

14. R. Krautheimer, in his standard work, *Ghiberti*, 1970, vigorously rejected the view that the women might be sibyls, saying they do not match the way they were normally shown at the time, "enthroned" and "in groups of six, eight, and most frequently ten." However, only one group of six and one of eight, cited above, is known, and the nearest model, Andrea Pisano's statues, shows two, not enthroned. Apart from Miriam (Exodus 15:20) and Judith, a third female figure is shown by Ghiberti, distinctively pointing her finger up to heaven, the gesture that identifies the Tiburtine sibyl for instance in the fresco in Florence by Ghirlandaio to be discussed below. Her costume is also classical in ways unlike the other women. A fourth figure by Ghiberti, gazing upward, has a very long scroll, normally signaling a prophet or prophetess who is linked to a text; the only well-known candidate seems to be Erythraea, with an allusion either to her *Vaticinium* or to her account of the Last Judgment cited since Augustine. The fifth figure does not have obvious distinctive gestures.

15. This saying is one of those quoted by Lactantius and then by Augustine without linking it to any one sibyl. However Antonino (in the passage cited in note 8 above) assigns it to Erythraea. That is of significance for the discussion of these frescoes by Angelico, which have generally been reasonably assumed to have been painted with personal advice from Antonino, the artist's fellow friar, but without any definite evidence. The most recent writer on the work says Angelico's probable source for the scroll was Augustine (W. Hood, *Fra Angelico at San Marco*, 1993, 317, note 70).

16. These are the two final episodes, apparently available for separate performance, of the vast, 50,000-line *Mistère du viel Testament*, first printed ca. 1500, with twelve woodcuts of the sibyls, and also ca. 1520 and in 1542; these books survive in a very few copies in France. The work is accessible in the six-volume edition of 1878. An earlier user of the second printing reported, presumably from it, that these

episodes had been performed for the entry of Queen Isabeau into Paris in 1385. (Many authors, *Histoire universelle des theatres*, 11:1780, 64–75; I am grateful to Annette Dixon and Stephen Mansbach for help with this also very rare work.) This and another medieval work, the seventh-century Byzantine *Chronicon Pasquale*, have been cited in studies of sibyls as anticipating the later twelve-sibyl sets, but without noting the names they assign, which only in this case anticipate the later ones.

17. E. Dotson, as in note 12, established the fundamental distinctive characteristics of these two traditions of groups of sibyls in the fifteenth century.

18. The sayings in French verse match, with allowances, those that the twelve sibyls speak about the Nativity in later works, notably the Revello play. The printed *Mistère* also presents the exact Latin sayings familiar in later twelve-sibyl series, but they may not have been in the original play. There seems to be no indication of the play's actual date, but the general placing in the fourteenth century seems likely, making this the earliest appearance of the twelve sibyls.

19. M. Reeves, *The Influence of Prophecy in the Later Middle Ages*, 1969, 163–164, 196. Mâle, followed by others, suggested that the twelve sibyls were produced to match twelve prophets, but in fact there is no set of twelve prophets except the minor ones, never found as a set with sibyls. See the article "Zwölf," *Lexikon der christlichen Ikonographie*, 4:1972, 582–583.

20. Mâle proposed that Agrippa was an error for Aegyptiaca, since he found that name used instead in one set of sibyls. This was not followed up, since Agrippa is found earlier and more often. But it supports Mâle's case that sibyls' names otherwise are invariably geographical.

21. These materials were reunited by W. Simpson, "Cardinal Giordano Orsini as a Prince of the Church and Patron of the Arts," *Journal of the Warburg and Courtauld Institutes*, 29:1966, 135ff. The work has further been studied by R. Mode, "Masolino, Uccello and the Orsini 'Uomini Famosi,' " *Burlington Magazine*, 114:1972, 369–378, but still has not been absorbed into the mainstream of Renaissance monuments.

22. H. Harth, ed., *Poggio Bracciolini*, Lettere, 3:1987, 280–282.

23. M. Hélin, in a fundamental study, "Un texte inédit sur l'iconographie des sibylles," *Revue belge de philologie et d'histoire*, 15:1936, 349–366, published two copies of the text of the Orsini list and rightly linked it to Poggio's letter, with the limitations indicated. Freund, as in note 11 above, in his thesis also published in 1936, had independently found the same text, in one of the same copies and in a third (see his note 4, p. 29); he also knew the date of the letter, its first sentence, and Valturio's identity. However, Hélin's more limited report is the one that has been followed, e.g., by Dotson, whose rendering of Valturio's name as "Roberto da Rimini," as of someone who was not there anymore, further distanced the connection with what took place in that town in 1454.

24. V. de Bartholomaeis, ed., *Laude drammatiche e rappresentazioni sacre*, 3:1943, 208–217. There are thirteen sibyls, Agrippa and Aegyptiaca being doubled.

Deborah then follows, but she evidently should be bracketed with the next group including Miriam and Huldah, as they are all Hebrew prophetesses.

25. F. Belcari, *Le rappresentazioni*, 1833, 23–43. The play is of the Annunciation. The prints differ in about three names, discussed by Hind, as above, note 7.

26. De Bartholomaeis, as above, note 24, 3:312–321.

27. F. Saxl, "The Classical Inscription in Renaissance Art and Politics," *Journal of the Warburg and Courtauld Institutes*, 4:1940–41, 27–29.

28. E. Borsook and O. Offerhaus, *Francesco Sassetti and Ghirlandaio*, 1981, 29–30, propose that the fourth sibyl may be the Cimmerian (a name variant of Cumana) because they find her with a similar hairstyle in the Florentine print. This method of pinning down a name certainly fits the standard puzzles of unlabeled figures, but here the artist's explicit removal from our view of the label that is there negates the underlying assumption that she was thought of by the artist as a particular nameable figure like the others whose labels we see. She is the leftover generic sibyl. In a brief survey of sibyl images the authors call this one of the earliest monumental sets and, citing the study by Simpson (as in note 21, above), mention Cardinal Orsini's room of three hundred men and women including two sibyls, but they surprisingly add that "it is unknown whether these sibyls appeared there by themselves or together with other types of figures," though the illuminated manuscript shows that the latter was the case. They wholly omit Orsini's other room with twelve monumental sibyls only, though Helin's study of 1936 presenting it had been cited by Simpson, briefly, and equally briefly absorbed into such a survey of sibyls as Tolnay's (as above in note 2, 152). This gap in the work of careful scholars is a token of how scattered the material has been.

29. A Pointner, *Agostino di Duccio*, 1909, 25–117.

30. Pointner, as above, note 29.

31. The useful discussions by Mâle and Dotson call the edition with sibyls alone the first and the one with added prophets the second, without explanation. The book with its many illustrations, discussed below, was costly to produce, and these variant versions suggest that someone, probably the author, was treating it as an expensive hobby.

32. The rare book by F. Ehrle and G. Stevenson, *Gli affreschi del Pinturicchio*, 1897, seems to be the only one to present all the frescoes and all the inscriptions in these rooms. They are all very much repainted, and the identity of some of the figures is dubious.

33. Excellent material on this overlooked work is provided by J. Byam Shaw, *Paintings by Old Masters at Christ Church Oxford*, 1967, 48–50.

34. The inscribed phrases come, in sequence, from Lactantius 7:24, 4:6, one unidentified, 7:18, 7:20, 7:18, 7:20, and 7:23.

35. Michelangelo, *Carteggio*, 4:1979, 265. To be sure, his specific phrase, that painting is the better the more it "goes toward relief" does not make a neat match with the pavement.

36. R. Cust, *The Pavement Masters of Siena*, 1901, transcribes all the inscriptions. A. Martini and U. Periccioli, *Il Pavimento del Duomo di Siena*, n.d., reproduces all the panels.

37. M. Slepian, "Merchant Ideology in the Renaissance: Guild Hall Decoration of the Renaissance," Ph.D. diss., Yale University, 1987, soon to appear as a book.

38. L. Venturi and G. Carandente, *Il Perugino: gli affreschi del Collegio del Cambio*, 1955, plates 10 and 12, provides the clearest view of the inscriptions; that of Delphica, LIBERABIT NOS, is in deep shadow. These texts seem not to have been checked other than in the brief mention by Dotson, as above, note 12, 406. Antonino assembles the three in the foreground in the same passage cited above in note 8. Of the very brief ones in the background, LUC may be from Lactantius 4:19, FLORESCET is from 4:13, and LIBERABIT NOS has not been possible to trace; this shadowed scroll may have been repainted.

39. G. Schiller, *Iconography of Christian Art*, 1:1971, 146 (Moses and Elijah as representing law and prophecy), 147 (Council of Nicaea), 146 (prefiguring the Last Judgment).

40. When Erythraea's saying shifts in the way indicated, her old text is given to Hellespontica instead of the latter's usual one; that is perhaps only one change, but for two sibyls. Phrygia and Tiburtina swap texts in a French manuscript. In Filippino's vault where Hellespontica gets Erythraea's text as indicated, she also gets another from Lactantius (5:5), a unique case in which that author drew not on the *Oracula* but on Ovid's *Metamorphoses* (1:111–112), further reinforcing the Roman classicism of this set. Ghirlandaio's one sibyl with no text and Pinturicchio's shifts at Santa Maria del Popolo involving new texts for Delphica and Cimmeria have been mentioned. It may be added that the Orsini list itself offers alternate sayings for three sibyls, those taken from Cologne; Samia gets part of the *Vaticinium* of Erythraea and Hellespontica gets the saying that *The Golden Legend* had quoted from the Oracula.

41. Dotson as above in note 12, 411.

42. Vasari, *Vita di Michelangelo*, ed. Barocchi, 1962, 1:46.

43. Byam Shaw, as in note 33 above, well informed on the usual sequence, found it odd that even after cleaning the fourth label, that of the sibyl who is presumably the Cimmerian, "still seems to be named Cumaean."

44. It is possible that Michelangelo has another precedent for showing the first five sibyls, in the set of Florentine drawings comprising a world chronicle of about 1490, known as the Florentine Picture Chronicle. It presents the Persian sibyl in folio 21v., Libica on 24v., "Eritea" on 26v., on fol. 43 two women with no label whom the editor takes to be two sibyls, and Cumaea on fol. 46r. If the editor is right, Cumaea is in her usual seventh place, but a viewer who did not make the same interpretation would see only Michelangelo's five. This cycle also includes Hermes Trismegistus at fol. 32. (B. Degenhart and A. Schmitt, *Corpus der italienischen Zeichnungen*, 1968, 1: nos. 566–620.)

45. To that list one should perhaps add a set that is equally balanced but very small,

in Jan van Eyck's Altarpiece of the Lamb, where the two prophets Zachariah and Micah match the two most standard sibyls Erythraea and Cumaea.

Cumaea is identified on the left by the scroll she holds, a unique choice of the line in Virgil's Aeneid (6:50) saying that she is divinely inspired. Erythraea on the right shows the familiar first line of her long prophecy of the Last Judgment. On the captions below, on the frame, their names are interchanged in error, and almost all scholars have followed this wrong identification; thus E. Panofsky reports "the Erythraean sibyl on the left" and "the Cumaean on the right" (*Early Netherlandish Painting*, 1964, 207), as do most recent writers. The mistake had been noted by the Dominican J. de Baets ("De gewijde teksten van 'het Lam Gods', *K. Vlaamse Akademie vor Taal en Letterkunde, Verslagen*, 1961, 549–558) as reported by L. Philip, *The Ghent Altarpiece and the Art of Jan van Eyck*, 1971, note 68. Though the error possibly occurred in later alterations, it may rather recall switches found not rarely in captions under newspaper photographs and in books. Its having been ignored signals that sibyls' distinct individual messages were not registered as interesting, again making them a uniform chorus.

A still different ratio of prophets and sibyls occurs in Feo Belcari's second and shorter Annunciation play, not printed in the period (Belcari as in note 25, 90–93). First three prophets speak a stanza each, as then do two sibyls. Six more sibyls share three stanzas among them. This is quite like the Rimini formula of prophets who are fewer but have the leading roles.

46. Biblia Pauperum, ed. Henry, 1987, scenes d, f, h, i, n, o, p, r, .f., and .h.

47. Dotson, as in note 12, rightly points out the same single text of Joel, as treated by Augustine, and its link to the Pentecost. She then calls it "perplexing," asking what it has to do with the incarnation, the theme that in her system it must symbolize. (It is adjacent to the Drunkenness of Noah, which she interprets as intended to explicate the incarnation.) A clue, she suggests, may be in Joel's last word, handmaids, because that will recall the word handmaid that the Virgin Mary applies to herself in the account of the Annunciation, the central event of the incarnation. Here as elsewhere one may ask why, if this message was meant, a more easily related prophet was not selected rather than Joel.

48. H. C. Agrippa, *De Nobilitate et Praecellentia Foeminei Sexus*, 1990, 87.

49. In remarks during the discussion at the Vatican conference of 1990 on the cleaning of the ceiling, expected to be published in its procedings.

50. In the book of Esther, 5:14, Haman prepares a cross, *crucem*, on which he plans to hang Mordecai, but then is hung on it himself. E. Wind, "The Crucifixion of Haman," *Journal of the Warburg Institute* 1:1938, 245–248, held that Michelangelo's image of Haman crucified is a "startling exception" to the tradition that usually shows Haman on a gallows, a tradition that he says "literally" follows the text. Wind did qualify his view in a footnote, saying that the word *crux* occurred in the text in "one single passage," but then added that "throughout the rest of the book" the scaffold "is called unambiguously a scaffold." That is dubious. Three other words are used: (1) *trabs* (again 5:14), a beam, timber, rafter, or tree in the standard Latin-English dictionary of Lewis and Short, though, like *crux*, gallows in the King

III

James Bible; (2) *patibulum* (6:4 and 7:10), a fork-shaped gibbet or yoke, evidently the precise object, hacked from a tree, to which the two thieves are tied in Antonello da Messina's Crucifixion of ca. 1475 (Antwerp, Museum), represented with side branches analogous in shape to Christ's cross, but again "gallows" in King James, as is (4) *lignum* (7:9) wood in general or tree, as in Genesis 3 where lignum is used for the tree in Eden. Thus Michelangelo's forked tree with Haman tied to it seems to give the literal reading, and if it is an innovation it may suggest attention to the text in a fresh way, perhaps by a theologian. The King James gallows, and Wind's, may well reflect the verb linked to these nouns, *appendere*, in two cases (5:14, 7;9) but the man is not said to hang from (as with a hangman's noose) but upon or on the tree (*super eum, in eo*); in the other cases also he is "affixed to" or "suspended on"—not from—it. Wind's treatment has been generally adopted, evidently accepting his report that *crux* was not the primary term.

51. Commenting on Matthew 4:1, Cornelius a Lapide writes that Lucifer tempted Adam by way of Eve (*per Evam*) and won, but was beaten by Christ (*Commentarii in IV Evangelia*, 1690, 101).

52. C. Beutler, *Meister Bertram, der Hochaltar von S. Petri*, 1984.

53. C. Jordan, *Renaissance Feminism*, 1990, 89.

54. Agrippa, as in note 48, 65–66, 71.

55. "Isotta Nogarola: Of the Equal or Unequal Sin of Adam and Eve," in M. King and A. Rabil, *Her Immaculate Hand*, 1992, 57–69. The writer lived from 1418 to 1466.

56. These two lunettes with few women are, besides, at the end of the room, where it has already been noticed that male figures dominate, as against the middle area where women are equal, both in the system of sibyls and prophets and in the nine stories.

57. Jordan as in note 53, 22, 57, 66, 122.

58. Jordan as above, 35, 71, 201, 259, 267

59. B. Castiglione, *The Courtier*, Book 3, Section 28. It will not be surprising that the sibyls are also cited here to support the high status of women. Women wrestlers are cited from classical antiquity, itself a token of respectability. That should not be taken to indicate that they did not exist in the period. The painting of this theme by Jusepe de Ribera must suggest that this role did not have the demeaned reputation it tends to have today.

60. Michelangelo, *Le rime*, ed. Girardi, 196, no. 235, cf. the note on p. 387.

61. Michelangelo, *Carteggio*, 3:1973, letter 594.

62. A text on the Sistine wall frescoes, written by the secretary of its patron, Pope Sixtus IV, overwhelmingly emphasizes its richness and artistic skill, with only a brief phrase on its message (J. Monfasani, "A Description of the Sistine Chapel under Pope Sixtus IV," *Artibus et historiae*, 7:1983, 9–18). The Florentine banker Filippo Strozzi, planning a family tomb in 1477, emphasized the choice of the right master for a work that will give the family honor. (E. Borsook, "Documenti relativi

alle cappelle . . . di Filippo Strozzi," *Antichità viva*, 9:1970, n. 3, Doc. 17; I hope to discuss these evocative records elsewhere.

63. K. Weil-Garris and J. D'Amico, "The Renaissance Cardinal's Ideal Palace," *Memoirs of the American Academy in Rome*, 35:1980, 45–124, published this text in Latin and an English translation; the passages are on pp. 91–97. Unluckily, Dotson had access only to this English translation.

64. Thomas's text and its echoes to 1500 are briefly surveyed in C. Gilbert, "Several of the Contexts of Savoldo's Dead Christ," *Bulletin of the Cleveland Museum of Art*, 79:1992, 23–25.

65. A. Marinoni, *I rebus di Leonardo da Vinci*, 1954, a study endorsed by more recent specialists, e.g., C. Pedretti, *The Drawings of Leonardo . . . at Windsor*, 1968, 1: nos. 12692ff.

66. In Bologna, the church of San Domenico had a "woman's side" (I. Supino, *Le chiese di Bologna, secoli xv–xvi*, 1938, 235, quoting a sixteenth century source) and similar documents for San Francesco are cited by P. Garani, *Il bel San Francesco*, 1948, 77). This was stated as a general rule by Honorius Augustodinensis (J. Sauer, *Symbolik des Kirchengebäudes*, 1924, 93).

67. W. Cohn, "Franco Sacchetti and die Gewölbcmalereien von Orsanmichele," *Mitteilungen des Kunsthistorischen Institutes in Florenz*, 8:1958, 65–77. The author's claim that the program was created by Sacchetti, who described it in a poem, is dubious. It is based on a line near the end in which he says that he has "disposed" all "this" so that all may know what composes it. "This" does not include all he describes, since that includes work done before his time, Orcagna's tabernacle. Since it refers only to a part, it may most naturally allude to the last comment previous to the cited lines, in which he tells of having reinstalled some discarded sculptures; he would have "disposed" them in his role as an official of the building. Alternatively, the words may refer simply to his having presented the list of images in his poem.

68. When Dante (*Paradiso* 32:1–12) presents Mary in her fixed place in heaven, she is accompanied in descending order by Eve, Rachel, Sarah, Rebecca, Judith, and Ruth. This may well have influenced the scheme in Orsanmichele, or may simply illustrate that this was an ordinary way of thinking.

THE ANCESTORS

Through the centuries since the Sistine ceiling was painted, the subset of the ancestors of Christ has consistently been given little attention. This is the more remarkable since it is one of the larger ones in scale as well as area, and one of the very few with figures in interactive groups (there are only two others, the nine Genesis stories and the four in the corners). This has in large part been due to their dark tonality, as it has been perceived by many. Tolnay in particular, in one of the more detailed discussions, called this part of the work "the sphere of shadow and death," making the claim that this was intentional.[1] Since the cleaning of the 1980s all this has changed. The color is not only bright but strange in its harmonics, and many have suggested that it anticipates the work a few years later by the younger artists called Mannerists. I am gratified to have anticipated this suggestion briefly at the end of an essay published in 1980 and reprinted in this book.

This part of the ceiling, as many observers have now noted, is also very different from the rest in its expressive tone. It is not heroic, grand, or ideal. The people instead are average, going about daily lives. They are not what we expect when we say "Michelangelesque," and that in itself may have helped to draw attention away from them; when we look at the ceiling, this has not been what we want to see. One young man leans far back and props up a leg on a footstool, while a young woman nearby meditates before her mirror. Another woman is cutting cloth with large scissors, while her child watches the process. Other mothers are nursing babies (in counterpart to the full-breasted mother in the *Deluge* who may have lost her child); another is testing a dish of hot food. Others are asleep, and indeed nobody is doing anything energetic, not to mention grand. There is a great deal of sitting about, as if waiting (fig. 1). A number of people have bundles or walking sticks beside them, and the idea

Figure 1: Michelangelo, *Ezechias, Manasses, and Amon,* lunette, fresco, Sistine Ceiling, Vatican

Figure 2: Michelangelo, *Asa, Josaphat, and Joram*, lunette, fresco, Sistine Ceiling, Vatican

Figure 3: Michelangelo, *Salmon, Boaz, and Obed*, lunette, fresco, Sistine Ceiling, Vatican

has often been invoked that they are travelers or pilgrims. Their everyday reality sometimes turns to the comic, when the faces are caricatured. One very thin man with a protruding lower lip and cap—not unlike some of Leonardo's caricatures—is writing with the intentness of a dedicated bookkeeper (fig. 2). One old man stares with quite crazy preoccupation at his walking stick, whose carved head stares back at him (fig. 3). (It is a type of folk carving that exists in reality.)[2] There are a great many children, and the mothers are all intent on them, but otherwise people tend to ignore each other.

It is common to compare Michelangelo to Dante for the epic power in both. As a poet, Michelangelo is in the tradition of Petrarch. But here he shifts, suggesting his universality, to a reading of the ordinary world that is closer to Boccaccio's *Decameron*—not its bawdy or trick endings, but its middle-class truths. In Michelangelo's time, this realist tradition is seen best perhaps in the two comedies written by Machiavelli, also a figure usually associated with quite different and grander issues than these. The *Mandragola* and the *Clizia* were both written close to 1510, the same time as these paintings.

The subject of the paintings is the ancestors of Christ. One could never guess that from the imagery. The emphasis on families seems logical enough, but it had never before been used in treating this theme. Here again Michelangelo is an innovator in addressing his subject, most obviously in including the women on an equal level. We know that these are the ancestors simply because large labels with their names have been provided, more emphatic than those for the prophets and sibyls and indeed dominant in the wall area where the figures appear. Forty names are provided as given in the gospel of Matthew, chapter 1.

This text, the very beginning of the New Testament, recalls some of the genealogies of the Old Testament, but it also has some quite special features. After the information is given in verse 1 that this is the book of the generation of Jesus, "son of David, son of Abraham," the detailed series follows in verse 2. "Abraham begat Isaac, Isaac begat Jacob," and so on, each name appearing twice. After Jacob and his son Judah we proceed to some relatively little known figures, then come Ruth and Boaz, Jesse who begat David the king, and Solomon. The series of subsequent kings continues in parallel with the stories of their reigns told in the Biblical chronicles until the end of the kingdom at the Babylonian captivity. The generations after that are totally obscure, and recorded only here, up to Joseph, "the husband of Mary, of whom was born Jesus." There is then an important summing up: "So all the generations from Abraham to David are fourteen generations, and from David until the carrying away into Babylon are fourteen generations and from the carrying away into Babylon unto Christ are fourteen generations" (verse 17). The story of Christ's birth then begins.

The neat series of three fourteens is achieved only with a little trickery, in that David is counted twice, in the first and the second group. There are thus just forty-one different generations, but these include Jesus himself, so there are forty ancestors, as Michelangelo shows. The figures forty, forty-one, and forty-two were thus all available for use. The reason for the insistence on fourteen in each unit is that the important middle subset of kings does indeed have fourteen royal names.

The history of images of this theme seems never to have received attention. Schiller, in her excellent handbook, points out only two kinds of medieval representations, the kings on the façades of Gothic cathedrals and illuminated manuscripts of the gospel of Matthew.[3] These indeed begin to have sets of the ancestor portraits at least as early as the ninth century. Not even this much was pointed out in the one reference to the matter in the Michelangelo literature, by Tolnay. He cited only the related theme of the tree of Jesse. In this, a tree grows out of the body of the recumbent Jesse, David's father, whose branches present a variety of human figures, from half a dozen to fifteen, including the Virgin Mary at the top. However, the tradition of the forty ancestors is broad. A survey will suggest ways in which Michelangelo used tradition and others in which he was highly original.

A few scholars have offered analyses of what Michelangelo meant to suggest by his images. It seems to have been taken for granted that it was not possible to connect religious messages with the appearance of these people, either as a group or separately. It is conspicuous that the most famous persons, such as David, are not rendered here in any recognizable way. None of the men near the label with his name seems to correspond to any notion we might have of David, either conventional or suggested as new. This only reinforces the larger difficulty that half the men have no traditional associations at all, being only names on a list. Instead, scholars have turned to the meanings of the names themselves. This has been encouraged partly as the one option left on the basis of the visual materials provided, partly by the emphasis on the labels by their central placing and size, and partly by the puzzling fact that they have seemed to be irregularly distributed. They are grouped in sixteen lunettes, the number permitted by the chapel architecture. Most lunettes show either two or three names on their plaques, but two show only one and one shows four. As Dotson further summarized, the four lunettes nearest the entrance, last in Biblical chronology, "and one other just short of the middle, have two names, and the rest three."[4] This irregular appearance might be explained, it has been argued, by the desire to place certain names at certain points, adjacent to elements in other subjects on the ceiling. This has been strikingly successful in a few cases, notably with the name Naason, pointed out in at least two theories of this type. The name is read to mean "serpent," and this figure is adjacent to the scene of the brazen serpent. However, it is not so easy with those adjacent to the Esther scene. The nearby names are read to mean either "my willing people" or "my desirable people" in one case, and "father seeing the people," "laughter" "supplantor," or "glorifying" in others. Evidently any of these could be made to fit, even reasonably, but not with any precision, and one also guesses that they would fit elsewhere too. After citing these and several other cases, Dotson frankly reports that "most of the remaining names present such a wide variety of possible interpretations as to be useless." Indeed, with forty names in a fixed order, the likelihood of finding such matches with the nearby images is small.

However, the irregularity in the labels is perhaps not so great as it has seemed. As noted, there are forty names in sixteen lunettes. It seems useful to inquire how they would be arranged if they were regular. There are two and a half as many names as lunettes, so a regular system would place two names in half of them and three in the other half, in some pattern that would have a balance or rhythm. One might think of twos on one side and threes on the other, or simple alternation. However, there is one such system that has a unique advantage. Half the lunettes are accompanied by spandrels, so that the group of lunette and spandrel regularly shows three groups of people; the other half of the lunettes lack such spandrels and normally show only two. Hence the former should have three names each and the latter two. The presence of spandrels is conditioned by the architecture, with windows along the sides but not at the ends; the spandrels are over the windows. Hence the eight lunettes at both ends of the chapel would have only two names each, while the eight in the middle would have three each, a neat arrangement.

Once this optimum regular system has been defined, it is noticeable that Michelangelo actually used it for one half of the chapel, the half painted first. There are, first, two two-name lunettes along the end, and then two more around the corner from them. After that, there are four with three names, arriving at the middle, with twenty of the forty names evenly distributed in a way that would give complete balance had it been continued. It cannot be denied that this was intentional. After that the irregularity begins; moving simultaneously along both sides, the next lunettes show, in the first pair, on one side three names and on the other two. Next there are two lunettes with one name each, and at the end one with four and one with three. Just before the middle one other irregularity is introduced. Whereas in all other cases the sequence of names moves from a lunette on one side to the corresponding lunette on the opposite side of the chapel, and after that in the next bay again from the first side to the second, once, after the twenty-sixth ancestor, Amon, we move to the next bay on the same side, and then continue as before by moving across, so that the last three sets start on the wall opposite that on which the first five began.

Unless all this is coincidence, it means that just before arriving at the middle, a change of intention occurred, calling for a different system. It is implausible to offer the only alternative, that such a shift to irregularity in the middle had been intended from the start. It is notable that at the middle some other shifts, independent of this one, also occur, which have always been noted. In the ancestor lunettes these include a shift in the design of the labels, which previously had been provided with side volutes, now dropped. In other subsets, there is a change to a larger scale in the prophets and sibyls. It seems clear that there was a pause here to reconsider matters on various levels, including the location of the names of the ancestors.

In the first half the regular rhythm of twos and threes, reflecting the architecture, suggests that the ancestors functioned as a chorus, each reinforcing the same point. That is consistent with the absence of knowledge about the personalities of half of them from other sources, and more so from the way they are painted, evoking characters that have no biblical ties and are indeed interchangeable. This factor of being a chorus may or may not have been part of what was shifted in the middle.

Michelangelo's most obvious originality is in the inclusion of the women, which had never been done before in the visual arts, apart from the special case of the Virgin Mary. It was to some extent suggested by the text in Matthew, which named the ancestresses in four cases: Tamar, who had a child with her brother Judah; Rahab, who with Salmon had the child Boaz; Ruth, who had a child with Boaz; and Bathsheba, (referred to as "her that had been the wife of Uriah") who with David had the child Solomon. To us it may seem obvious that they were chosen because they had been the themes of Biblical accounts already, and none of the other mothers had. Biblical commentators found other reasons for their presence, such as a lesson in the humility of Christ, with ancestors who were not virtuous. In any case, the text did not induce inclusion of them in images before, and on the ceiling these women are no more individuated than the men. It may also be added that many of the other women shown here could be named, although the Michelangelo literature has never treated the matter. In the books of Chronicles the names of twelve of the mothers of these fourteen kings are on record, with nothing else about them in most cases. They include, besides Bathsheba, Athaliah, known to us from the seventeenth-century masterpiece by Racine, and Hephzibah, who impressed that same era enough to have many namesakes in Puritan New England.[5] When to these we add the earlier Sarah, Rebecca, and Rachel, wives of Abraham, Isaac, and Jacob, and the four others named in Matthew's text, including the Virgin Mary, a total of nineteen of the ancestresses in these forty generations can be individuated by name. Yet it does not seem likely that Michelangelo was affected by this any more than he was in treating the men.

A survey of the prior treatment of the ancestors can illustrate how novel Michelangelo was and some traditions he used. The earliest monumental image of them may be that of the late eleventh century in Bethlehem, in the Church of the Nativity, in a series of inscribed wall mosaics in the nave. These have been little taken into account until recently for many reasons, including the grime that covered them.[6] They were produced in the context of the Crusades, when Western Christians arrived at the site. The topic is so obviously suitable to the place that one may think it was first given monumental development there. Of just about the same date is the remarkable series in Sigena, Spain, which perhaps first assigns the theme to frescoes in a vault (figs. 4a–b). They are lost but known almost completely from photographs.[7] The sequence assigns to each image the precise text including the word begat, thus, "Abram genuit Isaac." The corresponding image shows a man and a boy, and the next image shows that same boy as a man with his son in turn. Thus the images fully reflect the point of the words, including the presentation of every figure twice. The introduction of children as a basic element is a significant precedent for later works. These frescoes are notable in that the painter was English. The connection between Spain and England recalls that an English king of the time, Richard the Lionhearted, visited Spain and married a local princess while en route to take part in the Crusades; the two early ancestor cycles thus evoke a connected culture.

In Gothic France the theme was much favored, not only in series of kings like those between the doors at Chartres and above them at Amiens. Longer series not limited to kings also appear in the arches over cathedral doors, with the interesting feature that the figures are shown enclosed in foliage, which twists vine-like in a way that leaves an almond-shaped space inside for each figure. This pattern, underlining the notion of the family tree, was evidently evolved from the tree of Jesse, and makes a typically Gothic blend of diagrammatic system with a flexible organism. The most notable ones are at Laon, over the central portal of the west façade, and Chartres, over the central portal of the north transept (fig. 5). Like the trees of Jesse, they are incomplete, showing some twenty-five figures; again the individuals on the list are less important than the choric identity.[8]

123

Figures 4a-b: *Ancestors of Christ,* vault, fresco, Sigena, Spain. Photo: MAS

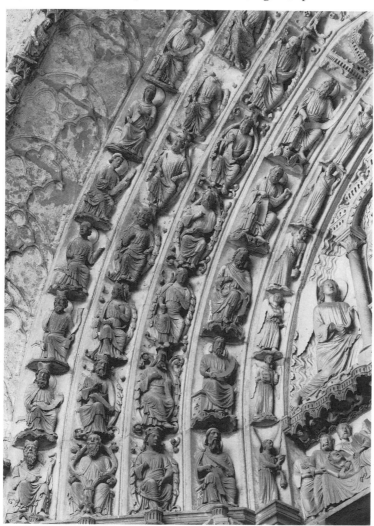

Figure 5: *Kings,* central portal of north transept, Chartres. Photo: Hirmer Verlag, Munich

Trecento Italian sculpture, often influenced by Gothic France, shows a similar development at the Cathedral of Siena, whose facade sculpture is probably most under French influence. Around the rose window we see exactly forty figures, thirty-nine men plus the top central Virgin Mary, who evidently replaces Joseph, quite reasonably, as the fortieth generation.[9] Such a shift was evidently not incompatible with Matthew's text, and relates to the dedication of the cathedral to Mary and a hierarchical arrangement of the figures, with Mary in the most noble place. It seems to follow that the sequence of figures is not chronological. This is also indicated by the use of three different sizes for the figures at the top, the sides, and in the curved triangles around the rose; architectural constraints are more powerful than historical order. Just a few others among the damaged figures are identifiable by attributes, David with his harp and apparently Jesse, his father, with his rod, the origin of the line leading to the messiah in the imagery with the tree.[10]

Another ancestor series from the same years has remained, astonishingly, unrecognized, in a monument no less than Giotto's Arena Chapel of 1305 in Padua. The portraits are in the barrel vault, where they enliven frame strips between and above the cycle of narratives of the lives of Mary and Christ on the walls. On the two lower tiers of the three that have the large scenes, windows on one wall separate the scenes, and on the other wall the corresponding painted frames are punctuated with little scenes, most of which show Old Testament parellels to events in Christ's life. All the other frames in the chapel are filled with little heads; these are at both ends of both long walls, all along the top tier of scenes where there are no windows, and in the vault above; there are sixty-five heads in all, including a few now lost.

On the level of the bottom tier of scenes the heads are found only at the ends of the two walls, in the outer frames of the first and last scenes. They are recognizable as the four doctors of the church, shown with their identifying headdresses as two bishops, a cardinal, and a pope (Augustine, Ambrose, Jerome, and Gregory); above these, still in the bottom tier, are the four evangelists, often bracketed with the doctors in imagery. Higher, in the frames at the ends of the second tier, are four female saints. In the top tier, where there are no windows, such heads fill all the

125

Figure 6a: Giotto, *Kings and Boys in alternation,* barrel vault at entrance door, fresco, Arena Chapel, Padua

Figure 6b: Giotto, *King David and King Solomon and a third ancestor,* barrel vault at center, fresco, Arena Chapel, Padua

Figure 6c: Giotto, *Abraham with Isaac, another mature ancestor,* barrel vault at choir end, fresco, Arena Chapel, Padua

frames between scenes, and there are ten on each wall. Those at the center are Saints Peter and Paul, and it is agreed that they are part of a set of twelve apostles, six on each wall, a few more such as Bartholomew also being recognizable. This accounts for all the heads on this level except eight at the ends, above the four female saints.

Apart from these four sets—of female saints, apostles, evangelists, and doctors—the other heads have never, with a single exception, been identified in more than a generic way. There are forty-one of them, the eight already mentioned at the ends of the top tier of scenes and thirty-three higher up in the barrel vault. These latter are in three strips, rising directly above the end frames, with those eight heads, and also above the middle frame with Peter and Paul. Each of these strips spanning the vault contains eleven heads; the strip at the entrance end shows alternating representations of six kings and five young boys (fig. 6a), the middle strip has six more kings and five mature men (fig. 6b), and the one at the altar end six more mature men and five more young boys (fig. 6c).[11]

The forty-one form a set of the ancestors, the exact number needed when Christ is included, which he appears to be as one of the young boys, one of the two at the crown of the vault. He may well be the one at the center at the altar end, since one unit down from him on the right is the only identified head of the forty-one, Abraham, shown in the standard way with his knife and his son Isaac. He would be the start of the series, just as the large narrative cycle of Mary starts just to the right of the altar end, and it would end with Christ to his left. Further, the cycle of forty-one also contains fourteen kings, just the right number among the ancestors. The boys as ancestors have been seen at Sigena, and they are enclosed in vines to suggest a family tree, as in France. The specifications all seem to match the ancestors and permit no other identification.

Yet it is understandable that this has not been offered. It is natural to think the thirty-three heads in the three strips of the barrel vault comprise a full set. Here eight more are seen accompanying them, the others that also have been only generically identified, continuing the strips down at the two ends and showing similar men. These eight figures cannot be grouped with those below them, the female saints, or those beside them, the twelve apostles, and so must either belong with those above or be a

127

set of their own. That they are the latter is shown when we note that the system in the vault at the entrance, with alternating kings, is continued down into this group where one of the two heads on each side is also a king, filling out the total of fourteen (figs. 7a–c). It is notable that the grouping of two heads here next to the top tier is unusual, since almost everywhere there is just one head in a frame next to a scene, except in special cases requiring two;[12] here the need was to have two extra kings and keep the alternating scheme. This factor thus seems again to confirm the hypothesis.

However, these two kings lack crowns, being recognizable as only by having the same type of scepters as the other twelve.[13] The difference may be explained in the technical process of the work, in which these kings would have been produced as part of the work on their level, otherwise involving the twelve apostles. The gold haloes would be executed first, and the assistant who made them, having made twelve others without providing crowns, might understandably have continued the same procedure here in a mechanical way and in error. The gold scepters, applied over the paint, are here worn badly, one being invisible in all reproductions, so that the figure has never been recognized as a king. (It is quite clear when a slide is projected.)

A larger difficulty derives from the five boys inside vines at the altar end. Whereas the ones at the entrance end (fig. 6a) wear haloes and standard robes, making them plausible as sainted youths, those at the altar, including the suggested Christ at the center, have wings and are tightly capped by the vine leaves, excluding any possible haloes (fig. 6c). They have been called angels, but Giotto's angels invariably have haloes. These figures are closest to a decorative motif he uses elsewhere, where foliage encloses a human face, but not, as here, a head and shoulders with the same clothing as the human figures nearby.[14] These forms seem to straddle between such vegetal ornament and the holy boys in the other set of five here, not happily definable as either. If we take them strictly as they look, we would call them a novel ornament, oddly alternating with the six holy men who, in the nearby strips, alternate with other figures, including boys dressed this way. Our vault would then be defined as showing a mildly abridged set of thirty-six ancestors, as certified by Abraham

128

Figure 7a: Giotto, *Scene One and adjacent ancestor heads*, at choir end, fresco, Arena Chapel, Padua

Figure 7b: Giotto, *Scene Six and adjacent ancestor heads,* at entrance door, fresco, Arena Chapel, Padua

Figure 7c: Giotto, *Scene Seven and adjacent ancestor heads,* at entrance door, fresco, Arena Chapel, Padua

and the fourteen kings, plus these five strange heads inserted within one part of it. The other option is to call these images too a mechanical assistant's product, as with the missing crowns, varying the holy boys seen elsewhere, while also under the influence of an ornamental formula. The missing crowns noted may support a view that such errors might have been left uncorrected in a place not likely to be noticed, as indeed these figures hardly ever are. Such error in a minor corner of a fresco cycle is demonstrably present elsewhere in Italian art.[15] To be sure, it is logically weak to rest the hypothesis of a set of ancestors in part on presumed error, so the matter requires mention. A third smaller error, however, which is not used as part of the basis of the hypothesis, may make this procedure seem reasonable.[16]

A different support for this reading, one of wider interest, is that the plan of the vault has subjected the images of the kings in general to an ornamental system that removes part of its biblical character. The text requires the fourteen kings to appear in sequence in one part of the series; here their alternation with non-kings, and the other alternations of boys and mature men, inserts the people instead into a decorative rhythm. The same was seen in the Siena façade. This is presumably allowed when the ancestors are seen as a chorus rather than as individuals, and such random order may occur too in larger figurations, as in the Siena pavement sibyls. It seems strange, however, when advantage is taken of it to transform these boys as we see here.

Giotto is at a crux. While using such older motifs as the Sigena boys and the French vines, he inaugurates later motifs. First we see ancestors favored in frescoes in Padua. A full such set of old men appears in 1382, in Giusto de' Menabuoi's chapel of Luca Belludi, each fully inscribed. The kings, like Giotto's, are differentiated with crowns, but the rest is more conventional.[17] An anonymous artist of 1523–24, frescoing a chapel at S. Francesco, shows almost all the ancestors, along with prophets and sibyls. He seems to follow Menabuoi in the odd, almost comic way in which the series of heads is packed into available corners as if at the last moment.[18] Both seem to imply awareness of Giotto's ancestors. So does the description of the Arena by the Paduan author Michele Savonarola; his remark that its imagery included all the Old and New Testaments would not work at all for the Old without the ancestors.[19]

Michelangelo follows a choice seen before only in Giotto, assigning some ancestors to be boys only (not showing them again as men, as in Sigena). He too distinguishes only Abraham and Isaac with individualizing attributes, to identify them as the first in the series; Michelangelo has Isaac hold the bundle of wood he carried up the mountain in Genesis. He is next to Jonah, the only one of the prophets and sibyls to have his standard attribute, the whale. (Isaac's appearance as a boy in a lunette, one of four male figures in it, matching the four names in the label, is the final proof that some ancestors are represented by boys only.)

However, Michelangelo also moves in very original ways. He not only first introduces the women; in a related procedure he shifts from simple portrait heads to groups in movement. Dotson is one of the few who has proposed a reading of their dramatic character, suggesting that there are two subclasses, respectively, in the lunettes and in the spandrels. Those in the former "turn away from each other" and are even "hostile, quarrelsome, suspicious or frightened"; those of the spandrels are "united," sometimes even "with tender concern." This does not apply, however, throughout the series. The women in the lunettes consistently do show tender concern with their children, more in fact than in the spandrels. A wife in the lunette of Jacob and Joseph seems to rub her cheek against her husband's shoulder, while in that of Eleazer and Matthan a husband intently watches his wife handle their child. Two other husbands, seated so that their backs are to the women, turn their faces around toward them, as do others who face forward. Conversely, the husband and wife in the Zorobabel spandrel ignore each other, as do those in that of Ozias (figs. 8a–b); in that of Roboam the wife turns away (figs. 9a–b), and in that of Jesse she is isolated for us as a single monumental protagonist, the man and child being irrelevant shadows behind. In the lunettes husbands do indeed most often detach themselves from the wives who tend the children. This may have a meaningful relationship to the biblical identity of these women, who, when not anonymous, were in the great majority not the queens of the kings but only the ones among their many concubines who bore the next king, starting with David's Bathsheba; their less important rank is suggested. A distinction

133

Figure 8a: Michelangelo, *Ozias,* fresco, spandrel, Sistine Ceiling, Vatican

Figure 8b: Michelangelo, *Ioatham and Achaz*, fresco, lunette, Sistine Ceiling, Vatican

Figure 9a: Michelangelo, *Roboam*, fresco, spandrel, Sistine Ceiling, Vatican

Figure 9b: Michelangelo, *Abias*, fresco, lunette, Sistine Ceiling, Vatican

in shape of surface field between lunettes and spandrels also tends to make the former work as compositions divided in two sections, the latter as centripetal triangles. Vasari, whose aesthetic was not remote from Michelangelo's, said the ancestor scenes showed "diversity" and "infinity of caprice," that is, whimsical inventions of wide variety, as one would expect from a chorus.[20] For Dotson, the two subsets she defines involve, as in St. Augustine's *City of God,* a contrast between sinners living in the historical world and people who pertain to the city of God. However that may be, no implication should be drawn that only the lunette figures, next to the labels, are the historical ancestors of Christ named in the labels. In two cases when the labels give three names, the lunettes show only two male figures, requiring us to assign the third name to the man in the lunette, and this same system would appear to function throughout [21] (figs. 10 a-b).

Certainly the figures' qualities as actors in groups depend in a major way on what they mean religiously, just as in the adjacent nine stories. It has not seemed possible to say what drama they were enacting, leading to recourse to their names. No biblical commentary on Matthew seems to help. As already noted, most of the men with names have no association with personal characteristics, and when some do, like David, they seem not to be applicable to the painted figure. Here a suggestion about the religious point being made will be offered, one that, hardly to anyone's surprise, again involves the tendency to associate analogies between the Old and New Testaments. Although Matthew commentaries seem not to invoke the Old Testament, the converse (as is usual) does happen, when a story in the Old Testament is stated to match Matthew, chapter 1. This is in the Book of Numbers, which deals with Moses' guidance of the Israelites out of Egypt to the promised land. The process of the journey gets its most thorough report in chapter 33, which says it took forty-two stages, each of one year. In verse after verse, we are told of the places where they halted, called camps or *mansiones* in the Latin. "And they departed from Rimon-parez and pitched in Libnah. And they departed from Libnah and pitched at Rissah. And they journeyed from Rissah and pitched in Kehelathah," and the list goes on until after the forty-second they reach Moab. The text never mentions

Figure 10a: Michelangelo, *Josias,* fresco, spandrel, Sistine Ceiling, Vatican

Figure 10b: Michelangelo, *Jechonias and Salathiel,* fresco, lunette, Sistine Ceiling, Vatican

the total number of camps, but of course the commentators counted and at once recalled the line in Matthew that adds up the generations also to forty-two. That specific quantity seems not to appear again in the Bible, so this linkage of the two texts may have been inevitable.

Of the authoritative commentators, none was more important than St. Jerome. He analyzed the 33rd chapter of Numbers in one of his epistles, so long that in the collection of the letters it is titled as a book, *Liber exegeticus.*[22] Most of it deals with the *mansiones,* one by one, but the introductory pages first dwell on the idea that food, so important on this trip, is to be interpreted as spiritual food. Turning to the chapter itself, he at once notes that the catalogue of the camps lists the forty-two "of which Matthew spoke," and quotes Matthew 1:17 in full. To the generations the camps are analogous:

> Through them the true Jew hurries, he is running to move from earth to heaven and enters the promised land, abandoning the Egypt of this world. No wonder, if we reach heaven in the sacrament of the number under which our Lord and Savior proceded, from the first patriarch to the Virgin, as if to the Jordan, which, flowing in a full stream, was filled with the grace of the holy spirit.

Jerome is evidently echoing an important earlier commentator, Origen, of the third century. Origen, who has been called "the most influential of all the theologians of the ancient church"[23] except perhaps for St. Augustine, is known to art history through a lively discussion as to whether Ghiberti's Doors of Paradise follows his description of Noah's ark. His homilies on Old Testament books, "edifying expositions," are known mainly through a Latin translation of the fourth century, and were notably printed in 1503 by the Aldine Press. Of the homilies on the Book of Numbers, that on chapter 33 is the longest, indeed three times the average.[24] It too focuses chiefly on the invididual camps, which, he writes, must be interpreted spiritually, either as the leaving of pagan life for knowledge of divine law, or as the leaving of the body by the soul. Until God sent us his son, we were in Egypt and in worldly error. Hence "the advent of our Lord and savior in this world through the forty-two generations" comes up, with a full citation of Matthew 1:17.

Therefore these forty-two generations that Christ fulfilled, descending into the Egypt of this world, that number is the forty-two camps which ascend from Egypt. . . . He who ascends, ascends with Him who descended to us. . . . Thus the children of Israel came to the beginning of getting their heritage in forty-two halts.

In the next paragraph, telling how the soul gets away from "the Egypt of this life," Origen also cites Psalm 120:6 on the way the soul wandered "in pilgrimage" (rather different from the English text) and then discourses at length on the pilgrimages of the soul.

The later continuation of these ideas is suggested by the major medieval theologian Peter Damian, who discusses them in almost identical ways in two works. One is a treatise on Lent, whose forty days with fasting make it a natural comparison. The other, a commentary on Numbers, was addressed to Pope Gregory VII, his close associate.[25] "As they ascended through the forty-two halts, so the Savior descended; where he began we end. The sequence is from Abraham to the Virgin, and if we begin with the Virgin birth we may in our pilgrimage get back up to God Father." Peter Damian's writings had not been published in Michelangelo's time, though one finds quotations from them. This citation simply suggests the long life of the ideas, of which Origen's and Jerome's statements would remain the chief vehicles. They seem to be the only vivid readings of Matthew 1 with any extended message to the faithful.

In these texts the Israelites, as a group, are seen as pilgrims, a quality often assigned to Michelangelo's ancestors—Dotson remarks that they are on a pilgrimage. Yet even more precisely, their counterparts in the Exodus are not literally journeying, but are resting at halts. So too we have seen the painted ancestors, who sit beside their bundles, sleep, prepare food, or do other chores as in camp. They also comprise the whole population, not just the named male ancestors. Artists would have been conscious of this through such well-established images of the Exodus story as the feeding with manna or Moses striking the rock, and his sister Miriam had her significant part in this journey too.

It has also often been noticed that one standard image provided a model for these resting families, that of the *Rest on the Flight into Egypt* by

139

Mary, Joseph, and the Christ Child. Of course one of the groups here represents that family.[26] The theme was only becoming established in Italy about this time, and works by Correggio around 1520 first give it major form. Earlier it was known among Northern artists, such as the engraver Schongauer, whose work Michelangelo had studied. This reference has recently been made more conspicuous by the reappearance of a drawing Michelangelo executed later, in the 1530s. It shows Mary with two young boys sitting on the ground, and Joseph sitting behind her in a secondary role. It plainly is a variation on some of the spandrel scenes, notably those of Zorobabel and Ezekias (fig. 11). In an essay about it, it is understandably called the *Rest on the Flight into Egypt,* but that is not correct.[27] It shows two children, Christ and John the Baptist, who are not newborn infants but perhaps four years old. This corresponds instead to the later story of the return from Egypt to the Holy Land, exactly the type of activity reported in Numbers 33. Images of this theme have been claimed to be rare, but that may well reflect a situation in which they have often been wrongly labelled as the original flight;[28] the theme is major enough to have been included in the *Biblia Pauperum,* as one of forty events in Christ's life and mission. That Michelangelo made this major drawing of it, using the motifs of the Sistine spandrels, tends to suggest that he was well aware that they too had represented such a return, the one described in Numbers 33.

The texts of Origen and the others have another interest in this connection, in their double direction. The main direction of Michelangelo's ceiling, manifested in the nine narratives of Genesis, moves from God's creation into the world of Noah. However, it has often been preferred to read it in reverse, for example in neo-Platonic interpretations that emphasize the ascent of the soul to heaven. This is not hard to do if one simply looks at the events in the opposite order. An unusual justification exists allowing scholars to do this, which is that we know Michelangelo painted in the opposite direction, from Noah to God. In emphasizing that, the artist's own participation becomes important. Skepticism about the validity of such readings may perhaps be reduced when noting that the early theologians instruct us to treat the historic reading, that of the generations through whom Christ "descends into the Egypt of the

Figure 11: Michelangelo, *Ezechias,* fresco, spandrel, Sistine Ceiling, Vatican

Figure 12: Michelangelo, *Aminadab,* fresco, lunette, Sistine Ceiling, Vatican

world" in the opposite sense, through the Israelites, who leave Egypt for the promised land. If we take Michelangelo to have been aware of this formula when he was working, one may well think that he could give the expressive qualities of his images this other suggestion of rising, which would match comfortably with his technical procedure as a painter designing and painting the work in that "ascending" order. It is certainly not something for which a theological adviser would be needed.

One last interest of the reference to Numbers is that it for the first time seems to explain the puzzle of the shift after the middle of the work to an irregular quantity of names per label. As noted earlier, the earlier phase shows a regular system, first four lunettes with two names each, then four with three each. We then proceed with two, three, three, three, one, one, three, four. One way of considering the odd rhythm thus set up is to treat each group as a musical measure, with differing numbers of notes. The reading, then, would be one-two, one-two-three, one-two-three, one-two-three, o-n-e, o-n-e, one-two-three, one-two-three-four. The doubles and triples seem ordinary, and of course retain the prior regular system; the quarter notes are a bit different, but perhaps not so much (and visually, the lunette with four generations does not look unusual). And there is only one such case. It is the two cases with whole notes that stand out, the more so since there are two of them and they are adjacent or, on the ceiling, opposite. The names of the father and son, Aminadab and Naason, seem to be favored with emphasis in this way.

This might seem to favor the earlier suggestion that Naason's name, interpreted to mean "serpent," is meaningfully placed next to the scene with the fiery serpents. However, this does not prove out if it is part of a system in which quite a few other names are thought to have such connections with nearby scenes, such as Dotson's in which this is applied mainly to the four scenes at the ends, including especially the David at the other end from this. Had that been the plan, it could also have been achieved with a regular pattern of quantities of names per label, though not with the optimum pattern actually used in the first half.[29] Hence we cannot be seeking an explanation for the emphasis on Aminadab and Naason that also involves the early part of the project. It must be one that involves the latter half only, and apparently Aminadab and Naason

142

Figure 13: Michelangelo, *Naason*, fresco, lunette, Sistine Ceiling, Vatican

Figure 14: Michelangelo, *The Story of the Brazen Serpent*, fresco, pendentive, Sistine Ceiling, Vatican

in particular, one that either had such importance as to make the later ir-regularity acceptable in the original plan, or, more likely, one that was decided on only after the early part had been produced.[30]

As observed, half the ancestor names are of people otherwise not known for anything. That is true of Aminadab, who appears elsewhere only as a patronymic, of his son and daughter, who married Aaron (fig. 12). It is different with Naason, who has an active part in events (fig. 13). He first appears when the Lord tells Moses to pick one head man from each tribe, "in the second year after they were come out of the land of Egypt," and the head of the tribe of Judah is "Naason the son of Aminadab" (Numbers 1:1, 7). In the next chapter the Lord further tells Moses and Aaron that each tribe is to pitch all its tents together, men-tioning first that those of Judah should be at the east, and "Naason the son of Aminadab shall be captain of the children of Judah" (Numbers 2:3). We then hear of the offerings of the tribes at the tabernacle set up by Moses, which the Lord told him should be done by "each prince on his day." The first one was "Naason the son of Amminadab," whose of-fering of silver dishes filled with flour and oil is then described (Numbers 7:12). It continues with gold and sacrificial animals, and concludes by re-peating "this was the offering of Naason the son of Aminadab" (Numbers 7:17). Finally, the Lord arranges a plan for the journeys of the children of Israel in which the tribe in the first place, Judah, has "over his host Naason the son of Amminadab" (Numbers 10:14). In later parts of the journey Naason disappears, having evidently died and been replaced by Caleb, an important figure but not in the line of ancestors.

It is Naason, then, who alone is both among the forty ancestors of Christ and also a part of the exodus from Egypt to the promised land. There had to be one point at which the two sets of forty-two generations of ancestors and forty-two halts of Israelites intersected, and he is it, thus giving him a special importance absent from all others. It is noticeable that he is never referred to simply by his name, but always with his fa-ther's, Aminadab, attached; thus the value given to these two names can be linked to the passages about Naason's participation in the travels as described. Evidently this was done by giving each name this otherwise absent value of the "whole note." If we suppose there is any reason at all for giving these two names the greatest prominence, and do not find convincing the hypothesis that it is because of the meaning of their names, it can only be in Naason's active role described in the Bible. That role appears only in the journey from Egypt. Hence this is a separate pointer to assign meaning to the forty-two halts on that journey in relation to the ancestors.

The same journey from Egypt to the Holy Land is registered on the ceiling in one other place, and that is of course in the scene with the children of Israel and the brazen serpent (fig. 14). Naason is thus equally relevant to that, and may be supposed to be one of the men and women seen in it. This then calls for him (more than Aminadab) to be represented adjacent to it. (The interpretation of his name as "serpent," which seems to fit the ceiling so much better than any other meanings of names, might indeed be a derivative from his connection with this incident, rather than the other way around.) However, to place Naason next to the scene of serpents, juggling was required; he is the ancestor of the ninth generation, and this is the second bay. Under the regular system used in the first half of the vault these two bays would show only the first eight ancestors; under other regular systems of twos and threes in balance they could show up to twelve, but only if Naason appeared as merely an equal in a lunette with two with others. To give him the place next to the serpents and also to give the extra emphasis of singleness to him and to Aminadab, the eighth ancestor, the only possibility is to squeeze the previous seven generations into the first bay and, afterward, to give the third and fourth bays, with the tenth through twentieth generations, one less name than the twelve that the previous regular system would have assigned to them.[31] And that is what was done. This odd schematic, minor in itself, is part of the larger interwoven set of demands by which the artist evokes character, action, and fate in this series, a theme that previously had been only a list of forty names.

1. C. de Tolnay, *The Sistine Ceiling*, 1945, 77–92. This section, with the title "The Sphere of Shadow and Death: Spandrels and Lunettes," is meant when Tolnay hereafter is named without a citation.

2. George W. Meyer, *American Folk Art Canes*, 1992, reproduces similar ones.

3. G. Schiller, *Iconography of Christian Art*, 1971, 1:14.

4. E. Dotson, "An Augustinian Interpretation of Michelangelo's Sistine Ceiling," *Art Bulletin*, 61:1979, 223–256, 405–429. The ancestors are discussed on pages 228–230 and 418–421; these pages are meant when Dotson hereafter is named without a citation.

5. Following David's Bathsheba, the woman who is linked to their son Solomon, the second king, must be Naamah, mentioned in 1 Kings 14:31 as the mother of the third king, Roboam, whom "Solomon begat." Similarly, the mother of Roboam's son and successor, Abia, is Michaiah (2 Chronicles 13:2), and that of Abia's son, King Asa, is Azubah (1 Kings 22:42). The list of fourteen kings in Matthew omits some of those who appear in Chronicles, and no mother is named for Achaz. The other mothers are Athaliah, Zibiah, Jerusha, Abijah, Hephzibah, Meshullemeth, Jedidah, and Hamutal, all named in either Kings or Chronicles.

6. The most helpful if slight report is by G. Kühnel, "Neue Feldarbeiten zur musivischen und malerischen Ausstattung der Geburts-Basilika in Bethlehem," *Kunstchronik*, 37:1984, 507–513.

7. W. Oakeshott, *Sigena*, 1972, passim.

8. W. Sauerländer, *Gotische Skulptur in Frankreich 1140–1270*, 1970, 109, figs, 48 and 49; 113, plates 80 and 81. The author labels them as trees of Jesse, but the thirty male figures in sequence at Laon exceed the number of generations from Jesse to Joseph. Hence one may instead think of this as the genealogy out of Matthew, abbreviated to fit the available space. The set at Chartres imitates it closely but has just twenty-six figures, and so might be read either way.

9. A. Middeldorf Kosegarten, *Sienesische Bildhauer am Duomo Vecchio*, 1984, 94–95, fig. 5, 164–189.

10. Middeldorf Kosegarten, as above, identifies the figure with the flowering rod as Joseph, and this is reasonable in itself, as it resembles the one he often holds. He is seen adjacent to Mary. However, in that case Mary (with the Child) would double the representation of the fortieth generation, or, if this figure counts as Christ, the forty-first would be represented, and then the forty figures are too few by one. Middeldorf Kosegarten indeed argues that there are thirty-nine ancestors, on the grounds that the constraints of the space did not allow more. Yet it seems implausible that, having got that far, the planner would have given up with only one to go, and indeed there is unused space under the furthest left and right figures of the top row. Somewhat puzzlingly, the author identifies one of the figures as Moses (p. 349) and a second, tentatively, as Melchizedek, though they were not ancestors. Jesse must be present, and if one wished to give him his attribute of the rod in the new

context where he is seated, not recumbent so that the rod issues from his loins, a borrowing of the formula used with Joseph would be natural.

11. Nearly all books on Giotto virtually ignore these heads in the frames. G. Previtali, Giotto, 1974, is a notable exception, providing helpful numbered diagrams of all the wall and vault images on p. 348, specifying each head and providing names in an accompanying key. This shows a few errors. He lists thirteen heads as apostles, and no. seventy-four should be omitted; it is at the end of the wall and has a different identity here discussed. His figs. 422 and 423 reproduce Paul and the apostle under him and not, as stated, the two apostles opposite them, Peter (not named in the key) and the one below him (who is reproduced in fig. 487, which is not noted). The key skips no. 76, the heads of Mark the Evangelist and Pope Gregory, who are reproduced in fig. 467. These are few errors considering the pioneer attack on this complex matter. Previtali also reproduces much more of this than any other commentator; the evangelists and doctors, except Ambrose, are all shown in his figs. 466–468 and plate 36, and one of the female saints in fig. 485; two others of these are reproduced by E. Baccheschi, L'opera completa di Giotto, 1966, 106. She reproduces only six of the heads in toto, suggesting that most are shop work without the master's participation, which may be so; see the text below. Four of the twelve apostles are shown by Previtali, in figs. 422 423 as noted above and 486–487. He shows the three eleven-figure strips spanning the vault almost complete, though in an unclear way; the one at the entrance requires one to follow figs. 469, 474, and 471 in that or the reverse order to go across, and the one in the middle likewise figs. 472, 473, and 475. Of the one at the altar, poorly preserved, he shows only part, in fig. 470; the whole seems to be shown only in the special number "Giotto a Padova" of the Bollettino d'Arte, 63:1978, plate 21. The major omission is of the eight heads at the end of the top tier, of which only two are in Previtali, fig. 421, those at the altar end (thus no kings). These eight can be found otherwise only as parts of reproductions of the adjacent big scenes of the life of Mary, scenes 1, 6, 7, 12, as photographed by Scala, for instance, in B. Cole, Giotto, 1993. As noted below, the corresponding Scala slides are the best source for these, as they are for all the heads adjacent to scenes (i.e., all except the thirty-three spanning the vault).

12. The only other such cases are, first, the doctors and evangelists in pairs in the lowest tier, and, second, the bracketing of Peter with an apostle under him and Paul likewise on the opposite side, both at the middle of the wall. This doubling made it possible for Peter and Paul each to appear at the center of a set of six of the apostles (the other five being placed two on each side and one underneath), which otherwise could not have had a central figure.

13. Of the twelve kings in the barrel vault series, two have crowns different from the ten others, but they do have identical scepters, and there seems no basis for Previtali's distinguishing them here as not kings but judges, apparently on the basis of the crown forms. These two appear, in symmetrical relation to each other, one unit down from the center in the middle strip (fig. 6b). Considering the analogy with Abraham's position one unit down from the center in the altar strip, these may be meant to inaugurate the kings, continuing downward from here and then in the entrance strip. They would then be David and Solomon, which seems consistent with

147

the fact that these are the most important of these kings, understood to be the ones we see when there are only two, and that one is old and one young, as seen for instance in the work of Nicola Pisano a generation earlier. David and Solomon are given this same type of crown in Andrea Pisano's sculptures, on the Florence bell tower.

14. Baccheschi, as in note 11, plate 53, reproduces such a detail from the Peruzzi Chapel cycle by Giotto.

15. In the monochrome dado of the frescoes in Orvieto of about 1500 by Signorelli, of the end of the world, a famous error was made in one of the scenes illustrating Dante. Where the text speaks of a *vasello*, a little boat, the painter showed a vase, taking another meaning of the same word. It is evident that the artist worked without supervision and, more interesting, that it was not considered necessary to correct the error. See also "van Eyck's mistake" in note 45 of the preceding essay on women.

16. This appears in the case of the two extra kings added below to the twelve in the barrel vault, discussed above, continuing the system of alternation with non-kings down into the top level of the narratives. On one side this is done correctly, since the last figure in the barrel vault was a king, the first upper one added on the wall is not, and the lower one is (fig. 7b). However, on the other side, by error this was reversed, and the upper added figure is a king, spoiling the alternation; as his scepter is also the one almost gone now, it is no wonder he has not been recognized (fig. 7c). Since this switch makes no difference in the number of fourteen kings, the presumption that this was an error is not being used to help the hypothesis that these are ancestors. The presumption that error is the cause also seems to be undeniable, as no intended message seems to be derivable from reading such a reversal. Hence this case seems to require that error in this area did occur and was allowed to stay, supporting the view that the same happened in the cases of the omission of the same kings' crowns and the transmutation of the boys.

17. C. Semenzato, ed., *La cappella del Beato Luca e Giusto de' Menabuoi nella basilica di Sant'Antonio*, Padua, 1988, 81–83.

18. In the multi-authored monograph *Il Complesso di San Francesco Grande in Padova*, Padua, 1983, the brief discussion of this chapel, pp. 130–133, mentions only "busts of patriarchs, kings, etc.," not recognizing the ancestors. Plate 2, however, reproduces part of the series with their names below, which viewers of the Sistine will recognize (Phares, Esron, and below, Eliachim, Salathiel, Abiud). An illustration on page 79 (right) shows others that extend out from the chapel into the aisle and the pier between aisle and nave. The heads seen on the piers are more ancestors; those above them on the underside of the arches are sibyls and prophets. Other ancestors are in dadoes. There appear to be thirty-eight, and after the first twelve they appear to abandon the sequence.

19. M. Savonarola wrote in 1447. His text is most accessible in C. Gilbert, *L'arte del quattrocento nelle testimonianze coeve*, 1988, 228.

20. G. Vasari, *Le vite*, ed. R. Bettarini and P. Barocchi, 1987, 6:45.

21. This happens in the lunettes labeled Jesse-David-Solomon and Salmon-Booz-

Obeth, opposite each other. In another instance, the lunette Ezechias-Manasses-Amon, we are shown a man and a woman with two infants, one swaddled on her lap and the other in a cradle at her feet. To apply the three names in the label to the lunette only, it would have to be supposed that one of these infants is the other's father, rather than his sibling.

22. Jerome, Epistola 78, De 42 Mansiones Israelitarum in deserto, in Migne, *Patrologia Latina*, 22:1845, 698–724; the quotations are on p. 700.

23. He is so tagged in the article on him in the eleventh edition of the *Encyclopaedia Britannica*, 1910, from which also the definition below of the word homily is taken.

24. Origenes, *Werke*, 7:1921, Homilia 27, De mansionibus filiorum Israhel, 255–280; the quotations are on pages 258–261.

25. P. Damiani, Epistola ad Hildebrandem, chapter 19 of his commentary on Numbers, in Migne, *Patrologia Latina*, 145:1853, 1052.

26. The lunette labeled Jacob-Joseph shows two families, of which therefore one must be the Holy Family with Mary and Christ. It has been usual to choose the one on the right, apparently with the idea that we read from left to right in the generations. However, the recent cleaning has shown that the child of about five in this group is female (F. Mancinelli and A. de Strobel, *Michelangelo: le lunette e le vele*, 1992, 19), and there was no such person in this family. The group on the left fits much better. There is one child, and the husband is unusually old, suitable for Joseph; he is even somewhat satirized, as Joseph has often been found comic. It has also long seemed to me that Michelangelo recycled the head of the wife here as Mary in the Last Judgment.

27. H. Chapman, "Michelangelo's Rest on the Flight into Egypt," *Christie's International Magazine*, June–July 1993, 8.

28. R. Sullivan, letter to the editor, *Art Bulletin*, 59:1987, 647–49.

29. This could have been done if, starting with Abraham, the number of labels in the first pair of lunettes had been three each, the same in the second pair (comfortably placing the ninth name, Naason, next to the scene of fiery serpents), the next four pairs had had two names each, and the last two pairs again three each, a dumbbell shape—the opposite of course of the best system since it does not exploit the spandrels, quite the contrary.

30. The latter option seems more likely on account of the unrelated other changes that also occur halfway along, mentioned earlier.

31. This factor also requires that Naason shall be not only in the second bay, but on this side rather than the other. That requires arranging the labels of the lunettes in the left-right order in which they do appear in the later part of the work, after the shift of sides in the third bay mentioned earlier. That irregularity is thus also explained by the two needs to put Naason in this position, and him and his father alone. As an irregularity, it seems to make it certain that this plan was developed only after some work had been done on painting the ceiling. This does not say that the correlation with Numbers was not present from the start, but only that it was decided only later to emphasize it in this way.

TITIAN AND THE REVERSED CARTOONS OF MICHELANGELO

In courses taught in the 1950s, Johannes Wilde made the comparison shown in figs. 1 and 2, and the deduction that Titian was borrowing here from Michelangelo. Earlier this had been suggested briefly and hesitantly,[1] and rejected as "not necessary."[2] To Wilde it seemed certain; before Titian painted the *Murder of a Wife*,[3] he "must have learned about the masterly solution" in the Sistine *Temptation*.[4] After one has noticed the general consistency of the two groups, with a wife on the ground and a husband leaning over her, it grows evident that the closest analogy is between the two wives, when one of them is seen in reverse. One may guess that in his classes Wilde exploited slides to show Michelangelo's fresco in reverse, as Titian presumably had looked at it when using it. The reversal shown is not done in the published form of his lectures, but has great interest (fig. 3). The women are represented in the *same* direction in both frescoes only in the lifted hand, as it bends back as far as possible and makes contact with the figure above, with the heel of the hand strongly lit and the fingers curling up. (In my Titian photograph, made prior to cleaning, the fingers are not clear.) Everything else in Titian's figure follows the other in reverse, from the upstretched arm, through the upper torso pulled to the right and seen on a diagonal, the buttocks at rest to the left, and the thighs toward the right, to the right leg tucked back to the same extent. Titian's only changes are to foreshorten the face more strongly and, more fundamentally, to make a new lower left leg (for a reason to be suggested shortly). When it is added that the figure as a whole relates in the same

Figure 1: Titian, *The Murdered Wife,* fresco, Scuolo del Santo, Padua

Figure 2: Michelangelo,
Temptation, fresco,
Sistine Chapel, Vatican

Figure 3: Plate 2 in reverse

way to the husband above, Wilde's "must" gains acquiescence. On a further level, Michelangelo's group was a drastic reorientation of the traditional subject, reducing the likelihood that other analogous images were involved.[5]

Wilde briefly alluded to only some of the art-historical paths thus opened up. A further one is the embarrassment that for a quarter century after this parallel had been seen by Wilde's students, all the rest of us discoursing on Titian failed to notice such a source. The reversal of the wife's pose might be an excuse, or even a basis for negating Wilde's proposal, but not, I think, for specialists in the area. Reversals of poses from sources in the same artist's or another's work in this period are quite often noticed in passing, though no special study seems to have been made.[6] A half dozen examples from about 1460 to 1530 are here collected in a footnote.[7] Besides the general familiarity of the practice, it will emerge below that Titian here had a double stimulus, since the model he used, the Sistine Ceiling, itself illustrated such reversals.

The stages of Titian's work on the *Murder of a Wife* can be reconstructed, as Wilde noted, with the lucky help of the well-known drawing in Paris. Its accepted status as the record of an early version of this design is not altered by its recent, convincing removal from Titian's canon and attribution to his Paduan admirer Domenico Campagnola.[8] It shows the husband's action in profile, which certainly makes it diagrammatically clear, and so perhaps, like many profiles, the natural or primitive approach to the motif. Once the group of husband leaning over supine wife existed, Titian could not possibly have failed to be put in mind of it, whenever he first saw Michelangelo's Adam leaning over Eve. When he did see that pair, he reacted by redrawing the wife in his own fresco version, evidently not only because he found it a better "solution of the artistic problem" (Wilde), but, in addition, because he could now allude to a powerful traditional association between foreshortened lying figures and victims of violent death. Mantegna's *Dead Christ* is the most famous instance of this connotation which was seen long before and long after.[9] If we lacked the Sistine fresco, it might well have been argued that Titian revised his depiction of the wife to make this other association, which certainly explains why his one large amendment of

154

Michelangelo is to foreshorten her leg. He thus alludes literally to a classic shock effect which is naturally absent in Eve's pose. It is an apparent paradox that Titian should have been pointed toward this imagery by the Eve, which does not have to do with the tradition. But it will be further illustrated below that the recurrent circumstance wherein Titian's literal borrowings of figures, limb by limb, remain long unrecognized and then appear with a shock, may derive from his habit of drastically reorganizing their function and meaning. He takes the pose only, and makes it do completely new work in the iconography. Whereas many less talented painters take form and theme together, and many talented ones revise forms they take, it is Titian's particular approach (in these cases) to see how some pose found in a remote context may be seized just as it stands. As of course he gives such a pose his kind of vibrant life, its derivativeness may long not occur to scholars, since they do not assume vitality will appear in a literal copy. His process appears in two other cases of ca. 1511, already listed (footnote 7). A Venus by Marcantonio, leaning over Cupid, becomes the Christ of the *Noli me tangere* leaning over the Magdalene, and a running soldier in the cartoon of the *Battle of Cascina* becomes Saint Dismas carrying the Cross in a procession. Wider inferences for Titian's approach to the body's life, to composing, and to subject matter will appear below.

The same three stages of composing the *Murder of a Wife* can be shown to recur, about a decade later, in the work usually cited as Titian's first and most literal borrowing from Michelangelo,[10] the *Saint Sebastian* panel of the Brescia Altarpiece, signed and dated 1522 (fig. 4). Titian first designed the pose in another way, then became attracted to a work of Michelangelo where a similar problem had been handled, the *Rebellious Slave* (fig. 5), and then produced the present revised form where some limbs follow those of the *Slave* quite literally. It is always noted that Titian's painting reflects Michelangelo, and usually it is noted separately that it embodies revisions from an early draft,[11] but not that the Michelangelism entered only along with the revisions. The first traces of the painting of any kind are references in letters of November and of December 1, 1520, to the duke of Ferrara from his agent in Venice, telling that a *Saint Sebastian* by Titian, painted for Brescia (and so certainly this

Figure 4: Titian, *Saint Sebastian*, panel, SS. Nazzaro e Celso, Brescia

Figure 5: Michelangelo, *Rebellious Slave*, marble, Louvre, Paris

Figure 6: Titian, studies for *Saint Sebastian,* ink, Kupferstichkabinett, Berlin

picture), was being praised by all Venice (and so was in a completed state).[12] The picture showed "one arrow only, in the middle of the body," and "one arm high and one low," just as it still does. But it differed in having the arms attached to "a column." That report of a column has, ever since Cavalcaselle, been treated as evidence of a different early form, whether on this same wood panel or another. A column is suggested in Titian's page of sketches in Berlin for the Sebastian (fig. 6), and Tietze reasonably suggested in 1954 that they belong to the same early form described with a column in 1520.[13] His idea, an aside in a study of other matters, has been largely overlooked, and the distinction may seem a trivial one if it only proposes that Titian changed Sebastian's column of 1520 to a treetrunk later. It may also seem that both kinds of evidence for an early column are dubious. The agent's report might be doubted, since he, as a political specialist, did not have a historian's concern for this point, and might very easily have been a little vague about a shape in the background when he wrote from memory. But this doubt is removed by independent confirmations that there did exist a column, both in an inventory of Charles I's collection describing a version of the *Sebastian*,[14] and in an existing copy.[15] As to the second kind of evidence, the identification of the sketchy lines in the Berlin drawing as column forms might also be questioned. The forms in question appear behind only two of the six variant figures of the saint. The form to the left has cross-hatchings that do suggest reflections off a polished cylindrical surface, though doubts cannot be ruled out.[16] The other form looks more like a square-cut post, and it suggests that no motif had been settled on when the drawing was made. But this doubt is resolved when the drawing turns out to match the letter of 1520 as to another motif in addition to the column. Besides the details quoted above, the letter describes how the saint is "completely twisted in such a way that one sees almost the whole back," and this motif too, as seems not to have been observed, recurs in the Berlin sketches and does not occur in the painting. The angle of the back view differs among the six sketches, but all show it more than the painting does, and two almost fully. Such a description would be wrong for the painting, where the small part of the back represented is in shadow. Since just the same two elements in the early description that conflict with the painting both appear in the Berlin drawing,[17] Tietze's idea that the drawing shows the early form of the painting, complete in 1520, was right.[18]

The drawing shows still further differences from the present painting. The agent nicely derived the visibility of the back from the body's twist, and it is specifically the result of the shoulders beginning to fall forward. Contrariwise, in the final version, where the back is nearly hidden, the torso rises straight above the waist, an arrangement consistent with the higher position of one leg and foot, lifted and resting on the large column drum. Correspondingly, in the early drawing with the visible back, not only the shoulders but the leg and foot were lower, resting on a smaller object. And of course it is this revised higher leg and foot which copy Michelangelo's *Rebellious Slave*. In the painting, the other leg shows general consistency with the Michelangelo too. But the arms and head do not do so at all, and it is now visible that they retained the original forms of 1520. An answer is thus now available to the question why, after 1520, Titian revised a finished and praised painting. To start (as the evidence did) at the top of the figure, with the more visible back, indeed leaves this matter baffling. But starting from the foot, one can see how Titian was first attracted to Michelangelo's way of solving a problem like his own (with respect to pose), the nude with arms held behind the back. Titian adopted very closely one graphic motif, the forward leg, and then modified the rest in accordance with it, hardly changing the angles among the various parts of the body.[19] An obvious irony is that Michelangelo's torso was far from upright, and Titian could therefore have copied the leg without altering his design otherwise. To guess why he did does not seem possible, especially without knowing the angle of the drawing of the *Slave* that he must have used. Titian may have wished to retain the original suggestion of the martyr's subsidence from stress, and not to introduce the "rebellious" effect that in the *Slave* is related to the sharper centrifugal angles. In his earlier Michelangelesque revision in the *Murder of a Wife*, Titian had maintained his own original degree of dramatic stress, different in that case from the lesser tension of the Michelangelo model.[20]

A different kind of art-historical problem opened up by Wilde's com-

159

parison is the relation in time between the Sistine *Temptation* and the *Murder of a Wife*. "You will rightly ask," he remarked to the students, "how could he know Michelangelo's fresco which was unveiled on 15 August 1511," but said no more. The *Murder of a Wife*, as is well known, belongs to a documented set of three frescoes in the Scuola del Santo, Padua. The set of payments, which can be proved to be complete, begins with an advance on December 1, 1510.[21] The second one, on April 23, 1511, starts a rapid series in the following weeks, and is thus reasonably believed to mark the beginning of the actual painting, after the wait to the end of winter that is normal with frescoes.[22] By December 2, everything was complete, as we know from Titian's autograph receipt explicitly saying that it is for the "three pictures I have painted."[23] This usually accepted completion date must indeed be pushed a few days earlier, on the basis of a less famous record of the same transaction in the Scuola's ledger of its expenditures.[24] The payment of December 2 was counted out to Titian in his house in Venice: "incontadi a luj a casa soa a venetia." Not only does this clarify why his receipt was required, and saved, but also that before the date he had packed up and departed from the job site. Hence even if this last payment came promptly on the completion of the frescoes, the time interval after Michelangelo's *Temptation* seems even slightly shorter.[25]

The *Murder of a Wife* was painted in five days' work (of the other two pictures, the *Foot* took nine and the *Speaking Babe* thirteen).[26] It might be claimed that *Murder of a Wife* was the last executed, because of its drastic revision, were it not that still more drastic revision preceded the *Speaking Babe*. Its place on the wall had been assigned to a different subject, one then dropped from the cycle.[27] Morassi's remark that we do not know the order of the painting of the frescoes reflects general opinion.[28] Valcanover has interpreted the documents as, in fact, placing the *Murder of a Wife* last (the *Speaking Babe* first and the *Foot* second),[29] but the evidence does not seem firm; rather, it appears to place the *Speaking Babe* last, though another way of interpreting it would prevent any deductions.

Since these differences of date are a matter of weeks, the speed with which the Sistine ceiling became known seems in any case to be impressive. To be sure, it is known to have produced responses in the painting of Raphael in the autumn of 1511, in the Stanza della Segnatura, evidently completed by November 25.[30] Indeed, it did so in two successive phases, more literally in the figure of Heraclitus and, in a more assimilated way in the *Three Virtues*.[31] Simultaneous responses to the ceiling in other frescoes in Rome will be noted. But to find it reflected in Venice at that same moment requires rethinking the general assumption that "international" influence is transmitted with such speed only in more modern eras, as well as the standard account of how Titian learned of central Italian art. This says that specific identifiable borrowings first appear in Titian's work about 1520, in the *Sebastian* and the Ancona *Madonna*, but that earlier the *Assumption*, around 1517, marks an "abrupt change" in him by showing qualities parallel to general Roman High Renaissance tendencies.[32] Although Panofsky accompanied his demonstration that Titian quoted Michelangelo in 1511, in the *Triumph of Faith* woodcut, with broader comments on Titian's already evolving awareness of Rome and Florence,[33] his remarks seem to have borne little fruit, perhaps because Titian's woodcuts are often somewhat discounted in discussions of his art.

Titian's rapid awareness of the ceiling may be made a little less astonishing through another modification of accepted views. There is complete acceptance of August 15, 1511 (actually the evening of August 14), as the date when a large portion of the Sistine frescoes was "unveiled," as Wilde likewise put it in this context.[34] But this is an over-definite reading of the sole document, regrettably illustrating the rule that texts are investigated less when they seem to bestow firm dates. This record is only of the festive mass on the vigil and Feast of the Assumption, performed by the *sacrista* or priest in charge of the chapel, at which the pope wished to be present, "for this chapel is consecrated to the aforesaid Assumption, and the pope came to it either so that he might see the new paintings newly uncovered there, or because he was drawn by devotion."[35] No event of uncovering or unveiling appears in this text, only the mass and the visit to see the "picturas novas noviter detectas." Evidently, "newly uncovered" cannot be claimed to assert newness on the same day, and Camesasca was surely right to paraphrase

161

"noviter" as "da poco."[36] For how long might the term "new" be maintained? Some weeks at least must be allowed. It is also necessary to avoid, by articulating, any art-historical assumption that a person like Julius made patronage his first interest in life, and would therefore have made his visit at the first moment possible. Julius's long campaigns away from Rome, their costs which no doubt delayed Michelangelo's pay, a reading of the most acute annalists of the age like Guicciardini and Macchiavelli, who never mention works of art, may serve to correct an image the more powerful as it is less explicit. In the present case, the image of the pope as art lover may be dimmed by the fact that he scheduled his visit on the one pair of days when attendance in the room was most suitable for another reason, whether the "devotion" was genuine or an excuse. There is then no ground to say that the frescoes became visible only on August 14–15. When the preceding weeks are surveyed, it becomes of interest that Julius had returned to Rome on June 27 after ten months' absence;[37] an exceptional amount of business must have awaited him there. Even more suggestive is the more obscure fact that throughout the trip he had been accompanied by Paris de Grassis, the source of the quoted record.[38] To Paris, whose professional concern was with rituals and liturgies, any paintings that had not existed when he left must have seemed new.

Thus the ceiling's accessibility to Raphael—who *would* have been eager and prompt—must be pushed back from August to an unmeasurable extent, and this in turn makes his response to the fresco in his work of 1511 a good deal less puzzling, reducing the tightness of the time along with the neatness of the apparent information. The same applies to Titian.

Discussions of Titian's later borrowing from Michelangelo, in the case of the *Sebastian*, have reasonably assumed that the transmission was through drawings.[39] This would also be the first possibility to consider for Titian's earlier years, which have been less explored on this as on other points. Speaking of Titian's central Italian contacts first in relation to the *Assunta*, Wethey suggested that Lotto might have shown him drawings, adding only that about 1516 "other Venetian visitors too whose names we do not know had seen the new masterpieces of the Vatican

palace and Michelangelo's ceiling."[40] This is to omit one Venetian in
Rome who was far more closely linked to Titian than Lotto was,[41]
Sebastiano del Piombo. He moved from Venice to Rome precisely in
early or middle 1511, the critical moment at both ends, and specifically
for Titian's revision of the *Murder of a Wife*. In Venice, he had been an important member of the same circle as Titian, and in Rome before the end
of the same year he had painted frescoes that also reflect the Sistine ceiling.

The latest trace of Sebastiano in Venice may be deduced from the reliable report that he completed an unfinished painting by Giorgione,
whose death took place in September–October 1510. The only other person who completed another of Giorgione's works was Titian.[42] Hence
Sebastiano belonged to the same group of young modern painters per-
sonally, as well as stylistically, at the very end of 1510. His trip to Rome is
generally assigned to spring 1511, and can scarcely be later than the summer in the tightest case, since his first set of frescoes in Rome is recorded in a poem printed on January 27, 1512.[43] These were the lunettes in
Agostino Chigi's Farnesina. All this fits nicely the report of Vasari and
others that Chigi arranged for Sebastiano to go to Rome. A recent suggestion offers interesting arguments for placing the journey in late
August,[44] yet that seems too late to allow for Sebastiano's execution of
the entire set of lunettes in the remaining months of the year.

Later on, from 1518, one of Sebastiano's best recorded activities was
the writing of letters to Michelangelo in Florence reporting on painting
in Rome.[45] Those letters owe their unusually lucky preservation to being
in the Buonarroti archive, which had no parallel among any other artist-
recipients. Already before 1511 drawings after works of Michelangelo
were being made by artists not in his shop; notable surviving ones are
Leonardo's tiny notation of the *David* and Raphael's finished study of
1507 from the *Matthew*.[46] It is here suggested that in 1511 Sebastiano was
writing to Titian in Venice the same sort of letters that he is known to
have written to Michelangelo in 1518, and, further, that he made and sent
with such letters the sort of drawings after Michelangelo that other
artists are known to have been making. The hypothesis that he did not
so write back to Venice and did not make such drawings is perhaps the

163

Figure 7: Titian, *Sacred and Profane Love,*
(detail of *Profane Love*), canvas, Galleria
Borghese, Rome

Figure 8: Michelangelo, *Prophet Joel,* fresco, in
reverse, Sistine Ceiling, Vatican

more implausible one; all that is new here is the suggestion that the two activities were one.

Although 1511 is the first year when paintings are found reflecting the ceiling, it drew special attention in another way in 1510, so that the influences are not so rapid as they might seem. Francesco Albertini gives the ceiling remarkable emphasis in his guidebook to Rome, whose colophon records the completion of the printing on February 4, 1510.[47] Writing as if addressing the pope, and after mentioning the wall frescoes of the Sistine, he continues: "Your holiness provided [the chapel] with iron chains, and adorned the upper ceiling part with very beautiful paintings and gold, the admirable work of Michel Archangel the Florentine, extremely admirable in the art of painting and sculpture."[48] This remark has often, unjustifiably, been dated at an even earlier and astonishing June 3, 1509, along with the whole book.[49] In 1510, Albertini evidently anticipated the completion of the frescoes out of a wish, understandable in a guidebook author, to postpone his text's obsolescence. Albertini made another allusion to a still incomplete work in a second major instance,[50] and it happens in earlier writing.[51] The strange reference to gold would also suggest that the author had not seen the frescoes he describes, where gold is particularly sparse, and that he was instead evoking splendor in a rhetorical way, as well as perhaps recalling the wall frescoes.[52] Yet Albertini's notice, in a book that includes no analogous reference to Raphael, shows that the ceiling frescoes were being awaited in an exceptional way.

Wilde drew attention also to a second case a few years later in which Titian painted a figure that "closely resembles" one from the Sistine ceiling "in shape and pose":[53] this is Profane Love (fig. 7) whose debt to the *Prophet Joel* is once again most apparent when the figure is reversed (fig. 8). It is, further, evident that this debt is significant only if a relation between the *concetti* or basic structures is allowed; if a reader holds that only specific details on the surface provide proof, Wilde's comparison in this case perhaps cannot convince. The kinship of the figures lies first in the rather special category which they share, both being of course grand monumental figures of imposing dignity, yet relaxing so informally that they lean far to one side. Though the category may seem rather general,

165

Figure 9: Titian, *Sacred and Profane Love,* (detail of *Sacred Love*), canvas, Galleria Borghese, Rome

Figure 10: Michelangelo, *Nude* above *Delphic Sibyl*, fresco, body in reverse, head original, Sistine Ceiling, Vatican

it may give pause that the vast numbers of images of seated majesty, like Madonnas and rulers, do not seem to yield, at least to me, any earlier example. The type involves a typical High Renaissance problem of form, to reconcile the heroically grand with the freely mobile, and Michelangelo's solution may have struck Titian for that reason. More specifically, both figures incline at the same angle, turn their heads back to the center, and share the foreshortening of their left arms and the upper halves of their right ones; Titian also places his figure's left leg forward and draws the right one back in the same pattern used for Joel. The parallel between the figures offers already a good deal more than many comparisons, to balance the looming unlikeness of the warmly created character types. Indeed, one might borrow a formulation from medieval studies and call Titian's figure a misunderstood copy, since in Joel the elbow's support justifies his leaning sideward, but Profane Love's elbow and arm seem to have no way of transferring weight, from the shoulders on down to the base; her fingers just touch the bowl when we might ask them to press on it. As to environment, both figures have a wide stone seat, whose strong horizontal accentuates the body's diagonal mass. In the Titian, the sarcophagus was presumably a given before the pose of the figure, and one could speculate, by analogy to the way Titian certainly was made interested in the cases already discussed, that what he liked about the pose of Joel was the help it gave him in relating the big figure to that horizontal. Also, Joel's putti hovering behind him are comparable to the Cupid at Profane Love's elbow. Not a twin by any means, the Cupid seems closer in his downward and frontward gaze to Joel's putti than he does to any of the numerous others on the ceiling. But this link is of interest only because its effect is cumulative with all the other more cognate ones.

It is hard to say why Wilde did not call attention to a similar debt to the ceiling in the one remaining figure of Titian's picture, that of Sacred Love (fig. 9).[54] It seems only natural that, as the richly dressed Profane Love reflects a robed and seated figure, the nude Sacred Love reflects a Sistine nude.

Once again the figure is reversed, or rather most of it is. As shown here (fig. 10), the head by exception retains the direction of

167

Michelangelo's, the same exception as the wife's hand taken from Eve, both times involving that extremity of the figure which connects it with its companion. Titian's source is one of the nudes above Delphica, in the same first bay of the ceiling as Joel. (One might think of Sebastiano starting a set of sketches at this end.) In both artists' figures, the bodies again lean to the side, and, as they do, share the same gentle turning of the torso so that the left shoulder is still a bit behind, whence in both the shadowed arm descends and touches the stone seat; meantime both left legs project the knees forward, while both right legs hang loosely.[55] The one major difference appears in Sacred Love's lifted arm, where Titian typically drew on another source, his own earlier work. As has often been pointed out, Sacred Love's head and arm echo those of a figure from his fresco cycle of the Fondaco de' Tedeschi,[56] also a nude turning left to look at her clothed companion. An attractive tentative reconstruction is possible, then, of the process of designing *Sacred and Profane Love* which is parallel to the one indicated with more direct evidence in the *Murder of a Wife* and with even more basis in the *Sebastian*. Titian's initial idea for a figure, in the two later cases a fresh handling of one he had completed not long before, was in each instance further reworked when he saw Michelangelo's solution of a similar figure problem.

Art-historical comparisons like these, alleging influence, of course always involve less than full identity of motif, and are thus very vulnerable to the simple allegation of being unconvincing, which is sure to be offered by some observers about every comparison. One would welcome any even slightly firmer test of sufficiency in comparisons, to keep those examples that passed it from being voted down (and those that failed it from being offered). In this case, such a test may be available. There is already a figural source for Sacred Love well established in the literature, a Nereid on a sarcophagus in the Campo Santo, Pisa. First proposed by Curtius in an article on Titian and the antique, this source was confirmed as "demonstrated conclusively" by Brendel in his well-known study of the same topic, and in turn was endorsed by Panofsky.[57] Whereas all comparisons are deniable, it is undeniable that Titian's figure has a less close likeness to this Nereid than to the Sistine nude. The Nereid is most of all an image of sitting, her body folded in three parts, near vertical, diagonal, and near vertical again, with a clear outline following these angles all around, in the plane. She is of course without foreshortening, as she is without Titian's single long contour. She faces and looks almost directly to the front, has only one arm visible, and, as Brendel noted, no other element in her sarcophagus relates to any other part of Titian's picture: such a factor, when present, is often a major aid in making comparisons persuasive. And whereas Titian's figure relates to Michelangelo's in each of the qualities missing in the Nereid, the converse is the case only with the uplifted arm already mentioned (which might evoke the hypothesis that the Nereid influenced Titian's first figure of this series, on the Fondaco). Since the high acceptance in our literature of the Nereid as a source is also undeniable, it would seem incontrovertible that it must accept also the more intimately related source, the Sistine nude.

All three of Titian's borrowings from the ceiling, discussed above, reverse the poses. This procedure is itself a borrowing from the ceiling, where over eighty figures are reversed. Yet the most thorough descriptions of the Sistine ceiling mention only individual cases or groups. No doubt Michelangelo usually exploited reversals in inconspicuous areas with a decorative aspect. The smallest-scale figures on the ceiling are the forty-eight nude putti in pairs which support the twelve thrones as caryatids. The pair at the left and the pair at the right of each throne are each other's mirror images, produced by turning a cartoon over. The same applies to the twenty-four bronze-colored nudes in the adjacent triangular fields. So are the putti with nameplates under the prophets and sibyls, in the first three cases: i.e., Delphica's putto is a mirror image of Joel's, Isaiah's of Erythraea's, Cumaea's of Ezekiel's. In the subsequent bays, the putti are individually drawn, a nice confirmation, if it were needed, that the work began at the entrance end. It is worth asking why Michelangelo retained the mechanical pairing throughout in the first two sets mentioned, but not here. It is not a matter of scale; the bronze nudes are seven-foot-tall adults, 211 cm, the nameplate putti are five-feet-five, 165 cm. The most obvious difference is that the latter are less strictly related to their frames, perhaps because they have a nearer approach to a real acting role.

This brings us to the one other set of pairs on the ceiling, the *ignudi* par excellence. Their painted heights are of the same scale as the other pairs', ranging from 150 cm to 180 cm, but they are physically larger in scale because they are sitting. The *ignudi* too, as is always noted, begin at the entrance end as mirror-image pairs but change later on (fig. 11). Yet except for Camesasca, often alert to technical considerations,[58] the literature does seem to have inferred here as it did with the other nudes that a single cartoon was used twice. Probably commentators have stopped short because in these famous *ignudi,* unlike the other sets, the symmetry is not at all mechanical. The figures have precisely the same layout, but they differ all over in details, to an extent increasing with the distance from the entrance end. That cartoons were used for them is known from Vasari, who saw some.[59] Are we to infer from the divergent details that each was painted from a separate cartoon used only once? Or, alternatively, did Michelangelo use a cartoon twice for a pair, letting it establish the contours—as he also let the still-visible incisions in the plaster do—and then only in the painting stage vary the details of each figure freely by hand? In the former case, two not quite identical cartoons would have been called for, a necessary implication of the usual view which seems not to have been considered. If Michelangelo had contemplated at all such a laborious extra step of repetitive work, the twice-used cartoons of the other nudes would have been there to suggest at once how to bypass that step. It is clear that Michelangelo welcomed mechanical aids to cut expenditure of time, not only such cartoons, but such another aid toward symmetry as the incisions in Delphica's face, which establish her level eyes and identical cheek contours.[60]

Mechanical symmetry is obvious throughout the outlines of the poses only in the pair of nudes over Joel. Within the outlines, the faces turn in different directions,[61] and other small divergences appear in the bodies. In the nudes over Delphica in the same bay (where one of them is lost and known only through copies), symmetry recurs in the same sense and nearly to the same degree, in body, head, legs, and one arm, but is rejected in the other arm, for a reason soon to be proposed. Yet even that arm, if seen as a unit with the festoon resting on it, has a general balance of outlined areas with the same unit in the other nude

170

Figure 11: Michelangelo, detail of section
including Isaiah and Delphic Sibyl and
Joel, Sistine Ceiling, Vatican

Figure 12: Michelangelo, detail of section
including Isaiah and Erythraean Sibyl,
Sistine Ceiling, Vatican

(and in a smaller instance, this same device of qualified symmetry had appeared in the nudes over Joel). When Tolnay observes that the symmetry of the pairs of *ignudi* breaks down in the second bay,[62] he might perhaps usefully have specified that it remains as strong on one side, over Erythraea. There the two bodies, arms, and legs are still contained in mirror-image contours to just the same extent as before. Symmetry diminishes conspicuously only on the other side, over Isaiah, where the arms of the two nudes (but no other parts) differ emphatically, and in that respect begin to resemble the ones of the later bays. The very interesting inference, not possible for any other bay, that Erythraea's side may be of earlier design than Isaiah's side, was duly drawn by Bertini,[63] but seems not to have been absorbed into the literature. (Even in the pair over Isaiah, the new asymmetry in the arms is much less emphatic if they are viewed as masses unified with their festoons, as before; when this is done, asymmetry is striking only in one arm raised over a head, among all the limbs of these two figures. See fig. 12.)

Five of these first six nudes on the ceiling, over Joel, Delphica, and Erythraea, and none anywhere else, share an approach to action in which just one arm works at the task, grasping the ribbon that holds the medallion, and the other arm simply descends in a general vertical to rest quite clearly on the front part of the seat, or on its cushion.[64] Work done with one hand is ordinary, but in combination with the use of mirror-image cartoons it obviously makes every second nude work left-handed. The nudes show this, and also show fascinatingly that Michelangelo took steps to diminish this evidently unwanted effect, with broad repercussions in his design which appear to have remained unsurveyed. It seems a natural postulate that in each pair, the right-handed nude follows the cartoon as drawn, and each of these right-handed, "original" nudes is painted to our right. The nudes to our left consistently undergo varying types of readjustments, which all tone down the impact of left-handedness. First, over Joel, in the most symmetrical pair, the one small asymmetry, as noted above, is the slight change in position of the hand holding the festoon. The right-handed nude actually pulls the ribbon toward himself, but the left-handed one merely rests his fingers on it. The work of the left hand is not shown as having the vigor of the other figure's right-handed work. This refinement might be held to be overread, if noted in isolation. In the second pair over Delphica, the one largest asymmetry is that the left-handed nude (the one known only in copies) holds his right arm at shoulder level. (This is the one exception, mentioned above, to the rule that the first six nudes all let their nonworking arms fall in a vertical.) His right hand then serves as a bracket or hook from which the festoon hangs. Even if, as a nonworking hand, it is in place and has no moving parts, it gains a functional utility. Thus, whereas in the first example left-handed work is deemphasized, by making that work milder in the mirror-image figure, in the second example it is deemphasized by increasing the role of the right hand, the logical complementary alternative method. Since both shifts, visually very different, involve the only asymmetries in those figures, and reach the same result, it would appear that this was their purpose. No other interconnected explanation of these variations appears to have been made.

In the third pair of nudes, over Erythraea, left-handedness is no longer allowed. The left nude still shares his partner's contour, but both his arms cross his body, and the right one crosses in front where it can grasp the ribbon. The left arm crosses behind him where it can rest on the seat, or rather on the cushion, for the first time. The cushion hides the hand and thereby the complexity of the arm position; a possible explanation is that Michelangelo did not want to draw attention to this virtuosity, induced perforce in this secondary figure. This nude with *contrapposto* arms is also the first with an emotional expression, suggesting pressure more acutely perhaps than any later one. It is easy to see how this results from his strained pose, whose source in turn in the problem of the working hands had not been so obvious. It seems evident that just this particular set of relationships among these six figures would not have happened without the twice-used cartoon as the point of departure.

The later nudes are diminishingly involved with the initial problem. In the nudes over Isaiah, Michelangelo found the rational solution, using a mirror-image cartoon that did not include arms. The arms here are perhaps more complicated and hard to follow in their actions, and more asymmetrical, than any others on the ceiling, an effect that might well result from the special attention required when they were separately

173

drawn. They inaugurate a rule of work with both arms which is then retained. In the third bay, over Ezekiel and Cumaea, mirror-image cartoons may still have been used in the bodies and part of the legs—each
time the lower half of one leg is outside the system—but if so, the free-
hand variations are much more prominent. The third bay thus shares
with Isaiah's nudes from the second bay the effect of symmetry apart
from the arms, not found in any other group, confirming their chronological unity. In the third bay, the nudes at our left, made from the reversed cartoons, have a new difficulty. Their shoulders are so placed that
their right arms are at the front, far from their ribbons. These arms fall
vertically, as before, but no longer passively. They hold onto the ribbons,
which must, therefore, wind around the far sides of their seats. This oddity has often been noted as an involuted design, without an exploration
of its genetics. In the fourth and fifth bays, Michelangelo abandoned the
twice-used cartoons, just where he is always observed to have abandoned those of the nameplate putti. No reason for the latter abandonment has been offered or is obvious, and hence it seems most likely to
have been made in tandem with the same change in the nudes. This
would be another confirmation that the nudes did have such cartoons
before. They had evidently been more trouble than help, and
Michelangelo made a great virtue of abandoning them. In the fourth
bay, he invented pairs that allude to each other's poses in the freest sort
of suggestion, and, in the fifth, pairs that are conspicuously dissociated.

One might take for granted Michelangelo's sensitivity to the left-right
antithesis, even before considering his daily work with his hands and his
unusual consciousness of his body.[65] A later poem beginning, "Now on
my right foot, now upon my left one. / Toward my salvation shifting in
my searches," seems to me to have been somewhat overinterpreted[66]
when the left foot is equated with "vice," introduced in the next line—
one surely does not search for salvation through vice—but the poet does
invoke in it the wrong "road" of those who "see no Heaven." And that
brings up the two most remarkable instances of left-handedness in the
ceiling, Delphica and Erythraea themselves. Again both work with the
left arm and let the right fall, and again the three later sibyls are equally
active with both hands. The surprising recurrence of the recessive trait,

in the two sibyls painted first, seems not to have been discussed.[67] It goes without saying that each is one of a pair of figures with a prophet, of course not in mechanical symmetry, and the prophets are right-handed. Left-handedness might here betoken inferiority in the sibyls, either because they are female or because they did not see the true religion, but that attractive possibility runs afoul of the abandonment of the device in the other three sibyls. It is now also obvious that the left-handed sibyls share their ceiling area with the left-handed *ignudi*, and are also analogous in that the device disappears among the later members of their series. The nudes cannot have derived left-handedness from the sibyls, since they derive it from the reversed cartoon. But the first two sibyls can have derived left-handedness from the adjacent nudes. After these first stimulated the possibility, it would have been reinforced by the additional factors that made it appropriate, but dropped when the nudes ceased to be symmetrical.

It need not be that Titian saw all this when he looked at drawings after the ceiling. But as a painter with really similar concerns for the figure, and as a woodcut designer, he might easily have registered at once the large role played by reversed cartoons in the ceiling. The length of the preceding paragraphs may be justified if they make that seem reasonable. And then the reversal in his copies from the ceiling may become not a doubt-inducing qualification of the proposed source but, rather, integral to its attraction for him. He certainly saw what was perhaps new in Michelangelo's use of the reversed cartoon, its application to the monumental figure. To be sure, expansion toward the monumental and the colossal was itself a vehicle of modernity at the moment when the Sistine ceiling was painted, and may have carried reversed cartoons along in its wake without special consideration. However that may be, it brings up the most important way in which the *Sacred and Profane Love* reflects Michelangelo. Starting with the truism that Michelangelo made sculptural paintings, Titian may be seen here putting such sculptural figures at their ease in a Venetian sort of painting. Like the Sistine colossi, and like no earlier figures by Titian, these two women are isolated statues, whose volume and stability produce their heroic inevitability. They then famously become *the* statement of their subject matter, a status

175

Figure 13: Titian, *The Three Ages of Man*, canvas, Collection Duke of Sutherland, Mertoun

Figure 14: Michelangelo, *Josias,* spandrel, fresco in reverse, Sistine Ceiling, Vatican

Figure 15: Sebastiano del Piombo, *Daughters of Cecrops*, fresco, Farnesina, Rome

shared with a few other images like the Sistine *Creation of Adam* and Leonardo's *Last Supper* (the first colossal one), and it does not matter in this case that the subject matter is arguable. Titian's "sculptures" contrast with their empty but airy world. Whereas Michelangelo had shown how such figures by themselves could be successful paintings, Titian makes that feat seem effortless by drenching them in Venetian colored and textured light, a living sensuous environment. Yet it is the Sistine ancestry that explains why the *Sacred and Profane Love* is a "classic," projecting itself to posterity as Titian had never done in any earlier work.

It is all the more unlikely that in Titian's work of these years and this type the *Sacred and Profane Love* would be an isolated homage to the ceiling. The *Three Ages of Man* repeats, again in reverse, one of the groups of ancestors of Christ in the Sistine spandrels (figs. 13 and 14). (Here Wilde is no longer a guide.) The group is the one between Delphica and Isaiah, generally known as the family of Josias. Titian's two figures embodying the second age of life, the young lovers, have a specially defined interrelation. As they look closely into each other's eyes, the young woman also leans far into the spatial territory of the young man, who is motionless, showing acceptance only in the stretching of his neck. Since the painting is generically a Giorgionesque pastoral, the figures may well have sat on the ground from the beginning of planning, whether or not the Sistine spandrel was already in Titian's mind. All eight of these spandrels show a man and woman sitting on the ground. But in the other seven, the man plays a secondary role, in shadow behind the woman. Thus the Josias group alone could be useful to Titian, and he borrowed from it in large ways and in some details. Already on the Sistine ceiling the man is passive, in fact he is asleep, and the woman presses into his space with her head, shoulders, and arm. Foreground details are especially alike, the woman's bent arm resting near one of the man's lifted knees, and his legs sprawling forward in such a way that they expend no energy and yet establish a wall, enclosing the woman behind it.

Once the reverse image of the Josias spandrel is introduced, the composition is found to have surprisingly wide links to other derivations. It will be recalled that in 1511 Sebastiano painted his first Roman works, eight lunettes in the Farnesina. Writers on Sebastiano have duly noticed

177

his particular awareness of Michelangelo's spandrels. Pallucchini suggested that the Farnesina lunette of *Flora* must be indebted to the Ezekias spandrel,[68] and Dussler, who preferred to link the *Flora* to the ceiling's other reclining nudes, saw the lunette of the *Daughters of Cecrops* (fig. 15) as derived from Michelangelo's "family scenes of the lunettes and spandrels."[69] The reversed view of the Josias spandrel makes more clear that Sebastiano's indebtedness is to this same group borrowed by Titian. One daughter of Cecrops, again sitting on the ground in profile, leans far over to the other, and in this case the same sprawling leg in front is transferred to that forward-leaning figure. It may thus be demonstrated that Sebastiano did, in 1511, make reversed drawings from figures by Michelangelo, such figures as, it was suggested above, he sent to Titian in drawings in the same year. A drawing by Sebastiano is preserved[70] which might be just one working stage away from such a copy.

It was also late in 1511 that Raphael was taking ideas from the ceiling for his Heraclitus and then, in a more assimilated way, for the *Three Virtues* of the Stanza della Segnatura. This general derivation is always accepted, but specific sources are less easily named, since Raphael's way with derived forms was not at all like Titian's. The seated Fortitude and Temperance certainly do suggest various seated nudes of the ceiling. But the central Prudence, in profile with her feet stretched out before her on level ground, matches the forms of the Josias spandrel, in reverse, more closely than any of the other relevant figures of the ceiling. It may therefore be that Sebastiano, Raphael, and Titian all paid special tribute to the spandrels, which generally have been the least noted part of the Sistine ceiling, and inspection of the reversed views may assist in arriving at this surprising conclusion.

The sculptural groups of the *Three Ages* and of the *Sacred and Profane Love*, generally similar within Titian's oeuvre, seem then also to have been closely connected in their working method. Since the *Three Ages* is now usually dated no later than 1513, with good arguments,[71] the new date of 1514 that Wethey offered for the *Sacred and Profane Love* for quite different reasons might be the more attractive.[72] (It would then seem ironic that the same writer seems not to lean to the usual 1513 for the *Three Ages*.[73]) These early dates may be even more attractive if considered together with the observation that soon after, from 1516, a traditional approximate date for the *Sacred and Profane Love*, Titian seems to have changed his approach to copying figures. He no longer lifted whole groups of actors from earlier images, but, if copying literally at all, he seems to have taken no more than a part of a figure, as seen in the *Saint Sebastian*, or a whole secondary figure, like the bacchante. Alternatively, he also made less literal use of his admired sources in the newest central Italian art.

1. T. Hetzer, "Vecellio," in Ulrich Thieme and Hans Becker, *Allegemeines Lexikon der bildenden Künstler*, Leipzig, XXXIV, 1940, 161, writes that Titian's woman "perhaps" derives from Michelangelo's. The sparse absorption of his point no doubt reflects scholars' non-expectation of original proposals in Thieme-Becker entries.

2. Rodolfo Pallucchini, *Tiziano*, Florence, 1969, I, 237, who unlike other Titian scholars did note Hetzer's suggestion, responded negatively perhaps as a result of being invited only to consider the single figures, and not in reverse.

3. From the starting point of hagiography, this fresco is a unit in a cycle of Anthony miracles, and its theme is "Anthony Resuscitating a Woman Killed by Her Jealous Husband." But the literature rightly notes that the preceding murder replaces the miracle as the chief concern in the fresco. (For the story see Antonio Morassi, *Tiziano: gli affreschi della scuola del Santo a Padova*, Milan, 1966, 7, 10.) In the fresco's second scene, in small scale in the background, the repentant husband kneels before the saint and is told to go home, where he will find his wife alive. The name usually given to the fresco, reflecting its visual center, appears already in the payment documents. It is the second of "duj quadri pizoli," namely "quello amazo soa mogiere" (Erice Rigoni, "Appunti e documenti sul pittore Girolamo del Santo," *Atti e memorie della R. Accademia di Scienze, Lettere e Arti in Padova*, N.S., LVIII, 1940–41 (issued 1942), 55, also repr. E. Rigoni, *L'Arte rinascimentale in Padova*, Padua, 1970). Titian's interchange of dramatic spaces, putting the official subject matter in the background in small scale, was a device that was in the air. He probably knew and exploited such a masterly example as Lucas van Leyden's engraving of 1508, *Susanna and the Elders* (B. 33). The two works share not only this layout (Lucas's tiny heroine is halfway up near the right edge) but also the same moral division (villainy nearby and large, good protagonist distant and small) and the same lighting (left foregrounds shadowed by a hill, upper right areas brightly lit, a similar line of division between them).

4. Johannes Wilde, *Venetian Painting from Bellini to Titian*, Oxford, 1974, 123. The posthumous publication of the class lectures is a tribute from students, and proves to be thoroughly deserved.

5. Erwin Panofsky, *Problems in Titian*, New York, 1969, 28, note. In an aside in a book on Titian, oddly enough, he observed that in earlier tradition Adam and Eve in the *Temptation* usually both stand, that in this period Adam but not Eve is sometimes on the ground, and that Michelangelo reversed that last arrangement.

6. Ernst Gombrich, *Norm and Form*, London, 1966, 95, discussed the phenomenon briefly as the base out of which nonmechanical symmetry evolves, and this aspect has been further explored by D. Summers, "*Figure come fratelli*, a Transformation of Symmetry in Renaissance Painting," *Art Quarterly*, N.S., I, 1977, 61.

7. Reversal in the copying of classical motifs in the Renaissance has been called "often the case" by P. Williams Lehmann, "The Sources and Meaning of Mantegna's Parnassus," in Phyllis Williams Lehmann and Karl Lehmann, *Samothracian Reflections*, Princeton, 1973, 74. The late 15th-century Italianizing French manuscript

illuminator, Jean Colombe, was recently described as often repeating a composition in reverse from a previous book of his own (C. Schaefer, "Les Débuts de l'atelier de Jean Colombe," *Gazette des Beaux-Arts*, LXXXIX, 1977, 146). Wilde, who is silent as to Titian's reversal of Michelangelo, in the same cited passage makes a telling case for Titian's having used a figure by Marcantonio in reverse, also ca. 1511. A print would obviously suggest such use, seen also when the derivative is a print. This is seen in Titian's *Triumph of Faith*, still again ca. 1511, where a figure is derived from Michelangelo's *Cascina* cartoon, one which is absent from the two early partial engravings after the cartoon (Panofsky, 58). The figure faces the same way on Titian's woodblock as in the source, but one may presume that the reversal in the print was taken into account. (It is often noted that in the *Bacchanal of the Andrians* Titian took another figure from the *Cascina* composition that is also absent from the engravings; Charles Hope, in "The Camerino d'Alabastro of Alfonso d'Este," *Burlington Magazine*, CXIII, 1971, p. 715, argues for a later than usual date for the *Andrians* on the ground, among others, that Titian almost certainly could not have seen the *Cascina* until 1519. This overlooks his earlier use of it, very likely from a copy, as Wilde assumed; p. 150.) Reversal in fresco painting is well established as to decorative borders and the like, with one cartoon used twice, from both sides of the paper; rich examples are in the Orvieto frescoes of Signorelli, begun in 1499 (good illustrations in Enzo Carli, *Il Duomo di Orvieto*, Rome, 1965, figs. 220, 238, 239, 240). Piero della Francesca's fresco of the queen of Sheba in Arezzo is the classic case of the twice-used cartoon involving larger figures in a scene, as Kenneth Clark first noted (*Piero della Francesca*, London, 1951, 31). As the queen moves to the left and to the right in the two incidents of the fresco, the profile face of one of her ladies recurs in reverse. Two canvases by Lotto of a *Madonna and Child* show a Christ Child traced from one cartoon reversed (William Suida, *Catalogue of Paintings in the John and Mable Ringling Museum of Art*, Sarasota, 1949, 65). Other than Lehmann, none of these authors suggests that something common is being exemplified, but it may be that this is one of the conventions known to a number of specialists that has never explicitly been brought out.

8. Konrad Oberhuber, *Disegni di Tiziano e della sua cerchia*, Vicenza, 1976, 123–24, with earlier literature. Tietze's original doubt of the attribution may then be confirmed, even without one of his grounds, a belief that Titian would not revise a composition so drastically. His powerful motivation for doing so is now visible.

9. Erich von Rathe, *Die Ausdrucksfunktion extrem verkurzter Figuren*, London, 1938, the standard study, is too narrow in its range of examples. The motif appears at the earliest date when corporal action became a vehicle of expressiveness, as seen in Ambrogio Lorenzetti's *Franciscan Martyrs*, at S. Francesco, Siena. Just before the date of Titian's fresco, the young Raphael is seen borrowing the device from Signorelli, as Oskar Fischel noted (the two works illustrated in C. Gilbert, "A Miracle by Raphael," *North Carolina Museum of Art Bulletin*, VI, 1965, figs. 20, 21, and citation of Fischel, p. 20).

10. Thus by Wethey, 1969, 18, who dates the figure 1522 here, but on p. 126 says it was already completed in 1520. The divergence is not resolved in the book, but can be, as will appear. The catalogue report that the Brescian patron "ordered the pic-

181

ture in 1520" (p. 127) appears to have no basis. It is known only that it was then in process. The patron had arrived in Venice as a papal legate in 1517 (Pastor, VII, 1923, 221–22), and it would hardly be unusual for Titian to be at work on a painting agreed on some years earlier. See Harold Wethey, *The Paintings of Titian, I: The Religious Paintings*, 1969; II: *The Portraits*, 1972; III: *The Mythological and Historical Paintings*, London, 1975. See also Ludwig von Pastor, *The History of the Popes*, St. Louis, 1923ff.

11. Wethey, 1969, 126, is a surprising exception, saying only that it was finished in 1520 and no more. His opinion justifiably reflects the report of 1520 indicating completion, but not the differences between that report and the painting we have.

12. G. Campori, "Tiziano e gli estensi," *Nuova antologia*, 9th year, XXVIII, 1874, 59. This hundred-year-old publication, summarizing the letters and quoting key passages, is still the most accessible source for this material, astonishingly so even though Campori was an admirable scholar. The sentences actually describing the *Sebastian* are relatively accessible, extracted from Campori, in [N. Barbantini], *Mostra di Tiziano*, Venice, 1935, 53. The slight availability of these texts for reading, as with many documents found only in 19th-century journals, no doubt explains in part why the inferences offered here were not made long ago.

13. H. Tietze, "An Early Version of Titian's *Danae*: An Analysis of Titian's Replicas," *Arte veneta*, VIII, 1954, 200. The suggestion was adopted by Valcanover, 1960, 80–81 of the English edition, but not noted by Panofsky or Wethey.

14. Joseph Crowe and Giovanni Battista Cavalcaselle, *Life and Times of Titian*, London, 1881, I, 253. Cavalcaselle proposed (pp. 345–46, 449) that among the lost replicas one had been autograph, the *Sebastian* Titian sent in 1530 to the duke of Mantua. Cavalcaselle also proposed that this was the one later recorded in Charles I's inventory; Tietze agreed. Wethey doubted that Charles's picture had come from Mantua, calling that an "assumption" by Cavalcaselle. It was indeed, but Wethey's doubt of it is reinforced more than it might be because his own list of recorded versions omits the Mantua record, so that Cavalcaselle is not credited with that much base for his proposal. Tietze further suggested that Charles's *Sebastian* with its column, already identified by him as the one Titian sent to Mantua in 1530, might have really been Titian's first version of 1520. But this is excluded since Charles's picture also had three arrows piercing the saint, as the inventory records; this was noted by Roberto Tassi, *Tiziano: il polittico Averoldi in San Nazaro*, Brescia, 1976, 11. It would also have been odd for Titian, if he had been induced by the praise of the figure to extract it from his commissioned polyptych, to keep it then for ten years before sending it to a duke.

15. Wethey, 1969, fig. 238. Apart from the column, this version reflects the final version, not the earlier variants discussed below.

16. Tassi, *Il polittico*, 11, sees a tree rather than a column in the virtually identical forms of the Frankfurt drawing (discussed in n. 18).

17. No further points of description occur in the letter. The description's only divergence from the Berlin drawing is that the latter shows no arrow. That should not be held significant for the identity of the version, since the function of the drawing is

evidently to establish the pose, as the six variants indicate. Props could well be held aside.

18. Tietze also assigned to this early phase Titian's only other known drawing for the *Sebastian*, in Frankfurt. But its "column" is rather more doubtful than the ones in Berlin, being broken at the top in a way that suggests a splintered bough. In any case, this drawing is different in purpose from the other, intended not to work out the pose, but for later, more pictorial matters, including the arrow. With respect to the differences between the versions discussed here, the Frankfurt drawing belongs to the later version, after 1520.

19. This reconstruction also gives a plausible answer to another (unraised) problem, why Titian not only signed the panel but dated it, 1522. So far as knowledge goes, he never had put a date on a picture before, and did not again at least for 20 years, more probably not ever. This unique act can reasonably be linked to the uniqueness of redoing a finished painting. The connecting term between the two might then be his feeling "Now it really is done!" Since the date is an inscription attached to his signature, a personal biographical interpretation seems allowed. An analogy would be to the "Laus Deo" added to the end of a manuscript.

20. After this close look at the forms in the Berlin drawing, and at its status, the story may be rounded out by pointing to this first version's derivation in turn from a work done just before. Titian's *Saint George* in the Cini Collection, Venice, is now identifiable, after cleaning, with a work put on public view on May 27, 1517 (F. Valcanover, "Il restauro del S. Giorgio Cini di Tiziano," *Arte veneta*, XIX, 1965, 199–200). Apart from the arm holding the sword, Saint George already shows the pose of the first Saint Sebastian. It is especially interesting to observe the very visible back and the small difference in height between the placements of the feet. The posited evolution from this figure of Saint George of 1517 to the final Saint Sebastian of 1521 22 would perhaps not be acceptable without the intermediate term of the Berlin drawing.

21. Rigoni (1970, 197–98) is more exact than the publication by Sartori usually cited, Antonio Sartori, *L'Arciconfraternità del Santo*, Padua, 1955.

22. Thus F. Valcanover, *Tutta la pittura di Tiziano*, Milan, 1960, also English ed., *All the Paintings of Titian*, New York, 1962, I, 51, places the start of the work on April 23. It is because frescoes need water that will not freeze that they are seasonal work, as unlikely to be undertaken at times of low temperature as outdoor cement work today. Though familiar to specialists (oral comment by Leonetto Tintori), this factor is not generally recorded in handbooks, and it is common to see arguments about fresco dating on a twelve-month basis. Individual recognition begins perhaps with Ernst Steinmann, *Die sixtinische Kapelle*, Munich, 1905, II, 226 (with poor technical explanation), yet the usual proposal for the beginning of the Sistine frescoes in January 1509 does not consider this factor. Thus it may be justifiable to draw attention to a small collection of documentary supports for the seasonal pattern included in an article of mine (C. Gilbert, "L'Ordine cronologico degli affreschi Bardi e Peruzzi," *Bolletino d'arte*, LIII, 1968, issued 1972, 196).

An additional case may be cited. In Prato in 1410, one patron warned another

183

not to allow wall painting in icy weather because the work would go bad and the money be wasted; it was a tip the patron had had from an expert, he said, "who told me these jobs in this weather are bad." (R. Piattoli, "Un mercante del trecento e gli artisti del tempo suo," *Rivista d'arte*, XII, 1930, 124.) The other painters besides Titian in the cycle at the Scuola del Santo began in spring, so far as records extend.

23. Bernardo Gonzati, *La Basilica del Santo*, Padua, 1852, I, clxiii, first published it, and reproduced it in facsimile. It was then the only document known for the cycle, and, aided by its rare status as a Titian autograph, it has remained the best known. The facsimile has led later writers to offer transcriptions, not all fortunate.

24. The records differ only in that the ledger records 24 lire, 16 soldi, and Titian acknowledges receiving just 24 lire. But he also writes the amount as 4 ducats, which are 24 lire and 16 soldi.

25. Since the second document appeared not to add to art-historical knowledge, except to a minute reading, it is understandable that it has not been noted.

26. Valcanover, 1969, 93. This book adds new material to his book of 1960, including an excellent Titian bibliography for 1959–1968. A contrary impression appears to have kept it from being checked, so this point seems worth noting.

27. The documents of Titian's work (Rigoni, 55) include an undated memorandum about the three subjects, their fees, and their locations on the wall. It starts with "the first picture on the right hand when one enters the hall above," which is to show "the miracle of the jawbone of Saint Anthony, how it was stolen and returned" ("lo miracolo de la maxella de messer santo Antonio, secondo la fo robata e renduta"), and it continues with the themes and locations of the *Foot* and the *Wife* just as we have them. In the first case, however, Titian did fresco that specific wall space, but with the entirely different story of the *Speaking Babe*. The Anthony cycle in the room also includes a fresco of 1512 by Montagna, representing the exhumation and formal "recognition" of the saint's body, including the incident of a cardinal arranging to donate the jawbone, seen in a reliquary, to another church. That two entirely separate Anthony stories should involve his jawbone will not seem strange to anyone who has dealt with cults of relics. Unfortunately, Morassi, while reporting the incident of the cardinal quite correctly (pp. 28–29), elsewhere introduced the error that the theme dropped by Titian was the one then painted by Montagna (p. 18); Morassi did this by giving both a short title, "Miracle of the Jawbone." Wethey (p. 129) compounded the error when, with Morassi as his base, he stated that Titian's original theme had been the *Recognition of the Saint's Corpse*. This report is now remote from the document, which, as Rigoni properly observed (p. 37), shows only that Titian's project got shifted away from the jawbone story. It is necessary to renounce the scenario in which Titian, by his patron's wish or his own, was taken off a job which was then reassigned to Montagna, in favor of the different interesting circumstance that one planned story was entirely dropped and a fresh one replaced it, again by Titian's wish or his patron's. (For the circumstances of an artist's proposing to change certain stories in a biblical cycle, Lotto's letters of 1524 and following are valuable; see his *Libro di spese diverse*, Venice, 1969, 272.)

28. Morassi, 10.

29. Valcanover (1969, 93) does not explain how the documents support this conclusion; the format of his book would not have permitted such discussion.

30. The Raphael literature regularly puts the completion of the Segnatura simply in "1511," or, in a fuller form, "the end of 1511." (Cf. Luisa Beccherucci in the many-authored *Complete Work of Raphael*, New York, 1969, 127.) All depend for this, as Beccherucci continues, on "the date marked twice on the walls of the stanza," under the *Parnassus* and the *Virtues*, dates identical in both places and thus reasonably held to refer to the room altogether. The inscriptions read: JULIUS II LIGUR PONT MAX ANN CHRIST MDXI PONTIFICAT SUI VIII. It needs to be understood that, just as much as MDXI includes anything to "the end of 1511," so the eighth year of Julius's pontificate includes only dates up to November 26, 1511, the anniversary of his coronation. Double dating systems with separate New Year's days, e.g., in the Fascist era, may serve to clarify the aid provided by the inscription toward a slightly narrower limit. The implication for the Segnatura was noted by Pastor (VI, 1923, 233, and footnotes; one reference has a misprint "November 28") and, following him, apparently only by M. Zucker, "Raphael and the Beard of Pope Julius II," *Art Bulletin*, LIX, 1977, 528, n. 34. Cavalcaselle noted the importance of the inscription but wrongly dated the pope's anniversary on October 31, his election. He is corrected by Pastor, but followed by Vincenzo Golzio, in *Complete Work of Raphael*, 587.

31. D. Redig de Campos, "Il Pensieroso della Segnatura," first published in *Michelangelo Buonarroti nel IV centenario del giudizio universale*, Florence, 1942, 205–19, first and definitively analyzed this relationship, and his conclusion seems to have been fully accepted. He showed that the Heraclitus was added to the *School of Athens* at the end of the work, not only after the cartoon had been completed but on a separate patch of plaster after the fresco was dry. This separate extra degree of lateness is at times overlooked, e.g. by Frederick Hartt, *History of Italian Renaissance Art*, New York, n.d., 402: the figure "is absent from the still preserved cartoon for the figures, and is therefore an addition inserted during the process of painting." The date of the Heraclitus, therefore, is independent of the date of the *School of Athens* altogether.

32. Thus Wethey, 1969, 17–18, began a section on "Titian and Central Italian Art" by observing that artistic interchanges between Venice and Rome increased rapidly during the late 1520s. Prior contacts had little effect, up to the *Sebastian* and the Ancona altarpiece, which prove Titian's strong awareness of Michelangelo and Raphael. Wethey, in 1975, 123, found Titian's newly gained knowledge of developments in Rome to be shown a little earlier, in the *Assunta* of 1516–18, marking an abrupt change. These views may be taken as standard.

33. Panofsky, 19; Titian's earliest work, from the beginnings to 1516–18, includes his "first preliminary contacts with . . . the Tuscan and Roman tradition, including Raphael and Titian's great antipode, Michelangelo."

34. Thus Charles de Tolnay, *Michelangelo*, Princeton, 1938–60, in III: "on August 14, 1511, the ceiling was uncovered for the first time."

35. The full text is conveniently accessible in ibid., 235.

185

36. Ettore Camesasca, intro. Salvatore Quasimodo, *L'Opera completa di Michelangelo pittore*, Milan, 1966, 69.

37. Pastor, VI, 332 (departure on August 17, 1510), 362 (return).

38. Paris's diary is the chief source for Pastor's full account of the pope's trip. Of the return, Paris remarked (Pastor, IV, 362): "This was the end of our toilsome and useless expedition."

39. Thus Wethey, 1969, 18.

40. Wethey, 1975, 23.

41. Lotto's occupancy of such a role is less plausible for several reasons. His only recorded presence in Rome was in 1509, too early to perform it. He might have remained there in 1510 and 1511, totally undocumented years, but this seems not very likely, both because the one known event about him in 1509 is that he was among the artists who lost their jobs to Raphael, and also because he would appear to have been in Jesi for some period of time when he dated his polyptych there in 1512. He had no known personal links with either Titian or Michelangelo in these years, and seems unlikely to have had any on a stylistic level. Indeed, Wethey's suggestion that Lotto was the linking figure might be regarded as made *faute de mieux*, running counter as it does to his own previous comments, which are to my mind better put: "Lotto had worked in the Vatican in 1509 at the same time as Raphael, previous to the completion of Michelangelo's paintings in the Sistine vault. Because of the early date of his visit the effects of his sojourn were not notable either in the career of Lotto or in any detectable reverberations in Venetian art in general" (Wethey, 1969, 17).

42. Marcantonio Michiel records the completion of the Giorgiones by the two painters (Theodor Frimmel, ed., *Der Anonimo Morelliano*, Vienna, 1886, 88). For Giorgione's death, cf. Lionello Venturi, *Giorgione e il Giorgionismo*, Milan, 1913, 3–4, 288–90.

43. The poem is only alluded to in most books on Sebastiano, but is conveniently printed in relevant part by Christof Frommel, *Der römische Palastbau*, Tübingen, 1973, II, 151. It describes three of the eight lunettes, which are spread through all parts of the cycle, permitting the inference that at the time of writing the cycle had been finished.

44. Frommel, *Palastbau*, 156, 168. The patron Chigi was himself in Venice in 1511, from February up to August 22. Since he is said in a 17th-century biography to have taken Sebastiano to Rome, it can be inferred that the latter's journey was in August too. The alternative possibility that Chigi sent Sebastiano ahead beforehand to start the work would, however, allow a more comfortable amount of time for his lunettes, would fit the evidence of the (quite late) biography in all but the most literal detail, and might well have been a practical thing to do.

45. See now *Il carteggio di Michelangelo*, ed. P. Barocchi and R. Ristori, Florence, II, 1967, 32 (first letter), 412 (index of all Sebastiano's letters).

46. For the Leonardo, Windsor 12591, see Kenneth Clark, *The Drawings of Leonardo da Vinci . . . at Windsor Castle*, 2nd ed., London, 1968, 118. Leonardo's transformation

of David into Neptune might be compared to the way Titian transformed Michelangelo's figures. For the Raphael, see Philip Pouncey and John Gere, *Italian Drawings in the . . . British Museum: Raphael and His Circle*, London, 1962, 10–11.

47. Francesco Albertini, *Opusculum de Mirabilibus Novae Urbis Romae*, ed. A. Schmarsow, Heilbronn, 1886, 69.

48. "Quam tua beatitudo ferreis catenis munivit ac superiorem partem testudineam pulcherrimis picturis et auro exornavit, opus praeclarum Michelis Archangeli Floren: statuariae artis et picturae praeclarissimi" (p. 13).

49. This untenable date is standard in the Michelangelo literature, e.g., Tolnay, *Sistine*, 110; Giorgio Vasari, *La vita di Michelangelo*, ed. P. Barocchi, Milan, 1962, II, 427. Such a date is given by Albertini in the last paragraph of his book as a record of when he finished writing. As Schmarsow already noted (p. iv), however, the author elsewhere at several points writes "in the present year 1506," proving that he let such references stand when they were no longer valid. Besides, the last page with the completion date 1509 is not part of his Rome guidebook, but of an account by him of famous men in Florence and Savona, printed in the same volume, and its completion date obviously has no bearing on that of the guide. The colophon of 1510 remains our only firm date for the latter; it is quite early enough.

50. He alludes to the Farnesina, finished in 1511 (p. 30). The Peruzzi literature has also treated this as a significant allusion during 1509, the only proof that the building was begun so early (Frommel, *Palastbau*, II, 149). Professor Frommel kindly informs me that he concurs with the revision to 1510 as here presented.

51. Donatello's Gattamelata, installed on its pedestal in 1453, is described there in a book on Paduan glories that is firmly dated 1446–47; compare H. W. Janson, *The Sculpture of Donatello*, Princeton, 1957, 152–54, with Arnaldo Segarizzi, ed., intro. to M. Savonarola, *Libellus de Magnificis Ornamentis Paduae*, Città di Castello, 1902, vii. Janson naturally concluded that the book on Padua must have been later. The motivation of guidebook writers to insert such anticipations is as clear as the distressing trap for art historians, who are naturally ready to accept the apparently firm evidence of definite *termini ante*. Such an insertion is especially risky when it is the only evidence; where there is better evidence (which would provide a control for such situations), our methods tend to bypass the secondary documents.

52. Tolnay, *Sistine*, 110, gives no grounds for saying that Albertini had by June 3, 1509, "certainly seen the frescoes" before any other outsider, a proposal from which he draws further inferences about how much Michelangelo had painted by then. Steinmann, as cited in n. 22, 224, pointed out that the presence of the word "gold" made it questionable whether Albertini had seen the ceiling. Tolnay perhaps did not notice the problem since his citation does not include "gold," *auro* being misprinted *aura*. (*Testudineam* is also misprinted *testudine*; both errors may have been in his source, the second edition of the guide, of 1515.) He also omits the first phrase quoted above in n. 48, including the subject of the sentence, "your beatitude." The subject thus appears to be "opus," and the writer appears to credit the work of Michelangelo for adorning the vault rather than crediting the pope for adorning it with that work. The honor given the artist is exaggerated, and in Tolnay's version of

187

the sentence the author seems to evoke impressive artistic activity, hence something which he had seen, more than to evoke impressive papal acts. Stress on the latter is more consistent too with work not yet complete.

53. Wilde, 130.

54. Wilde's lectures are fascinating for the brevity of their proposals, which were sometimes followed up by questions and sometimes not at all. The richness of the results that may be uncovered by extending these lines of inquiry makes one ask why he did not. A former student of Wilde's suggested to me that this may have been a teaching method, that Wilde actually had the further points in mind, but hoped to stimulate his listeners to find them. It may then well be that the present deductions have been anticipated, but if so they have not been made public.

55. A recent writer's lapse in calling Sacred Love a "standing nude" (David Rosand, *Titian*, New York, 1978, 80) is probably a tribute to the power of Titian's basic image of figures in contrast, which the artist, however, interplays with samenesses.

56. C. Nordenfalk, "Titian's Allegories on the Fondaco de' Tedeschi," *Gazette des Beaux-Arts*, VI, 40, 1952, 101–8.

57. O. Brendel, "Borrowings from Ancient Art in Titian," *Art Bulletin*, XXXVII, 1955, 117; Panofsky, 110–11, both with repro.

58. Camesasca, 92.

59. Vasari-Barocchi, I, 68.

60. See the excellent diagram in Camesasca, 95, which also shows the nail holes of the cartoon. The incisions are clear in good reproductions, e.g., Tolnay, *Sistine*, fig. 84, but only if one looks for them.

61. In a previous study, I suggested a similar case in two figures by Piero della Francesca, in that instance found in different buildings but representing the same saint. The structural parts are the same but forms "are freely modified in painting surface details" (Creighton Gilbert, *Change in Piero della Francesca*, Locust Valley, 1968, 111). A reviewer, not otherwise peremptory, rejected the proposal of a re-used cartoon as "wrong" on the sole ground that the second "head is turned further to the side," as indeed it is, within the same contour (G. Robertson, *Art Quarterly*, XXXIV, 1971, 357). The reviewer then discussed his own dating of the two figures, one which a single cartoon would have tended to countervail. Since he offered no other basc for rejecting it (and was silent on the stipulated surface modifications), a postulate or principle appears to be implied, that re-use of a cartoon cannot be claimed if interior sub-shapes are divergent. If there is such a principle, then readers must discount the analysis in the text above. On the other hand, if Camesasca is right, as he seems to me plainly to be, helpful materials for many studies may emerge.

62. Tolnay, *Sistine*, 65.

63. Aldo Bertini, *Michelangelo fino alla Sistina*, Turin, 1945, 80–81.

64. Heinrich Thode, when grouping the nudes of the ceiling in clusters, made one of his groups from just these five. None of his other clusters consists of figures adjacent to each other on the ceiling (*Michelangelo, kritische Untersuchungen*, Berlin, I, 1908, 423).

65. This is well treated by Robert Clements, *Michelangelo's Theory of Art*, New York, 1961, 355–56.

66. Michelangelo, *The Complete Poems*, trans. C. Gilbert, New York, 1963, No. 160; Michelangelo, *Le Rime*, ed. E. Girardi, Bari, 1960, 345.

67. The left-handedness of each is separately considered by Tolnay in his full descriptions (*Sistine*, 58).

68. Rodolfo Pallucchini, *Sebastian Viniziano*, Milan, 1944, 33.

69. Luitpold Dussler, *Sebastiano del Piombo*, Basel, 1942, 31. Dussler's and Pallucchini's books were written simultaneously, so that views of this kind were reached independently.

70. This is the *Venus* in the Ambrosiana, most recently discussed by M. Hirst in Konrad Oberhuber, *Disegni di Tiziano e della sua cerchia*, Venice, 1976, No. 9, with bibliography and reproductions. It precedes his *Death of Adonis* of 1512, always recognized as the painting closest to his Farnesina frescoes. Venus sits in profile and leans forward intently. Hirst suggests a derivation from the Sistine nudes, which may be a closer source than the spandrels; she is on a seat, not the ground. On the other side of the drawing ("recto") is a rendering of an ancient river god; the sheet thus documents the artist's interest in copying figures he saw on arriving in Rome.

71. The group of babies is imitated by Romanino, in a work contracted for in 1513, as first noted by Roberto Longhi, *Viatico per cinque secoli di pittura veneziana*, Florence, 1946, 65.

72. Wethey, 1975, 177–78, drew attention to a second coat-of-arms in the painting, besides the one always observed. Since the two families in question were joined by a spectacular marriage in 1514, it is certainly plausible to see in this event the reason for ordering the painting. To be sure, the date gained is only a *terminus ante* beginning when the marriage was planned. Wethey's listed date (p. 175) "about 1514" may be assumed to be based on this information, but he does not discuss it, e.g., he does not state why the painting should be assumed to have been promptly produced, rather than delayed to perhaps 1516, which has been the date most often suggested on the basis of style. Hence the findings here, linking the picture with one commonly dated not after 1513, have additional attraction in reinforcing the new observations.

73. Wethey, 1975, dates the *Three Ages* "about 1512–1515" in a catalogue entry (p. 182), but "about 1515" on two captions of plates (color pl. opposite p. 8; pl. 13). The evident preference for the late end of the range may reflect the omission from the catalogue of the argument for the early date offered by Longhi, and of Longhi's study from its bibliography. The catalogue mentions that a dating "ca. 1512" has been proposed only in citing writers who were following Longhi, and indicates no reasons for their views.

ON THE ABSOLUTE DATES OF THE PARTS OF THE SISTINE CEILING

Michelangelo began work on the Sistine ceiling in May 1508 and finished in October 1512. A slight refinement of the earlier of these two dates will be proposed in the course of this essay, but to all intents and purposes both are firm beyond question.

The relative dates of the parts, i.e. the sequence in which he executed them, are also agreed on by almost all observers. In this view, he began near the entrance end of the chapel, in the laymen's part of the room, and progressed toward the altar end, in the priests' part. Whenever he painted one of the nine main scenes, he also painted the figures to right and left of it—prophets, sibyls, and others—before going on to the next scene and the figures adjacent to it. This procedure continued over the entire vault surface, in the strict sense of the term vault. When it was done, he then painted the upper parts of the chapel walls, i.e. the lunettes, in a separate campaign. This usual view is much modified by a few scholars, notably Wilde,[1] and qualified in details by many, notably in the frequent suggestion that the scene in the first bay was painted after the one in the second. Ambiguity and debate appear in the context of the spandrels over the windows, as to whether they belong to the vault campaign or the lunette campaign. But the general lines are very generally agreed, and here will be taken as given.

In view of the settled relative order of the parts, and the settled absolute dating of the whole, it logically remains to determine the absolute dating of the parts. Obviously it is a smaller question, and variations of more than one year are most unlikely. Yet in such a monument even such details are significant, and the present study proposes first that they can be better determined than they have been, and then points in a brief conclusion to surprising further deductions that thence emerge. The question has been little explored both because of this minor role and also because the matter appeared to be accounted for, wrongly in my view.

In what follows, Tolnay's statements will be equated with standard current opinion.[2] His work not only obliterated all similar preceding studies, while giving proper notice to nearly all of them, but has been adopted ever since, often uncritically, as if it were equatable with the facts. A few other citations will be offered, either simply to illustrate this nearly unanimous acceptance, or for the rare arguments against it, which are by no means necessarily improvements. No doubt some objectors have been missed, but the continuing status of Tolnay as standard authority may even so justify this arrangement.

What follows consists mainly of reexamining words in documents. At two points the results depend on findings of two other sorts, the kind of scaffolding used, and the relations of his fees to his other money. It is convenient to take these up first, rather than digress when they touch the primary argument.

I: THE SCAFFOLDING. The anecdotes about the scaffolding in the sources emphasize that it was Michelangelo's own inventive design, so it is the more tantalizing that facts are so scanty. The best-known story got recorded because it showed Michelangelo scoring off Bramante, who, according to the same report, had just forced his transfer away from the tomb sculpture to the chapel. It is well summarized by Tolnay: "Bramante was commissioned by the Pope to erect the scaffold. If the accounts of the old biographers are reliable, he made one of beams suspended from the ceiling by ropes. Michelangelo was dissatisfied and, according to Vasari, asked Bramante how the holes in the ceiling would be filled up when the work was finished. Therefore the Pope permitted him to have Bramante's scaffold taken down and to have a new one erected according to his own design. Michelangelo's scaffolding touched neither the ceiling nor the walls."[3]

The concluding reference to walls explains why this scaffolding had presented any special problem in the first place. It had to avoid the walls, because of the older frescoes there; beam ends rubbing them could not be permitted. This constraint, by the way, is surely the basic reason why Renaissance frescoes were normally painted from the top down, rather than because of possible dripping paint as the matter is ordinarily explained. It is evident that any drip problems were avoided when this chapel was painted from bottom to top, and presumably could have been anywhere; likely enough drop cloths were used, as they are today by housepainters doing ceilings. But to make a scaffolding without side support was evidently perceived as an obstacle, baffling to Bramante, but solved by Michelangelo to general acclamation. It is in this context that emphasis was given to the scaffolding and the need for unusual specifications.

Bramante's absurd scaffolding hung from ropes also stimulated the only concrete element in Condivi's description of Michelangelo's amended one, that it was *"senza corde."* "He made it without ropes, so well put together that it was only the firmer the more weight it bore."[4] Tolnay translates too narrowly: "without suspension cords";[5] a reconstruction with no cords of any sort seems indicated. Vasari's main anecdote is related to the same factor. The poor carpenter who executed Michelangelo's scaffolding received a gift from him of "so much rope that, when he sold it, he had enough for a dowry for a daughter."[6] Michelangelo's economy in materials and money is being contrasted with Bramante's foolish extravagance.

The only more descriptive detail provided is Vasari's report that the scaffolding was *"sopra i sorgozzoni."*[7] Tolnay is implausible in interpreting this rare term, saying that the scaffolding was "built from the ground" (on *"sorgozzoni"*).[8] They are not ground-borne objects. Barocchi rightly cited the definition of the term in Baldinucci's dictionary of art terms, written in Florence in the later seventeenth century. It means a plank or beam projecting from a wall so as to support a balcony, in short a cantilever.[9]

Understandably, few students have offered to describe the appearance of the scaffold, and even Tolnay, generally fuller on all questions than others, only alludes to it in partial ways at various points. He proposes that three scaffolds would have been required "at one time," respectively for the central row of scenes, the side figures, and the lunettes, of which the last would have been "probably movable."[10] Unmovable scaffolding would, then, have spanned the width of the chapel at all times. The length would have been equal to that of several bays of frescoes, so far as one can judge from Tolnay's only relatable remark, that it was "probably not very different" from the one set up in 1935 during a restoration, which had such length. (It was also of the full width.) The original would, however, at first have extended only the length of the laymen's part of the chapel. That this is Tolnay's view emerges from a comment elsewhere, in which the scaffolding is mentioned as an aid in fixing the chronology of the paintings. It is argued that "up to 17 August 1510, the date of departure of the Pope, it is not likely that Michelangelo finished the whole ceiling because masses were held regularly in the priests' area."[11] His departure created a "favourable moment" for painting in this area, the vaults of which, he thinks, were painted between then and about the time of the pope's return to Rome on 27 June 1511. In support he writes that "in fact, he received money for the scaffolding about 7 January 1511 (Appendix No. 46)," i.e. a new scaffolding which would correspond to the vault of the priests' area of the chapel, heretofore left alone "because Masses were held," which in turn reflected the pope's presence. In fact, the writing quoted in Appendix 46 says nothing of scaffolds. It mentions receipt of some money, which Tolnay identifies with money mentioned earlier on 7 September as due and expected "to make the scaffolding."[12] Aside from the indirectness of evidence, we are being given a coherent hypothesis about the location and general character of new scaffolding proposed around this date. Clearly there was one, but the evidence for this location is very shaky.

That records of masses exist up to 17 August 1510, as they do, and then cease does certainly seem to imply that thereafter they were not held, and Tolnay must be drawing that inference. But so far as our knowledge extends all that really happened then was that the departing pope took away from Rome in his suite Paris de Grassis, the writer of the diary that is our sole source about the holding of any masses. Paris returned with the pope on 27 June 1511, and masses reappear in his diary as before.[13]

There is no evidence about either the holding or the suspension of masses while he was away.

In the absence of information, it might be thought reasonable to suppose that scaffolding and masses in the same space would be incompatible, and hence that the vault frescoes of the priests' area, and a scaffolding for them, might be best dated in the only period when masses are at any rate not known to have occurred. The idea is attractive, even if inevitably bound up with the common risk in art history of retaining an idea after the disappearance of the supposed evidence which had produced it, transferring it to a grounding in general reasonableness, a view which actually gains unmerited support from the previous habituation to the idea when it had been based on supposed evidence. The common opening: "I still feel that . . ." is often a signal of this dubious pattern. In the present case, however, the idea of the incompatibility of painting, scaffolding, and masses in the space has to be given up because it conflicts with the painting of the lunettes, to the extent that half of these are in the priests' area. These are dated by Tolnay and all observers in the last year of the project, 1511–12, a time when masses were certainly held, although Tolnay does not note their resumption. Hence the whole hypothesis about the nature and location of the scaffolding recorded in September 1510 as to be built fails, dependent as it was on a link to the proposed relevance of the proposed disappearance of masses at that time.

Steinmann, in his chief discussion of the masses and the scaffold, took for granted that masses went on while the pope was away. Indeed the idea that they were suspended, attractive mainly because it would then give us something with which to help date the frescoes, is in itself not a probable speculation. Motivation for having masses would appear to depend little on the pope, who rarely attended Sistine masses,[14] and had another fine chapel within his own apartments for his needs, and mainly on the Sistine's own officiating priests, who may be assumed to have had a self-interest in their continuation, and who did not leave Rome. When one thinks, therefore, of the masses as continuing in the presence of scaffolding, as a quite likely case in 1510–11 and a certain one in 1511–12, one welcomes as a help in envisioning its design Steinmann's comment that it had to be the kind of scaffold that would not impede the floor, "despite the posts."[15] Certainly as between two arrangements, one (Tolnay's) holding that masses were omitted for ten months during which there was a scaffolding, and the other (Steinmann's) calling for a scaffold design that permitted masses to continue, we must prefer to think that those deciding would have opted for the latter,[16] only assuming that such a design was a practical possibility. In the context in which Michelangelo is described as an innovator in scaffold design, able to avoid the usual contact with walls, it seems a dubious argument (but the only one left) that he might not have been able to meet that requirement. Tentatively then the list of characteristics of the scaffold can be given an addition, the minimizing of floor occupancy.

These constraints are fortunate ones, in reducing the possible designs to a few. Still another limiting fact has almost always been overlooked. A scaffold running the full width of the room and having even a few bays of length is impossible because it would have left the artist in darkness. Its working floor level, no more than about seven feet below the peak of the vault, is far higher than the window tops. When the large scaffolding was set up in 1935 it was equipped with a forest of electric lights.[17] Only one writer seems to have taken this into account in reconstructing a scaffold design. The Victorian biographer Charles Wilson, whose account of the scaffold seems more detailed than any other, did presume a large deck filling the whole chapel, but with removable trapdoors to provide light above. The proposal has been suitably ignored, but so, less suitably, has been the impossibility of the deck on any other terms, and the working requirements in general.[18]

It can surely be hypothesized that Michelangelo wanted as much light as he could get. He may therefore be thought to have planned a scaffold as narrow in section as it could be made. Rising almost sixty feet, it then would have been a tower of wood, doubtless in openwork, perhaps narrowing to the top like an obelisk. Once this form is envisioned, it remarkably matches the known small facts, just as the large deck fails to do. The tower is obviously economical of materials and of money, as Michelangelo's design is known to have been. Such a form, when competently built, will indeed gain firmness from being weighted on top, as a deck will not. And it will easily avoid the impeding of the masses, as the deck will not, since it can be stowed in a corner when they take place (assuming, as is probable in any case, that he did not work on the actual feast days). Best of all, it has a neat potential for *sorgozzoni,* quite unaccountable in a deck, though they are the one recorded structural characteristic. At the top of the slim tower one could indeed wish to have a working platform of somewhat greater area, and such a top would certainly become at once the most striking visual motif, and the first one cited by the biographer. Condivi says that the *ponte* was upon the *sorgozzoni.* Though *ponte* is translated scaffolding without important error, the word is a *pars pro toto*, since its basic and never lost meaning is the platform element. Hence it is properly described as being *on* the cantilevered beams; when Tolnay deduced that the *ponte* on *sorgozzoni* was resting on some ground-based element, he presumably was thinking of the generalized use of the word *ponte* for the whole structure.

Any other design appears to be in conflict with the known factors. It was therefore pleasant after this conclusion was reached to note a photograph of the scaffold used in the chapel in a restoration of 1904, which was of just this sort.[19] This is helpful since it removes any arguments against this proposal on the ground that it might be technically impractical in some way.

This hypothesis plainly includes the idea that the scaffold was moved about. Its platform area would correspond to a unit of work, perhaps to the largest, that of the four larger narratives. If it is felt, as is true, that such moving would be quite laborious, it can only be debated against the alternatives, which are nonmoving: either the big deck, which gives access to the whole vault but cuts off light, or a small deck, which if nonmoving would have to be dismantled and rebuilt frequently; there seem no other options. The moving of the narrow tower is cumbersome except in comparison with any other system. As to a technique for the moving, it happens that one was well known to Michelangelo. In 1504 the *David* had been moved from the workshop to its permanent location inside a crate, which was pushed and pulled along resting on oiled logs.[20] An easier version of the same scheme would have done for the chapel. It is even quite plausible that this earlier experience helped

197

Michelangelo in being able to resolve the problem of inventing the scaffold when he was faced with it in 1508, something not otherwise explicable from his known background.

Such a tower could move freely through the chapel except where the marble balustrade partitions the lay and priests' areas all the way across the room. For it to pass this barrier, one might think that it was disassembled and reassembled on the other side, thus meriting the name of a new scaffold, or that it was lowered to a near horizontal and then lifted over, like Domenico Fontana's obelisk eighty years later. A simpler procedure, suggested to me by Christian Otto, would have been to disassemble some part of the balustrade, widening its door to let the scaffold go through intact, as today house movers may remove struts between windows to admit pianos. Indeed the one best known fact about this balustrade is that it was itself moved in the late sixteenth century to a line about five meters nearer the entrance.[21] The still visible traces of its old location in the floor design prove that it had at first merely sat on the floor, not bonded to anything; it was church furniture, not architecture. Thus the disassembling of a unit of it would not seem to offer problems.

To envision the small tower and its platform in relation to the curved vault may also resolve a famous small puzzle about the painting process. The very popular story that Michelangelo painted lying down has a respectable origin in Giovio's writing in the 1540s. Yet Tolnay has called it "incorrect"[22] because still better evidence from Michelangelo's own writing about 1510 shows him standing up to paint. Surely in reality he did both, standing at mid-vault, and shifting when the curve came down to the level of the *ponte*.

II: THE FEES. This part and part III depend on three kinds of written evidence. The earliest is in letters of Michelangelo, and related writings, of the years 1508–12, obviously the best material, but fragmentary. The second is the letter he wrote in 1523 to his business adviser Fattucci, which survives in two drafts. It reports his whole financial relationship with the pope in 1508–12, and other years, and is the most useful single source. The third source is the lives by Vasari and Condivi, where caution must be greater, but which have some helpful further materials.

Five payments to Michelangelo are certainly connected with the Sistine ceiling by their own specific references. The first is the 500 ducats on account that accompanied the signing of the contract on 10 May 1508, "for the painting of the vault of the chapel of Pope Sixtus,"[23] known from Michelangelo's surviving memorandum. Then follow:

(2) 500 ducats received on 25 October 1510, "from the pope's datary," therefore for work for the pope, reported in a letter of the following day from Michelangelo to his brother in Florence.[24] He explains that he is forwarding 450 of them through his Roman and Florentine bankers for deposit to his account in the Hospital in Florence.

(3) 400 ducats received on 1 October 1511, which the pope "caused to be paid to me," reported in a letter of the 4th to his father.[25] He is forwarding 300 of them in the same procedure as before.

(4) 500 ducats received in June, apparently 1512. The source is an anecdote by Condivi.[26] Michelangelo asked the pope to be allowed to go to Florence for the feast of St. John, which is 24 June, and also for money. The pope asked when he would finish the painting. Michelangelo answered "when I can"; the pope became angry and struck him with his stick, but then apologized by sending 500 ducats after him. Ramsden[27] has shown that this could not have been in 1510 as Tolnay and others had thought, and in 1511 the pope was away from the city until after St. John's day, leaving 1512.

(5) 2,000 ducats received at an uncertain date, not far from the completion of the painting in October 1512. Michelangelo in his letter of 1523 to Fattucci recalls that his complaints of having no money "to finish the work" met response from friendly officials who arranged for him to get this sum.[28] As to the date of this event, Tolnay's hesitant suggestion: "before 31 (?) May 1512 (probably end of 1512)"[29] depended on a letter now redated some years later in 1514,[30] and so must be discarded. Ramsden's view[31] that the payment only followed the completion of the work seems not likely in view of the statement in Michelangelo's account that his hope for money "to finish" was fruitless until "one day" he lamented that he "could not stay in Rome longer, and had to go" whereupon one of the officials told the other to remind him of the matter and "had the 2,000 given to me."

This fifth payment soon became the theme of bitter dispute, when papal representatives told Michelangelo it was not intended to apply to the ceiling but to the tomb, for which Michelangelo was therefore not a creditor as he had supposed. It was this dispute that occasioned his survey of the finances in his letter of 1523.

No one supposes that these five records correspond to the total received by Michelangelo for the painting. This emerges from a survey of the varied reports about what that total was. Vasari in 1550 wrote[32] that the pope had first budgeted 15,000 ducats to paint the ceiling and repaint the walls of the chapel, a project whose area would have been roughly three times as large as the surface covered by his work of 1508–12. The whole story may be fabulous, as are other points in Vasari's account of the ceiling. Condivi in 1553[33] wrote that Michelangelo received 3,000 ducats in all; his informant was doubtless Michelangelo. If this is correct, then of course the fifth amount above, the 2,000 ducats, would have to be excluded, which could be quite simply on the assumption that by 1553 Michelangelo had come to accept that it was for the tomb. Tolnay, for reasons to be discussed, thinks the total was 6,000.[34] Ramsden, in the only more recent independent analysis, disagrees vigorously, and accepts Condivi's 3,000.[35] The two agree in adding to the above five records two other documents as payments for the ceiling. These two documents, which are central to the present discussion, account for a minimum of 578 and a maximum of 1,000 ducats, taken together. Both writers also in different ways add a further 100 ducats. These items, along with (1) to (4) above, could add up to 3,000, and thus Ramsden thinks everything is accounted for. Tolnay thinks two other money documents concern other payments for the ceiling, and they add another 3,000, so he similarly thinks that existing records account for all of Michelangelo's receipts, which for him are 6,000 ducats.

One of these last two documents of Tolnay's is of course (5), which he assigns to the ceiling, and makes a basis for calling Condivi's total "erroneous." Ramsden can rightly complain that Tolnay here omits to mention that this money was later claimed to be on account of a different job. Tolnay's last added item is 1,000 ducats which Michelangelo, in an undated letter to his family, said would be owed him on completion.

Since Tolnay dates this letter (?) January 1512, which is later than the dates he assigns to all other payments, he can logically make it an added item in his total. But others reject his dating of the letter, in favor of June 1511,[36] and have also changed some of the other payments to later dates, so that this money could be appearing twice, once as pledged and then as paid.

Hence Tolnay's increase from 3,000 to 6,000 is shaky in respect of the claims to find the money accounted for in specific payments. But for him and others it has an additional basis, the best possible one, Michelangelo's own letter of 1523 surveying the finances. In the earlier of the drafts,[37] Michelangelo has been discussing the initial agreement with the pope that he would get 3,000 ducats for "simply a few figures" on the ceiling.[38] But when, in the famous change of plan, that project came to seem "a poor thing," the pope "made another assignment over again down to the stories below, and that I should do what I wished in the vault, which added up to about as much again" (*mi rifcce un'altra alloga-gione insino alle storie di sotto, e che io facessi nella volta quello che io volevo, che montava circha altretanto*). In the second draft this part becomes: "he gave me a new commission, that I should do what I wanted, and that he would satisfy me, and that I should paint down to the stories below" (*mi decte nova chommessione che io facessi cio che io volevo, e che mi chontenterebbe, e che io dipignessi insino alle storie di sotto*).

Since the first "poor" plan called for a fee of 3,000 ducats, the phrase in the first draft "about as much again" is Tolnay's basis for assigning 6,000 to the definitive project. But problems about this seem to have been overlooked. (1) The word *circha* in any case excludes a specific fig-ure, such as 6,000. It also seems hardly possible that Michelangelo was being vaguer than he had to be in a letter whose vital goal was to make a case for the money owed him. So at best the pope is being said to have made this promise in general terms. Supposing such a general pledge of approximate doubling of the fee to have been made, the least vague in-terpretation possible would call for a range of at least 100 ducats up or down. But this conflicts with the next phrase in the same draft, when Michelangelo estimates his credit balance as "several hundred ducats" (*parecchi centinaia di ducati*). This calculation is incompatible with a base admitted to contain a variable factor of that same amount. (2) The whole statement conflicts with the other draft, which alludes to a revision of the "poor" fee only in saying that the pope promised he "would satisfy me." That formula is recognizable as a familiar one, in which lordly patrons do not contract for any particular fee with their artists, but assure them that they may rely on their liberality. How could Michelangelo describe the promise in the two drafts in such directly conflicting ways? He might have done so in statements remote from each other in time, but it is agreed that these two drafts were made in very close succession, with repetitions of phrases indicating that, in a common way with drafts, one was made from the very text of the other. The sum of money being the primary theme of the letter, one cannot understand a variation between "approximately doubled" and "left for the patron's goodwill." Tolnay cites only the former, perhaps as alone offering quantitative evidence.

A resolution of these difficulties can be had from a close reading. When we read *che montava circha altretanto,* "which added up to about as much again," it is obviously required to identify the noun or other pronoun that is the antecedent of the relative pronoun *which*. Scholars' interpretations indicate that it is assumed to be *allogagione*; although that would indicate a loose-knit grammar, such could well be present. An alternative, assigning the antecedent by strict grammar to the nearest preceding noun or pronoun, would make it *quello*, which by grammar is in turn to be expanded into *quello che io volevo fare nella volta*. The analogous expansion of *allogagione* would make it *un'altra allogagione insino alle storie di sotto*. No other possibilities seem available. When we substitute for *che* either of these alternate antecedents, in the most expanded form, for the purpose of learning what is meant by the sentence, we then have either: "that which I wanted to do in the vault added up to about twice as much" as the previous project had, or: "another assignment down to the stories below added up to about twice as much." This simple if drawn-out exercise makes it quite obvious that, in either alternative, Michelangelo is saying that the revised plan is about twice the *scale* of the first one. It has nothing to do with money at all. The letter about the money due him reasonably includes the point that after making the contract he agreed to do twice as much work. The only statement about revision of the fee is the one saying the pope would satisfy him. It is

202

located, in the draft where it appears, before the discussion about the new extension down to the stories below. The phrase about "twice as much" is located, in its draft, after the discussion about the extension downward. Thus the two phrases are not parallel and need not be equivalents of each other in their varying drafts. And only the last mentioned is an extension of the remarks on more wall surface, which precede it; the first-mentioned, referring to money, precedes the remark on wall surface and so of course does not allude to it.

Some other points are now also more clear. Michelangelo's drafts are responses to Fattucci's written request to him on 22 December to prepare such an account, to aid him in his negotiations with others. He had, it seems, told someone that "as to the chapel, the Pope had always said he would satisfy Michelangelo."[39] This confirms the reading above, even adding an "always" to show that the undefined liberality was the only formula, there never was a 6,000 ducat figure. Fattucci further asks Michelangelo to put in writing how "you told me that, as to the chapel, there was no contract." That is not a contradiction of the known contract of 10 May 1508, but simply makes clear that it was for the original "poor" scheme; there was only a verbal revision for the definitive scheme. At the end of Michelangelo's summary we learn that when he finished his painting, and it came to being paid (*quando veniva l'utile*), the matter did not go forward (*la cosa non ando inanzi*). The "matter" is the promise of liberal extra pay. Hence Michelangelo's claim, in the next and final sentence, that he is still owed several hundred ducats, can only relate to the first, "poor" contract, the only one with numbers in it and hence the only one allowing such a calculation. He had then got several hundred less than 3,000 ducats, or, at most, than 3,000 ducats plus expenses. This in turn dovetails with Condivi's report that his pay was 3,000 ducats. None of the sources has to be dropped as erroneous.

It was seen above that of these approximately 3,000 ducats, with or without expenses, 1,900 were firmly accounted for in four particular records or reports. Apart from those, Tolnay and Ramsden concurred in arguing that reports of 578 to 1,000 other ducats in Michelangelo's hands belong to other partial payments for the ceiling (in Tolnay's case this is argued for an additional record of 100 ducats). When it is held that the fee was 6,000 ducats, this argument is attractive, since one would tend to expect the survival of more than one-third of the records, where any survive, the more so where the fame of the artist and the work have clearly encouraged the survival of papers. On the other hand, with the total at 3,000, the picture changes. Tolnay's total of 1,100 more recorded ducats seems not possible, and even the other figures would indicate a most unusually high survival rate of the papers in a case of this sort where the sources are a miscellany of various kinds of records.

These reports are: (a) On 15 September 1509, Michelangelo in Rome remitted 350 ducats to his father, sent to be invested, through his Roman and Florentine bankers, in the way discussed above.[40] (b) On 11 January 1511, he remitted 228 ducats to his brother in Florence, to be deposited in his account.[41]

Tolnay and Ramsden agree that these are not only payments for the chapel, but that they can be assumed to represent larger amounts of 500 ducats each time paid to Michelangelo, the installment he received in three other cases. (It is thus that the 578 ducats are held to signify 1,000.) Tolnay, but not Ramsden, adds: (c) In a letter currently held to be of June 1511[42] (for Tolnay it was of January 1512) Michelangelo wrote his father that he had not long before sent him 100 ducats. This is the same letter in which he mentions expecting 1,000 when the work is done, as already discussed. Ramsden holds that "in point of fact" the 100 ducats is part of the hypothetical 500 out of which 228 had been sent earlier, that is item (b) above, and so has already been counted. No reason is given for saying this is a fact; it appears that it rests on a general reconstruction of a fairly regular payment pattern. Although Ramsden rejects this 100 ducats, she comes out with the same total of a round 3,000 by saying "we must add the outstanding 100 ducats, which we must assume he received" in 1512.

It is evident that these records a, b, and c differ from those previously considered, 1, 2, 3, and 4, in not mentioning any source of payment, the pope or another. To be sure, one cannot argue that papal payments would regularly be identified as such, and hence reject these unidentified ones, since the regularity is strictly found only twice, in 2 and 3. However, when 2 and 3 mention the papal source, there is a substantive reason for doing so, that it was family news. Michelangelo told his family that the money he was sending came from the pope not merely to explain its availability, but referring back to other letters in which he had dwelt on not being paid by the pope as he was supposed to be. Thus he wrote his father on 27 January 1509 that "it is a year since I have had a penny from this Pope," then, in one assigned to 1509: "I have not had money from this Pope for thirteen months," and shortly thereafter he cannot act "until I have money from the Pope." To his brother in a letter generally dated summer 1510: "I believe I will have money" very soon, and in a fifth case on 5 September 1510, to his father, it is that he was supposed to have money but "the Pope has gone away and left no order."[43] To say the least, one may expect that when the disappointments are finally reversed, and he *can* send money to Florence, he *will* mention the unusual good news that the pope has now indeed paid, and in just that way the fifth of these letters is shortly followed by (3), which does mention it. It may then be at least a bit surprising to find it claimed, as in the hypothesis about a, b, and c, that he would pass over this point when dwelling on the very theme of money which he is sending. Once this oddity is broached, it is noticeable that a, b, and c all have contents involving more or less explicitly other bases for sending money than having just been paid by the pope. In a, he is responding to his father's "last letter"—that would normally have been only a few days before—which had reported some major loss of money, by sending some to repair the loss. Since he was paid by the pope only at very long intervals, it would have been a powerful coincidence if such a rare remittance had arrived at just the time to solve that problem, and all the odder if it was not mentioned in the course of solving it, omitting to say what was said in nonurgent cases.

In b, the money is newly received by Michelangelo. He has obtained it on returning to Rome from a trip to Bologna and Florence, "as it had been written to me there that I would." It is natural that the source is not mentioned, since he had seen the correspondents to whom he was now writing in Florence a few days before when he had got that written message, and they had no doubt talked about it. The biographers have taken the source of the money to be the pope, on the reasonable ground

205

that the trip to Bologna, like a previous one in September, had been for the very purpose of getting money from him. However, it will be shown below that he had obtained none on the second try any more than on the first. Letter b has another theme, to send thanks to the Gonfaloniere of Florence, for an unstated reason; a letter of the previous 2 November from a Florentine to Michelangelo in Rome had mentioned giving a message to the Gonfaloniere, no doubt in the same connection.[44] Letter b's two items of business might be unconnected, but there also might reasonably be a connection between getting money and giving thanks. The last previous tie between Michelangelo and this Gonfaloniere, Piero Soderini, had concerned the bronze *David*, commissioned from the former by the government headed by the latter.[45] After an advance in 1502 and two small payments in 1503, no further payments for the work are recorded. It was finished in late 1508, in Michelangelo's absence from Florence. His first return to Florence after that time was on these two brief stops of late 1510 en route to and from Bologna. It would thus be plausible that this money was the balance still due him; it certainly is more suggested by the context than is the papal payment generally cited. A desire by Michelangelo to get back to Rome where he could best pursue his campaign for a papal payment, and to end his brief stop in Florence before these ducats were ready to be paid him, would explain why they were arranged for at his Roman bank.

In letter c the money is explicitly sent from the stock that "I had kept here for myself to live and work." Hence if this were papal money it would, as Tolnay indeed says, be from an earlier remittance in any case. This establishes at a minimum that the sending of money is not to be correlated with receipt of papal money in any direct time sequence.

Letters a, b, and c differ on still another level from the others which cite a papal source, that is in the kinds of numbers that appear. To summarize, items 1 to 5 are of 500, 500, 400, 500, and 2,000 ducats, items a, b, and c are of 350, 228, and 100. All of the former are larger than any of the latter. All the former are in even hundreds, but the latter are not, except for the *one* hundred that is part of a stock. The only qualification to the even hundreds of the former is that in two instances the amount sent is not the whole, but a part, 450 and 350 respectively. This calls attention to another constant difference, that in the former set when there is a send-ing, both the larger figure received and the smaller amount sent are mentioned; in the latter, only the single amount sent is mentioned. The former set differs again in being more internally consistent, involving the figure 500 and its multiple to such an extent that Tolnay thought the one exception, 400, was a slip of the pen for 500, and both he and Ramsden, as noted, thought that the irregular sendings of the latter set reflected receipts of 500.

It is hard to see how the first-mentioned difference, i.e. that in the lat-ter set no reference is made to a papal source, could be a dependent vari-able: that is, why Michelangelo would consistently mention the pope when the sums were larger, more consistent, and in hundreds, and con-sistently not do so when they had the opposite characteristics. One might then consider the other alternative, that the former set is larger and more consistent because it is of papal payments, and the latter is smaller and irregular because it is not. As noted, they not only show no evidence of being such, though appearing in contexts where there would be some pressure to say so if they were, but further involve suggestions of other sources or reasons for sending them.

Since these amounts are not credited to the pope by evidence, what grounds have led to the hypothesis that they should be? The biographers have found this so axiomatic that they have not given their reasons, al-lowing one to speculate what they were, with the clue that they must in-volve something obvious. The reason appears to be the belief that at this period Michelangelo did not have any other source of money. If so, that would certainly suffice, and the idea certainly finds support in state-ments that Michelangelo made. On 22 July 1508, he wrote, "I don't have a farthing"; the same in either May or early June 1509; soon after, as noted, that he could not do anything until he had money from the pope; and on 5 September 1510, that "I am without money."[46]

The statements are so plain and so consistent that they do seem de-cisive. What makes them less so is that each letter cited (and these seem to be all cases of such statements in 1508–12) contains other contradicto-ry statements. In the first, after saying he doesn't have a farthing, Michelangelo goes on to say he can't assist his brother because he has to

207

pay his rent. In the second, while still without a farthing, he instructs his brother to withdraw sums from Michelangelo's savings account in Florence. In the third, he advises his father that he should not feel anxious about what he may have to spend in a current legal problem. In the fourth, he tells him to draw from Michelangelo's account "fifty or a hundred ducats, what is needed, do not worry about it." Even if there were no such evidence, Michelangelo's good financial condition at this period would emerge from his having received 3,000 ducats in 1505 for the *Battle of Cascina*,[47] combined with the certainty that he did not spend on any such scale in the following years. There are far more records showing that he had, than that he did not have, money; the series of letters above is incomplete on the former count, though complete on the latter.

How could he then say he had none? The available answer is not based on historical evidence, yet seems the only possible one and also an obvious one. He was behaving in a familiar human way. In our own culture, in social intercourse, it is not strange to find a person in comfortable circumstances saying he doesn't have any money, specifically in response to a proposal that he make some expenditure, including a loan. We are generally so far from demanding thoroughgoing factuality in the statement, that we do not even notice the paradox with the well-being of the speaker; it is a convention that listeners share, and the rebuffed asker for money, who alone is likely to note its oddity, is impeded from objecting. The statement indeed probably flourishes regardless of its falseness because it effectively ends proposals. Its only claim to rationality, that the person may have no cash in his pocket—often as irrelevancy—may be combined with a social understanding that he may then well spend his illiquid money for goals desired by himself, say to buy land, withdrawing it say from a bank deposit. Michelangelo in this period did have several bank accounts and bought several plots of land. A notable document is his letter of January 1514, in which he asks whether some might be for sale, since he has 2,000 ducats "here in the bank of Balduccio, and they are not bringing me any return."[48] The rich survival of the Michelangelo correspondence, in contrast say to the cases of Raphael and Bramante, has as is well known made us see him in his own way, and in this case we have perhaps gone especially far in seeing him as penniless.

208

It is clear that sum c above, the 100 ducats he had been keeping to live on, is the sort of money in the hands of one who says he has no money, and there is no reason at all to link it to papal payments. Sum a, sent promptly to his father when needed, may plausibly be the same; certainly its existence does not imply any papal remittance. The complexity of sum b is discussed above; though there is no firm alternative explanation about it, a tentative one is at least better supported in its context than is the papal payment.

Scholars quite often note that Renaissance artists' and others' expostulations of poverty are unreliable, particularly in tax returns, yet others as often take them at face value. Thus it is necessary to go beyond the logically adequate statement "there is no basis for calling these papal payments" to claim that they should then not be treated as such. By showing that the only basis for so treating them—Michelangelo's apparent lack of other money—is without merit, the reasons why it is unlikely that these were papal payments may come to the fore.

III: THE DATES. Although the official starting date of the work on the ceiling, 10 May 1508, when Michelangelo wrote "I begin today to work"[49] is always rightly presented, Tolnay and others hold that thereafter there was a long delay before painting started. Yet other evidence suggests, to the contrary, that earlier preparation might be emphasized.

Payment documents show that the scaffolding and plastering had been done by the following 27 July.[50] Yet Tolnay writes that "in January 1509 the actual work on the frescoes was begun."[51] His date has been widely adopted, e.g. by Hibbard in his recent well-grounded monograph, who puts the start in "winter,"[52] though others have more cautiously written that only then is work known to have been in process. Both the delay of some six months and the beginning in winter, a bad time technically for fresco work, are surprising.

Tolnay explains that after the plastering was done in July, and still in August, Michelangelo was without painting assistants, and that in addition his receipt of colors sent from Florence in early September shows that he "could not have begun at that time."[53] These are his sole bases for proposing the wait until January, and both are unjustified.

209

The idea that there were no helpers in August is based on a letter to Michelangelo from Florence, dealing with arrangements to send helpers to him.[54] Tolnay and others have dated it August 1508, but restudy has shown that it was of the previous April. The proof is a phrase in the letter to the effect that it is now getting on to Easter. How the point escaped earlier readers is puzzling. The process of collecting helpers was, then, not delayed until August, but, interestingly, preceded the contract signing on 10 May.

As to the colors, Michelangelo had written to his brother in Florence asking him to buy some, and a reply of 2 September mentions that they are being sent. An ounce of lake is mentioned in the first letter, two and a half pounds of colors in the reply. Yet the purchase of colors hardly need imply that the purchaser lacked and had lacked colors; it may only mean that he is about to use up those he has. Indeed, on the previous 13 May, long before plastering and scaffolding were done, Michelangelo had written a similar letter to buy azure.[55] Thus the August and September documents have been granted a richer value for art-historical deductions than they merit. The next useful document is a letter of 27 January 1509, which refers to painting being done, and similarly this reference to activity taking place becomes for Tolnay the date of beginning, as noted. In a note he repeats the point even more firmly: "In the text we have shown that the actual work could not have been started before January 1509."[56] Not only is there no reason to doubt that it began months earlier, but any scheduling to start fresco work in January would be improbable because it is impossible when water freezes. Indeed that is probably the explanation why, in the case of the *Last Judgment*, after the preliminaries had been finished in the autumn, frescoing only began in the spring, a season when many other fresco projects were started.[57]

It need not surprise us that Michelangelo was seeking assistants in April before he signed his contract in May. It is familiar enough that official contracts are often the end point of long negotiations, during which the parties have in practice arrived at assurance about a plan. Such a situation in this case is consistent with the fact, often noted in isolation, that the ceiling project had been under consideration already in May 1506.[58] The buying of azure three days after the signing also suggests that he was proceeding with promptness. During the two and a half months of scaffold building and plastering, one may suppose with probability that he was at work on his drawings. Hence the best date for the probable beginning of the painting is around 27 July, when (if not earlier) the plastering was complete. The whole dating of the Sistine frescoes should then be moved about six months earlier than the accepted time.

The next records are of July–September 1510. They record a completing of some phase of the work and a pause while arrangements are made for a different phase. Three letters from Michelangelo to his family allude to this. The first has usually been dated August, but Ramsden's shift to July is well based, at least for the last days of that month, and the recent editors mark the letter "July–August."[59] Ramsden points out[60] that Michelangelo's father received a political appointment beginning 22 September 1510, that appointees were notified about two months beforehand, thus in this case about 22 July, that the family wrote this news to Michelangelo, and that he acknowledged it, saying: "I understand from your last that . . . Ludovico has got another office." This acknowledgment might then be as early as about 27 July, otherwise a few days later, and it is this same letter that also gives his news about the painting: "I shall have finished my painting by the end of next week, that is, the part that I began, and when I have unveiled it, I believe I will have money." Looking ahead from 27 July, a Saturday, the "end of next week" would be Saturday, 3 August, so that day is a bare possibility as the one when Michelangelo expected to finish, if everything in this sequence was quite prompt. But Saturday, 10 August, seems more likely. On Saturday, 17 August, Pope Julius left Rome for his ten-month trip,[61] and that scheduled date was certainly known somewhat in advance to Michelangelo, who would surely be trying to finish the work before then, since he wanted the pope to give him money.

In a second letter dated 5 September, Michelangelo wrote his father that a trip to Florence was not then possible, because "I am to have five hundred ducats on the basis of an agreement, which are earned, and the Pope was supposed to give me as much again to get started on the other part of the work, and has left here and did not leave any order." He sent a second version on 7 September, with the variant: "He was supposed to

211

give me as much again to make the scaffolding and continue with the other part of my work."[62] Michelangelo had, then, not got money before the pope's departure, but thought he had had some sort of assurance that before leaving he had given instructions to pay Michelangelo the two equal sums, for what was done and what was to be begun. Then, when he checked, it turned out there was no order. The formula "Pope did not pay before leaving, but was understood to have left an order" is an interesting detail. To be sure, it might merely represent procrastination. But when combined with the first letter, "I believe I will be paid when I have finished" suggests that perhaps Michelangelo took a little longer to finish than he expected, and was not done until after the pope left, so that he was not then entitled to be paid but thought he was told there was an order to pay him as soon as he did finish.

What was this completed part of the ceiling? The answer is available once again in the financial summary of 1523, in the passage that refers to this departure of the pope's. "At this time, the vault being almost finished, the Pope returned to Bologna.[63] As seems not to have been noticed, this dovetails with the letters, in that both make a connection between the departure and the completion of a part of the ceiling, and the latter tells us what part. Michelangelo finished the whole vault in late August 1510. The evidence is rich and without opposition.

Tolnay and others believe that what was completed up to the pause in August 1510 was the first half of the vault, including the first five narrative scenes through the *Creation of Eve*.[64] Of course the primary reason is stylistic; there was a real shift of pictorial means after that. But why date the shift 1510? Tolnay connected this with the one most concrete allusion in the letters, to a new scaffolding. As noted, he supposed with little analysis that there was a large unmoving scaffolding, and, even though at one point noting that it could be built where the masses were held, supposed that it was not, and also supposed that masses were held in the chapel only up to August 1510, thereafter leaving the field to this scaffolding. Hence, even while quoting the statement that the "vault was almost finished" then, he immediately adds that it really was not, his sole specific reason being the apparent evidence about the masses. How imprecisely he read the letters of 1510, when convinced that what happened

212

then was a move to the second half of the vault, emerges when he quotes in Italian Michelangelo's words about making a scaffold for "the other part" of the work, and translates them, even in quotation marks, as "the other half."[65] His link of the style change after the *Creation of Eve* to a pause to put scaffolding in the priests' area also has an internal contradiction. While of course the *Eve* belongs stylistically to the moment before the pause, it is physically within the priests' area, as Tolnay himself notes elsewhere,[66] and so, on the hypothesis about a pause related to masses, would belong to the moment *after* the pause. Since the stylistic linkage is sure, the proposal that the pause of 1510 with a new scaffold was at the entrance to the priests' half of the room falls on this separate ground too.

The numerous bases for assigning the completion of the *whole* vault to August 1510 include (1) the summary of 1523, recording that on 17 August the vault was "almost finished." That must mean well over half, and may mean that a day or two was left to work. Though it might reflect faulty memory, it is confirmed by evidence from the time. (2) The letter of July–August 1510 saying that in the next weeks he will complete a part that will be unveiled and paid for. Our emphasis on style history obscures the fact that a style break is not the type of pause mentioned here; five-ninths of a ceiling would normally not be the end of a section for unveiling and payment purposes, and a whole vault would be, (3) the second letter saying that he was to be paid and to begin a new part of the work, and (4) the other draft of that letter, saying that the new part involved a new scaffold. The analysis of the scaffolding above would indicate that, on the basis of the only possible design consistent with what is known, a new scaffolding would not be required at any point up to the shift from vault to lunettes. Thus the same conclusion results, even if the summary of 1523 "vault almost finished" did not give independent confirmation. (5) That the middle of the vault was regarded as *not* a natural break is, by remarkable luck, directly demonstrated by an anecdote of Condivi:[67]

> [The pope] being vehement by nature and having no patience to wait for things, when half was done, that is from the door to middle of the vault, wished him to unveil it, although it was unfin-

213

ished and had not had the final touches. The opinion and expectation that was had about Michelangelo drew all Rome to see this thing, and the Pope went there too, before the settling of the dust that had been raised by the dismantling of the scaffold.

The details of this story diverge from the situation of August 1510, so that they appear to describe two different events, as indeed is permitted by the fact that Condivi identifies a locus but no date, and the 1510 letters do the opposite. In Condivi, it is the pope who is pressing a resisting artist for the unveiling, in 1510 it is Michelangelo who presses, hoping to get money from a resisting pope. In Condivi, what is unveiled is unfinished, in 1510 Michelangelo works toward an unveiling in ten days or so "when I have finished." The Condivi unveiling occurred when the pope was in Rome, but cannot be later than August 1510, since the pope's next presence in Rome was in June 1511, undeniably much later than the completion of mid-vault. The Condivi unveiling is therefore earlier than August 1510, another confirmation, then, that in August 1510 the painting had gone further than mid-vault. To be sure, Condivi's story can be discredited as novelistic, but it is likely like most of Condivi to have some real basis, even if there is risk in selecting what parts to adopt.[68] (6) It is often noted that Condivi said the Sistine was done in twenty months, and as often pointed out that this is absurd for the project of 1508–12. It has therefore been proposed, since Condivi has some authority, to interpret this as referring to the vault only, even when the figure seemed to work only very approximately.[69] The present findings, of its having been painted from about the end of July 1508 to late August 1510, or in somewhat over twenty-four months, must in fact be reduced by about four months, because of the normal winter suspensions in two years, which are each likely to have been of about two months, on the basis of the best single evidence on this question, Pontormo's diary.[70]

This dating of the vault is not new, but is that reached by Wölfflin, in the study that also proposed the relative chronology of parts now universally accepted.[71] Tolnay's rejection of it was presumably influenced by his proposal that painting only began in January 1509, hardly leaving time for completion of the vault in August 1510. Thus the disappearance of the former date from evidence helps to confirm further the consistent evidence for the latter date. The net span allotted is about the same as Tolnay's.

In further confirmation, it can be shown that the later date offered by Tolnay for the second half of the vault, his alternative to completion of it in August 1510, is excluded by the evidence.

Turning to this later period, it is agreed by all that Michelangelo did no painting from September 1510 to January 1511, a time during which he traveled twice to Bologna to seek money. In Rome on 26 October he got the 500 ducats which are agreed to represent the first of the two sums he had said on 5 September were due, the one for completion of the painting so far done, still leaving him with "no money" to begin the second phase. Consistent with this, a Florentine correspondent alludes on 2 November to his having received "part of the money earned."[72] Arriving in Rome again on 7 January from his second trip, he wrote to his family on the 11th as discussed above that he had got 228 ducats. Whatever the source of these funds, it was not the pope, as is shown by Michelangelo's letter to his brother of 23 February:[73]

> I think I will have to return to Bologna in a few days, since the Pope's datary, with whom I came from Bologna, promised me, when he left here, that as soon as he was in Bologna he would have me provided for so that I could work. It is a month since he went; I still have heard nothing.

He dates the letter "On the twenty-third, 1510" and his brother endorsed it on the back "From Rome, on . . . February, 1510" which is of course 1511 in non-Florentine calendars. Michelangelo had, then, complained to the datary, before that official left Rome about 23 January, of having not had working provision; it follows that he had not received any such provision on 7 January. The money he then got was certainly not papal. It was shown above that there was no reason to suppose it was papal. Ramsden's rebuttal is to deny the accuracy of the date February inscribed on the letter, on the sole ground that the funds of 7 January are assumed by her to be papal, and so this complaint must precede them; she dates this letter 23 November. That would be just as awkward for the hypothesis.[74] No one else rejects the date written on the letter, however. Tolnay has a different solution to the problem of supposedly papal

215

money in January, followed by complaint still in January of no papal money: he argues that "it must be concluded that in January he did not get the entire amount."[75] That is in conflict with Tolnay's own hypothesis on another page that Michelangelo did get the usual 500 ducat fee from the pope as the 7 January payment, of which the 228 sent to Florence is the recorded trace.[76] If that hypothesis is abandoned, receipt of only 228 ducats from the pope would still be in conflict with the insistence in the following days that he had not had the wherewithal to go to work. The hypothesis that the 228 came from the pope has no support, then, even from these explanations, as it has no basis generally, aside from the general impression that such was the source of all money. What remains is the direct statement on 23 February that he had not had papal money to start work. And again this conforms readily to the financial summary of 1523, in the passage that follows at once after the sentence about having almost finished the vault at the time the pope left for Bologna: "So I went there twice for money that I was due to have, and I did nothing, and lost all this time until he returned to Rome."[77] The previous evidence indicated that Michelangelo was in suspense from September at least until 23 February, when he was still waiting. This statement says the same, and only adds more, that the suspense without work continued until the pope's return to Rome, on 27 June 1511. As before, the summary of 1523 faithfully matches the fragmentary references in the letters of 1510–11.

But a difficulty seems to arise when we proceed to the next point in the summary of 1523: "Having returned to Rome, I started to make cartoons for the said work, that is, the ends and sides around the chapel." This appears to contradict the immediately preceding statement that he was doing nothing at this period up to June. One could consider possible contradictions perhaps even in different drafts of the same letter, as discussed above, but contradictions in two directly successive statements in the same letter are surely so implausible that it is more probably our interpretation which is at fault. The simple answer to the difficulty can again be found by close reading of the text, in this case taking into account the original punctuation, or rather lack of it. All modern editors have treated the above two points as two sentences. But Michelangelo does not indicate sentences in his letters, either by punctuation (his only punctuation mark is a dot in midair, which may be a comma or anything else, and that at rare intervals) nor by capital letters (he even tends to write proper names with lowercase letters in most cases).[78] Turning to the original Italian, and using only a liberal allowance of such dots as punctuation, we have:

> ond'io v'andai dua volte per danari.che io avevo avere . e non feci niente . e perde' tucto questo tempo.finche ritorno a rroma . ritornato a rroma.mi missi a far chartoni per decta opera . cioe per le teste e per le faccie actorno di decta capella

It is evident that, before punctuation forecloses alternative interpretations, two are available. One is that Michelangelo did nothing until the pope returned to Rome, in June 1511, and that after Michelangelo returned to Rome, in January 1511, he started making cartoons. This is the same as before, when the passage was punctuated in two sentences, and is an internal contradiction. The second interpretation is that Michelangelo did nothing until the pope returned to Rome, and when the pope did return to Rome, Michelangelo began making cartoons. This latter interpretation is not internally contradictory, and so is evidently the correct one. It also conforms to the basic sentence patterns, since the first "ritorno" has the same person as subject as does the immediately following "ritornato": this happened until he returned, after he returned that happened. It also conforms to the social and financial realities: when the pope got back, Michelangelo at last could get money or a lively expectation of it, so then he went to work. Michelangelo did not work at all on the Sistine ceiling, then, from August 1510 until the end of June 1511, a startling amendment of conventional ideas, but the only one not calling for straining of the evidence.

It may be noted that even with the editors' two-sentence construction, in which "ritornato" begins a new thought, it may still refer to the pope as here suggested by a grammatical form which is indeed incorrect, but common among educated people. Thus a university newspaper article of 6 November 1979 describes how a senior official, Kahn, had appointed an economist to assist him, and then begins the next sentence:

217

"An economics professor from California, Kahn described Russell as
very able."[79] By the rules of grammar that require *ritornato* to refer to
Michelangelo (and so to say contradictorily that he made cartoons from
January 1511), here "professor" would have to be Kahn, but in fact it is
Russell. It is the same looseness that might be read in 1523.

It should be noticed that there are only two interpretations of this passage; from January Michelangelo either did cartoons for the lunettes (the
self-contradictory one) or nothing. He did not complete the painting on
the vault. Tolnay, however, writes that in spring 1511 "it seems that he
also executed the rest of the curved parts of the ceiling, i.e. the remaining parts of the presbyterium."[80] This has no support, and is in conflict
with both readings of the financial summary. It is forced on Tolnay because it is clear that these frescoes existed in the following August, when
the pope saw them on Assumption Eve, and he does not accept that they
were already done by the previous August. The evidence that all the
vault was done by August 1510 seems further confirmed when it appears
that the rejection of this idea necessarily leads Tolnay to an untenable alternative denied by the 1523 report. This part of Tolnay's chronology has
also been widely accepted, however.

IV: THE FURTHER IMPLICATIONS. The whole vault was painted between July 1508 and August 1510, with two presumable interruptions, in
the winter months. Its stylistic development shows both a rapid evolution and a special break after the fifth scene, as discussed, as well as other
shifts and an overriding unity. It seems quite possible that the break in
style corresponds to the winter break of 1509–10. It is often suggested
that Michelangelo began rather slowly and quickened his pace as he
worked, so that the division of about a year and four months for the first
five-ninths, plus preparatory work for the whole, and about seven
months for the last four-ninths, need not be askew. The break in style
does suggest a break in time, and this has been a strong basis for the
chronology arriving only at mid-vault in August 1510. But that was not
the only break in time that occurred. A briefer one, if combined with a
readiness to change, is entirely sufficient to explain what happened.

But the truly large break separates the vault from the lunettes. They took a year and three months to do, including the drawings (not in addition to the drawings, a hypothesis of very slow work which is another implausibility in Tolnay's chronology). The lunettes have been passed over very briefly by almost all writers, beginning with Condivi. Among other reasons, this may be precisely because the style break between the vault and them is tremendous, indeed it is so great as to make the break in mid-vault seem a small variation. They do not even correspond to our idea of what is Michelangelesque, being painterly, bizarrely inventive in color in a way rather like Rosso later, psychologically subtle and immensely individual, even eccentric, and not heroic, muscular, aggressive, or sculptural. When as often we look for demonstrations of what we well know Michelangelo did, we do not look there. Wolfflin is one of the few writers to have emphasized them. In seeing that they represent the next phase of the style of Michelangelo at an interval after he completed his Sistine vault, we may be led to look more closely at a great pictorial achievement.

It was a particular pleasure to present this essay to Peter Murray, who gave us pioneering models of studies using the method of intense reading of documents combined with awareness of their siting in historic contexts. The present findings, now only slightly modified, were first presented in public at a small but international symposium on Michelangelo, held at Cleveland (Ohio) State University on 2 March 1978.

1. See now J. Wilde, *Michelangelo, Six Lectures*, Oxford, 1978, 48–84. For an interesting variant, using pure stylistic argument, see M. Wundram, "Beobachtungen zur Chronologie der Malereien M.'s an der Sixtinischen Decke," *Zeitschrift für Kunstgeschichte*, XXXVI, 1974, 235–47.

2. C. de Tolnay, *Michelangelo, II: The Sistine Ceiling*, Princeton, 1945. Hereafter references to Tolnay and a page are to that volume.

3. Tolnay, 4, largely repeated on 187.

4. Condivi's text is conveniently quoted in full in relation to other materials by P. Barocchi, in her edition of G. Vasari, *La vita di Michelangelo*, Milan, 1962, II, 409,

5. Tolnay, 187.

6. Vasari, *Vita di M.*, ed. Barocchi, I, 37.

7. Loc. cit.

8. Tolnay, 187.

9. Barocchi, II, 410.

10. Tolnay, 187.

11. Tolnay, III.

12. Tolnay, 110.

13. E. Steinmann, *Die Sixtinische Kapelle*, II, Michelangelo, 1905, 180: "Denn während der ganzen Zeit, die der Meister in der Sixtina malte, wurden hier die Gottesdienste nicht ausgesetzt." This is immediately followed by a footnote: "Der Umstand wird durch Paris de Grassis bezeugt, der die Gottesdienste nach wie vor in der Capella maior beschreibt und niemals erwähnt, sie seien der Malereien wegen ausgesetzt oder verlegt worden." The accuracy of Steinmann's reading of Paris's diaries has been kindly confirmed to me by Professor John Shearman, who has worked extensively with the manuscripts. Steinmann at a later point, when discussing the chronology of the paintings (p. 219) suggests that Michelangelo started at the entrance end so as at least to postpone the problem of congestion in the priests' area, and in that connection mentions the records of masses being continuous up to the pope's departure. Tolnay, also discussing the chronology of the frescoes, unfortunately cited only this briefer report by Steinmann on the mass records being continuous up to 1510, temporarily overlooking the longer report about their also being held later, and hence was more naturally drawn to think of their having been suspended.

14. This may be deduced from Paris's report on the mass held there on 14 August 1511, quoted by Tolnay, 235. He notes that the pope "wished to attend vespers and the Mass celebrated in the chapel by the resident priest" and explains that he came either because he wished to see the new paintings, or out of devotion to the Virgin assunta. It hardly seems that he would have brought up possible reasons for his coming, if he came often. F. Hartt (*History of Italian Renaissance Art*, n.d., 456) incorrectly reports that the pope "said" the mass of 14 August, thus assigning him a more active involvement with the chapel than is evidenced.

15. Steinmann, ii, 180, immediately following the remarks quoted in note 13.

16. Tolnay does indeed at one point (p. 187) take note that the scaffolding did permit masses to continue, but does not apply this when discussing the chronology, indeed the contrary. He writes that it "had the advantage of being so constructed that it was possible to hold Masses while work was being done on the ceiling, as is attested by the Diarium of Paris de Grassis," but gives no citation of any particular statement by Paris that would describe such a structure, or any secondary reference, which presumably would be Steinmann. And it is hard to see how the type of scaffolding envisioned by Tolnay could be compatible with masses. One may think that this is why he proposes elsewhere that, in the event, a scaffolding was not built in the priests' area until masses were not being held, and that painting was not done there earlier "because" of the masses, a contradiction of the reference to the Diarium just cited. Evidently it is only when the structure of the scaffold is determined that the contradiction can be resolved in application to the chronology.

17. Personal recollection. I was privileged to be on the scaffold in December 1936 through the kindness of and in the company of Edgar Wind.

18. Tolnay, 103, writes that for Michelangelo it was a handicap that, while working, "he received light only from the sides." This passing reference, apparently the only one to the light problem, assumes the large scaffold as a given, and then deduces the light quality. In the present study it is suggested that the sequence should be reversed. Analogously, other observers envision Michelangelo unable to see his work from a suitable distance for gauging its effect, and make this an element in the "difficult" character of the work. It may be suggested rather that he would have made the provision of a good viewing distance a specification in his scaffold design, in the same way as the provision of adequate light discussed infra.

19. Steimnann, ii, Abb. 73.

20. Vasari, *Vita di M.*, ed. Barocchi, i, 21, with additional details.

21. Tolnay, 18.

22. Tolnay, 185.

23. *I Ricordi di Michelangelo*, ed. L. Bardeschi Ciulich and P. Barocchi, 1970, 1.

24. *Il Carteggio di Michelangelo*, ed. postuma di G. Poggi, by P. Barocchi and R. Ristori, 1965, I, III.

25. Op. cit., 121.

26. Michelangelo Buonarroti, *Rime e lettere, precedute dalla vita dell'autore scritta da A.*

Condivi, 1908, 91–92.

27. E. Ramsden, ed., *The Letters of Michelangelo*, 1963, I, Appendix 9, "Payments for the Painting of the Vault of the Sistine Chapel," 242–43.

28. *Il Carteggio*, III, 1973, 9.

29. Tolnay, 191.

30. *Il Carteggio*, 148; the reasons for this are indicated ibid., 385, 389.

31. Ramsden, I, 243, 245, "probably toward the end of October 1512."

32. Vasari, *Vita di M.*, ed. Barocchi, I, 36.

33. See the discussion by Tolnay, 191.

34. Tolnay, 191, section XXII, "Notes on the Salary." Unspecified allusions in what follows to Tolnay's views on the fees are to this section.

35. Ramsden, I, 240–46, Appendix 9. Unspecified allusions in what follows to Ramsden's views on the fees are to this appendix.

36. *Il Carteggio*, I, 118. Tolnay's date of January 1512 is shared by no one, because it argues that the word "giugno" on the letter is a slip of the pen. Ramsden's argument for June 1511 is accepted by Barocchi, loc. cit. Other opinions are cited by her; to these should be added that of H. Mancusi-Ungaro, *Michelangelo: The Bruges Madonna and the Piccolomini Altar*, 1971, 94–95. His date of 1508 is, however, a unique aberration.

37. There is some disagreement on the order of the drafts. Barocchi places later the one that seems to me earlier, in all probability, because it breaks off sooner; the other fills in much more detail of Michelangelo's arguments on behalf of his case. However, this matter seems not to have significance for the present discussion. The repetitions are so close that the later one was evidently written in the actual presence of the earlier one, and within hours or days.

38. *Il Carteggio*, III, 7–11, is the best text of the two drafts.

39. *Il Carteggio*, III, 4.

40. *Il Carteggio*, I, 97.

41. *Il Carteggio*, I, 113.

42. *Il Carteggio*, I, 118.

43. *Il Carteggio*, I, 88, 91, 92, 106, 107.

44. *Il Carteggio*, I, 112.

45. C. de Tolnay, *The Youth of Michelangelo*, Princeton, 1943, 205–9.

46. *Il Carteggio*, I, 73, 91, 92, 107.

47. In the financial summary of 1523 he wrote that he had taken on the commission for the *Cascina*, and "n'avevo tre mila ducati" (*Il Carteggio*, III, 7). He adds that when he did the cartoon he felt that they were half earned. Tolnay seems wrong in paraphrasing that he "was to get" 3,000 ducats (*The Youth*, 209). Ramsden translates "was getting" (*The Letters*, 148). That is certainly an idiomatic rendering of the word *avevo*, but the implication created that he was only paid a part seems to extrapolate

wrongly from the statement. It seems possible that both writers work from a belief that Michelangelo did not receive such sums.

48. Ramsden, I, 83.

49. *I Ricordi*, 2.

50. *I Ricordi,* 3.

51. Tolnay, 110.

52. H. Hibbard, *Michelangelo*, 1975, 118.

53. Tolnay, 110.

54. *Il Carteggio*, I, 54–65.

55. *Il Carteggio*, I, 66.

56. Tolnay, 188.

57. For a small collection of examples, see C. Gilbert, "L'ordine cronologico degli affreschi Bardi e Peruzzi," *Bollettino d'Arte*, LIII, 1968, 196.

58. Tolnay, 3.

59. *Il Carteggio*, I, 106.

60. Ramsden, *The Letters*, I, 54, 203.

61. L. Pastor, *History of the Popes*, VI, 1923, 332.

62. *Il Carteggio*, I, 107, 108.

63. *Il Carteggio*, III, 9.

64. Tolnay, 111.

65. Tolnay, 187.

66. Tolnay, 11.

67. Buonarroti (as in note 25), 87–88.

68. Unless Condivi is novelistic, this reference to dismantling the scaffolding will indeed seem to conflict with the arguments above that no new scaffolding was needed at mid-vault. One may risk discounting Condivi's phrase perhaps if one can persuasively reconstruct his purpose in writing. Admittedly in such storytelling, some points are central and are exact evidence, while those tangential to the writer's motives reflect less care by him and so deceive anyone who takes them as exact. It is often observable in art-historical analysis of brief vital texts that they are weighed word for word in ways unlikely to match the relatively unfocused intention of the original writers. Condivi's interest is to prove the pope's eager haste. The dust is a vivid motif in support, and we may incline to think the description is exaggerated; the dismantled scaffolding in turn is, after all, simply a tertiary point to show how much dust there was. So it may have been invoked for the storyteller by the image of the dust, rather than vice versa. If there was dust, but not really so much, its cause could have been the moving about of the smaller scaffold. The above may seem less like special pleading when it is added that in this very circumstance of a temporary unveiling, to dismantle a scaffolding would be a dreadful idea, since it would have had to have been rebuilt to continue the unfinished work on the same

frescoes. So it is less likely to have happened than to have been imagined. A moving aside of a small scaffold, on the other hand, would really be appropriate for the particular purpose named.

69. C. Seymour, *Michelangelo, The Sistine Chapel Ceiling,* 1972, XX, 120.

70. See J. Rearick, *The Drawings of Pontormo,* 1964, I, 350–54. Pontormo's diary of 1555–56 records two things daily, what he ate and what he painted, but after such an entry on 27 November describes only what he ate daily, until on 6 February he writes "cominciai a lavorare" and resumes the two reports.

71. Cf. Tolnay, 188.

72. *Il Carteggio,* I, 112.

73. *Il Carteggio,* I, 116.

74. E. Ramsden, *The Letters,* I, 203. On this dating Michelangelo would have complained to the datary before and about 23 October, when that official departed, but obtained 500 ducats on 25 October from the same datary, but still complained on 23 November of having had nothing. It is true that he probably made a sharp distinction between the sums due for separate purposes, but such a precedure would seem extreme.

75. Tolnay, III.

76. Tolnay, 191.

77. *Il Carteggio,* III, p. 9.

78. The reader may easily check this in the photographs of letters reproduced by Ramsden. In her volume I, fig. 18 reproduces a letter close in date to 1523, of September–October 1521 according to her, or February–March 1521 according to Poggi (*Il Carteggio,* II, 274).

79. *Cornell Chronicle.*

80. Tolnay, III.

PART TWO

THE ARTIST AMONG OTHER ARTISTS

A NEW SIGHT IN 1500: THE COLOSSAL

Let us first look at two photographs side by side, of Donatello's bronze *David* (fig. 1) and Cellini's *Perseus* (fig. 2). To do so is to exploit the most distinctive quality that is familiar in slide lectures when regarded as a genre of communication. The implication is that the two sculptures are significantly comparable, and everyone would agree, for they share a series of qualities perhaps never again found together in combination. Both present single figures, in bronze, of male youths, in the nude, shown with the cut off heads of persons they have killed, and the swords with which they killed them; both were produced by leading artists in Renaissance Florence. As to differences, they were made about a century apart, so we can use the comparison to think about any changes of attitude or style that occurred in the interim—a kind of thinking much eased by choosing objects that are alike in almost all other ways. The resulting observations would then focus on qualities associated respectively with "the early Renaissance" and "Mannerism." The later sculptor, while starting from the assumptions of the earlier one as to vitalism and ideality, the combination of the real and the beautiful called for by Donatello's contemporary Alberti, would move toward a more artificial and a more ornamental quality in the whole and in details.

In this often repeated introductory reading, one extremely elementary difference between the two works seems to be usually omitted. That is scale. The *David* is about five feet high, and hence may be classed as life-size, recalling how the Bible text suggests that he was not quite full-grown when he killed Goliath. *Perseus* on the other hand is more than ten feet high. He may be called colossal, a vague term for which here a working definition will be over-life-size to the extent of belonging to a different category, or order of magnitude. It is a rather rare class of sculpture, and its size is generally supposed to be intended to impress. And yet

Figure 2: Cellini, *Perseus*, Loggia dei Lanzi, Florence

Figure 1: Donatello, *David*, Bargello,
Florence

the description of the *Perseus* in the book most often used on the period of sculpture that includes it does not bring up this factor, even though it refers to Donatello's *David*.[1] Nor does Cellini himself in his autobiography seem to have articulated the matter in the detailed account of the *Perseus*. He calls it a big statue, but always in comparing it to its own preliminary models.

Two questions are thus suggested: what led to the shift to the colossal in comparison with Donatello, and why was the circumstance then not emphasized? The matter is of greater interest in that it seems to be not limited to this one comparison, but to be typical of the two eras. Here some of the circumstances will be explored, as a start toward answering these questions, but no more. The puzzle for me began with the impression that around 1500 a shift took place, in the context of Florentine art and to some extent more broadly, in that before then artists produced no colossal works at all, whereas after that these became fairly normal. On a little further reflection, it came to seem that the truly unusual circumstance was, rather, the lack of the colossal in the earlier era, the *quattrocento*. Many cultures produce colossal works in fair quantity. They are not, it is true, absolutely absent in the *quattrocento*, but it seemed and continues to seem valid to argue that all the exceptions were works attached tightly to older projects, so that their scale had been preestablished in a late Gothic context. This is obvious in the case of the cathedral of Florence and sculptures associated with it. Hence the independent appearance of the colossal around 1500 would seem to be intended, and to have a meaning or meanings.

Our two photographs evoke one very basic reason for remaining unaware of the scale of the *Perseus*. It is well known that looking at slides of works of art commonly provides no sense at all of their scale. The fact is constantly being reflected in students' questions, and in lecturers' efforts at approximate responses on the spot, which nevertheless do not seem to have stimulated much in the way of systematic reform.[2] In the case of images of a human body, especially when some degree of natural imitation is involved, our own body image of ourselves seems to become a factor, and we tend to adjust the perceived scale of the sculpture toward that of the real body, as more comfortable and even more

Figure 3: Paris, Notre Dame, west front

Figure 4: Rome, St. Peter's façade

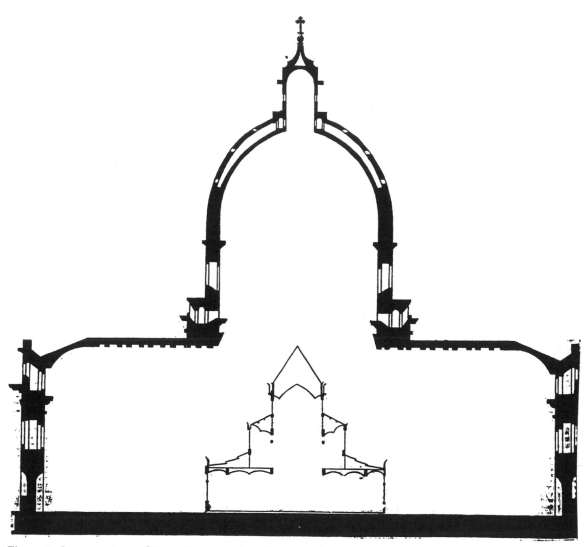

Figure 3: Cross sections of Notre Dome and St. Peter's in the same scale

ego-bound. Something of the sort happens with the slide image, when the absence of any information seems to make people tend to think of all the images as of a middling size, smaller than the projection. The approving term "human scale" used about very different kinds of things such as cities suggests the power of such internal points of departure. A median scale may also be inferred when all the parts of a thing have proportional interrelationships that are familiar or normal, whereas colossality or tininess is only evoked through "disproportion." Ruskin, in complaining of St. Peter's in Rome, mocked the great effort to make it grand, arguing that the effect is all lost, in view of the equal enlargements of all parts, capitals, foliage, etc.[3] It does seem true that we do not see many things as internally colossal, but need a gauge in a different scale. Cellini's *Perseus* lacks such a gauge, since in its setting (which is the original one) it is adjacent to similar, indeed slightly larger works, Michelangelo's *David* and Bandinelli's *Hercules*. That may have made the *Perseus* seem of a quite ordinary scale, nothing special, both to him and others. On the other hand, the earliest of the three works, Michelangelo's *David*, was known as "the giant" from the start. It may be that, along with other factors, a gauge creating the needed contrast may be a temporal one, when an object exceeds what we expected on the basis of comparable ones familiar previously.

Our sense of the colossal may work with respect to the same object in some situations but not others. As we approach Nôtre Dame de Paris (fig. 3) or St. Peter's in Rome (fig. 4) they loom as enormous, and the photographs continue to give the effect. The gauge is our own size, which may get help from such "human-sized" surrogates as windows in nearby houses. It is also a matter of triangulation, the angle from our eye up to the top of the object. Hence our distance is critical. From immediately under a facade the colossality is awesome, but that is not photographable; miles away the effect nearly vanishes. There seems to be a standard distance for photographing facades of monumental buildings. It embraces all of the facade, but not more, and sets up an effective angle to the top. In this normal system both Nôtre Dame and St. Peter's seem impressively gigantic in much the same way, but that is incorrect in an important respect. To our astonishment, a measured drawing (fig. 5)

233

makes Nôtre Dame look rather tiny—on the gauge of St. Peter's, which when looking at the drawing we seem to accept as the gauge. If instead we assign the role of gauge here to Nôtre Dame, with an effort, St. Peter's seems incomprehensibly vast, or it may seem less comparable to Nôtre Dame than to the Eiffel Tower, that other vast gauge for Nôtre Dame which is conveniently visible not far from it. Thus to stand in front of St. Peter's makes Ruskin seem wrong. I think he is also wrong for the interior, at least for the moment of entrance, for one's own scale makes all those forms seem immense until one adjusts to something medium, as one does after a while to darkness. After that has happened Ruskin seems right, but only as he would for other cases, where his special factor of retained proportions of all large objects was not present. He is also right in the context of our not supposing St. Peter's to be larger than Nôtre Dame. There Nôtre Dame gains from our notion of colossal height as inhering in Gothic cathedrals and primarily in them, whether this is something we have picked up from our culture or whether it is experienced directly. Yet it fails the test of measuring, at least with St. Peter's as a gauge.

All these elementary, and partly very familiar, observations are by way of suggesting that the artists of 1500 faced a somewhat complicated challenge, if indeed they were purposefully setting up a new trend to the colossal. That is, it was not just a matter of making big things. Besides the problems of winning major commissions, coping with costs, and solving technical problems, they would need to end up with objects not only truly colossal but also looking that way. One recourse for them of course, helpful because it bypassed some of the other problems mentioned, would be to create the perception alone of the colossal without its physical actuality. If, as indicated, colossality is dependent on perception, perhaps it can be perceived where it is not as well as failing to be perceived where it is.

It will not be surprising to start with Michelangelo, whose *David* was mentioned as being already nearby when Cellini installed his *Perseus*. The *David,* begun in 1501 (fig. 6), was in a sense also a model for the third colossal work in the same area, Bandinelli's *Hercules,* and so evidently had some sort of pioneering role. To be sure, this may have been in good

234

Figure 6: Michelangelo, *David*, Accademia, Florence

part accidental. As is well known, the *David* was produced as a renewal of an old project.⁴ It was connected with a plan to place appropriate sculptures on Florence's cathedral, a colossal late Gothic structure of the *trecento*. The specific plan of installing statues high up on its roofline first emerges in planning records of 1408. However, the first sculpture produced, Donatello's life-size marble *David*, was seemingly brought back down to the ground in 1409, and was soon after installed indoors in the city hall of Florence.⁵ No one explained the change of plan, but it is generally supposed to have concerned such matters as its being too small to be seen from below, or too good to be left where it could not be examined, or of too heavy and breakable material to risk uncertainty about its underpinnings. While its eventual location suggests the second possibility, the first and third are evoked in the next effort to fill its original one. For this Donatello received another commission, but for a work of colossal size to be executed in terra-cotta, assembled from pieces like bricks, and then painted white. The effect of the paint on the clay was probably a less sharp-cut surface than marble, such as is seen in later Florentine terra-cotta figures, whether painted only or also glazed.

This colossus, obviously conceived in terms of a Gothic church buttress as its setting, though by a very modern Renaissance artist, remained in place for some two centuries until it disappeared, probably from disintegration through weathering. What is remarkable is that the fairly rich literature of praise for Donatello written in these centuries by Florentine artists and connoisseurs seems to ignore this largest work by him entirely. The rare exception is a memorandum by Donatello's doctor, who recorded receiving a gift from him and added a reference to the colossus, and it alone, by way of identifying his patient as a famous artist. It is rightly noted that he showed a layman's viewpoint. It does not, in my view, however, imply as has been suggested that all Florence knew the colossus. "Unsophisticated" Florentines have left no trace of response to his works otherwise, and when this one comes from a personal associate of the artist, one may agree that the colossus would be an unsophisticated choice, but think even it would only have been remembered if the person had that added stimulus to think of such works at all. The colossus's disadvantages for the connoisseurs may have included its cheap, non-noble materials (unlike bronze and marble) and their blatant function of avoiding the difficulty that was prized by the age in artistic achievement. Cellini's boastful account of how hard it was to cast his *Perseus* so successfully is a good case of that attitude. Donatello began a second similar figure, but did not get far with it. Then in the following decades, for whatever reasons, there seemed to be no interest at all in colossal sculpture, even when there was much work being done on the cathedral. The emphasis on "human-size" works even in that gigantic structure seems to suggest the strength of that preference.

A small revival of interest occurred in the 1460s. The minor sculptor Agostino di Duccio was paid to produce a figure to make a pair with Donatello's, very likely utilizing what Donatello had begun fifty years earlier. It was presumably installed, but attracted no attention afterward. (Vasari's remark that Donatello had done two such figures is the only probable trace of it.) The cathedral authorities at the time were enough encouraged by it, however, to give Agostino a second commission immediately. This was more ambitious, for it reverted to marble, but maintained the same colossal size. It was cautiously specified that it would be in four pieces—not so awkward as it sounds, since the head and arms accounted for three. Ancient Roman marble figures were often produced in this way, a fact that may have been coming to notice at the time. Agostino then responded still more ambitiously by coming up with a single block for it. Then, however, he did not finish the carving; his whole career had been spent in doing small panels in low relief, and the (unrecorded) explanation of this new setback for the colossal may have been that it was simply too much for this individual. Yet none of the other available sculptors who might have handled the matter, such as Verrocchio, became involved. Ten years later there is only a single record of an approach made to another relief sculptor, Rossellino. Thus if it is true that some sort of feeling about the pleasure of colossal sculpture did not totally die in *quattrocento* Florence, it seems to have run in a stream that was not only very thin but almost calculated to fail. During all this period, as Florentines certainly knew, the cathedral of Milan was acquiring colossal stone statues. They functioned beautifully, partly because they tacitly continued to accept the idea of a Gothic encyclopedic program, figures all over the sides decoratively integrated into the structure—though their figure style moved into modern Renaissance modes.

Perhaps it was only one more such little spurt which, in 1501, led the authorities to assign Agostino's block, unfinished and perhaps hardly begun, to a promising local twenty-six-year-old carver. The result was of course Michelangelo's *David*. The effect was not as spectacular as that when a hundred years before Brunelleschi became a civic hero for solving the colossal difficulty of vaulting the cathedral dome—in a scale specified long before, but left unfinished for want of a practical method—yet it certainly did set his career on its road to unique success. Two closely related circumstances that quickly followed are of special interest here. One is that Michelangelo immediately went on to do some more colossi, as if he had opened a welcome door. I am not referring to his famous tendency to accept impractically large commissions for sets of sculptures, the famous bad decision of his life. Much less noted is that even before he got mired in the problems of the twelve apostles for the cathedral, not to mention the Julius tomb, he first went on to the colossal bronze statue of Pope Julius and to the *Battle of Cascina*. The first is variously described as having been fourteen or twenty feet high, the latter mural is usually reported as 22 by 54 feet. The loss of both works is of course largely responsible for our not thinking of them a great deal, especially the former which is not even known from drawings. It is like being able to know them solely from slides, that is, through filters that severely exclude the sense of scale. Nevertheless, Michelangelo swiftly became an artist for whom the colossal was a standard vehicle. The fact that these three works were conspicuously in three different media—all major and noble—adds still further to the effect of a master able to do anything. This is not the long-sought key to explain Michelangelo, but it seems a basic addition to other observations and an oddly underemphasized one.

The second circumstance, following even more closely, was the special response to the *David* by its patrons, the Florentine authorities, and their public. It consisted of calling a meeting of advisers to decide where to install it. There has been much comment on the minutes of the meeting that followed, including the reasonable one that it showed great re-

238

spect for the artist. What seems not to have been emphasized was the oddity of conducting such a meeting in the first place; scholars seem to begin by accepting it as something "there"—after all, it is a document— and immediately going on to details. We learn first that the work had been produced without anybody having determined where it should go, and that means without any sense of its purpose. The authorities are saying: we have this big thing, what are we to do with it? It sounds like a gift, a white elephant, not something they had ordered. To be sure, this is hardly likely to be the first occasion of a work of art ordered with no distinct idea of where to put it—precedents nearby, in great probability, are the small bronzes of Pollaiuolo, Bertoldo, and others, desired for admiration and possession, without any sense of fitting in any more definite place than in a good spot in one's house for display. But they did not generate the problem that was now involved with a non-site-specific colossus. The new problem clearly had crept up gradually. The first colossi in the cathedral series had of course been designed for an exact place; it had then been found unworkable, without drawing the conclusion of either ceasing to produce such figures or finding a new site. The issue is charmingly reflected in one of the comments at the meeting by a modest woodcarver. He said the figure had been meant for the top of the cathedral, and "I don't know the reason why it isn't to be put there"; neatly enough he had begun with the general principle: "I believe all things are made for some purpose." Purpose, he clearly felt, had been bewilderingly lost to view. A few other members of the committee favored placing the figure on the ground next to the cathedral, but nearly all wanted it next to the city hall. The reasons articulated had to do with weathering, traffic patterns for viewers and for officials, and vandalism; it sounds much like a committee of curators debating the installation of a large sculpture in their garden, with arguments chiefly mundane.

The choice made, to place it in front of the city hall facade, is the more interesting since it had not been supported by many speakers—only four, as against twelve who thought it should go under the Loggia dei Lanzi nearby. Four or five others proposed putting it either in the city hall courtyard or in a room there.[6] The position inside the loggia had great appeal for protecting it from the weather, and it has recently been

239

supported with an interesting photomontage and the hypothesis that this is what Michelangelo wanted (fig. 7). The comparison with the montage strongly suggests that the present position has the special virtue of making the colossal work look colossal. Under the loggia, fitting inside a big arch, it would have strikingly harmonious relations to its framing forms, and indeed seem a bit small for its opening. Inside the courtyard, surrounded by four high walls, it could hardly have been seen at all. That is the spot later effectively assigned to Verrocchio's small fountain with the putto. As it was, the *David* was seen along with the palace door, windows, and masonry blocks, gauges that measure its grandeur with great success. That the Florentines were conscious of the siting value of the wall treatment behind the figure is nicely shown from a record of 1416, when Donatello's *David* was being moved into the city hall. A painter was paid for painting lilies—the Florentine heraldic fleurs-de-lis—on a blue ground "on the wall where the said *David* is placed."

Almost as soon as the *David* of Michelangelo had been installed outside the building, the artist began work on a mural to go inside it. This was the *Battle of Cascina,* which was never finished, so we know it only from drawings, copies, and descriptions. It is usually thought to have been planned for a wall area 22 by 54 feet. The room, later remodeled into the Sala dei Cinquecento, contains murals of the later sixteenth century with colossal figures that may well give some impression of the earlier effect of scale quite faithfully, and were probably meant to do so (fig. 8). Here of course Michelangelo shared the project with Leonardo, who was projecting his *Battle of Anghiari* beside him, on the same scale. The subjects alluded to Florentine victories, just as *David* alluded to Florentine political ideology of freedom against tyrants. But *David*, we have seen, was only connected to the politically important location after the fact, and in this case too it is likely that the well-known specialties of the artists in horses and in active male nudes were strong factors at least in deciding which patriotic scenes to present. (They had not been favored before, as *David* had been.) The colossal scale is keyed to the size of the room, which in turn was intended to accommodate the mass meetings of citizens set up by a new democratic regime. Thus a fluid group of forces was involved in generating these works.

240

Figure 7: photomontage of *David* in the Loggia dei Lanzi, by Charles Seymour

Figure 8: Sala dei Cinquento, east wall, Palazzo Vecchio, Florence

Figure 9: After Leonardo,
four engravings of leaping horses

Figure 10:
Leonardo, *Leaping Horse,* drawing,
Windsor Castle,
Royal Library.
Reproduced by gracious permission of
Her Majesty Queen
Elizabeth II.

The presence of Leonardo reminds us that Michelangelo was not the first artist in this context to involve himself in the special qualities of the colossal. It is not surprising that it fascinated Leonardo, as one of his many experimental concerns with unsolved challenges. In any case, if we suspect that the new interest in colossality is in some way linked to the emergence of what we call the High Renaissance, then Leonardo would almost necessarily be found as a pioneer. When Leonardo left Florence in 1481–1482 for his long stay in Milan, he was specifically purposing to work for the duke on major jobs, and the equestrian monument of the duke's father and predecessor was already in question. Around the same date Florence's two leading older artists, Pollaiuolo and Verrocchio, also left never to return, with similar intentions; Pollaiuolo went to Rome to work on a papal monument, Verrocchio to Venice for an equestrian bronze. Big scale, in general, if not the colossal in particular, had an association with career distinction as well as better income.

The monument that Leonardo worked on in Milan is alluded to by contemporaries as colossal, without any indication of its specific measurements. The work remained uncompleted after many years, so that Leonardo here failed more visibly than Agostino di Duccio had, and it remained to haunt him though it certainly did not spoil his career. Even his processes were so fascinating that (fig. 9) reproductive engravings were done after his drawings for the ducal horse, probably the very first case of such a public relations effect of a work of art in progress. It evidently seemed natural that a colossal sculpture would involve a horse. The image of the ruler or general immediately suggested both, and the type had recently had striking success on a slightly lesser scale, first in Donatello's *Gattamelata* (the horse and man together about ten feet high) and then at this very time in Verrocchio's *Colleoni* (thirteen feet). Leonardo evidently wanted to outdo them in every way, starting with scale. The most immediate stimulus he found for surpassing them in difficulty and in liveliness certainly came from an area usually not found important for Leonardo, in classical antiquity. There he could find the motif of the leaping horse, forefeet in the air, which we see in the most beautiful record we have of Leonardo's project, the drawing of the leap-

243

ing horse trampling an enemy (fig. 10). The brilliant fusion of tremulous vitality and effective power is typical of Leonardo at his most intense. It was understood at the time that he was aware of the marble horses of the Quirinal (fig. 11); the comparison was made, as to Leonardo's second equestrian project, by Luca Pacioli, the best reporter we have on Leonardo's years in Milan, but has played little role in recent thinking about him.[7] The ancient Roman horses are eighteen feet high. Once anyone became interested in them, it would probably become soon noticeable that a high proportion of the few Roman sculptures known and admired at this date—before the explosion of archeology after 1500—were colossi. Well treated by Virginia Bush[8] in relation to sixteenth-century sculpture, this group of ancient works also included the bronze statue of *Marcus Aurelius* on his horse, twice life-size. It may be underlined that the scale of these classical works seems not to have been interesting, a few years earlier, to Donatello and Verrocchio when they planned their bronze equestrian figures, suggesting again that the *quattrocento* was different on this score.

When Leonardo gave up his plan for the leaping horse, he shifted to one with an ambling horse. He was surely aware then not only of all these models, but of another great classical model, the bronze horses of St. Mark's. (These are life-size, six feet high.) That these figures could nevertheless also inform his exploration of the colossal is suggested by Leonardo's other project being carried out at the same time as the monument, his *Last Supper* (fig. 12). In it the sense of scale, with figures looming larger than ourselves, is emphatic. Heydenreich has put it well in his little book on the work.[9] "The figures who throng around the table," he writes, "are mighty ones; if they were to rise there would not be room enough for them." And again: "Leonardo made use of over-life-size figures. Within the given space they possess a supernatural size." It seems instructive to see how this relates to the *Last Supper* by Castagno of 1450 (fig. 13), Leonardo's greatest predecessor in representing this theme, and always compared with him (though not in this respect). Castagno offers us people to whom we respond comfortably as "human-sized." They are on a par with us, while Leonardo's are indeed overweening, stronger, and grander. The difference in height on the wall is part of the effect.

244

Figure 11: *Leaping Horse*, Rome, Piazza del Quirinale. Photo: Cesare D'Onofrio, *Gli Obelischi di Roma*.

Figure 12: Leonardo, *Last Supper,* S. Maria delle Grazie, Milan

Figure 13: Castagno, *Last Supper,* S. Apollonia, Florence

Thus Leonardo's mural was naturally part of the theme when I began to think about the phenomenon of the emergence of the colossal at this date, especially among the greatest artists and in their most famous works. Hence it was a surprise when, on being checked more carefully, its measurements did not turn out to be of that kind at all. At 14 feet high and 30 feet wide, it is of the same scale as Castagno's, which is also 14 feet high and a bit wider, 31 $^{1}/_{2}$ feet. This is modified only in a mild way if we examine the measurements of the figures alone. From the point where they emerge above the tabletop, to the tops of their heads, Castagno's people average 2 feet 4 inches, Leonardo's 3 feet. The effect, though, is very different indeed. Heydenreich pointed to this as a matter of effect when he spoke of Leonardo's people not having room, and then that they are large proportionate to their space. Another way in which Leonardo is different, as he points out, is that his "painted border surrounding the scene cuts off so much of the ceiling and also the side walls that the table and figures appear to spring forward in front of the setting and so form part of the refectory itself." I am not prepared to agree with all of that, and it is perhaps a little overstated. The figures do appear to be part of the refectory, but that is usual in perspective frescoes including Castagno's, and does not account for the quite special quality here. It is not clear whether Heydenreich means the figures come forward of the frame (as they in fact do in the much earlier *Last Supper* by Taddeo Gaddi), but they do not. However, the cutting off the sides of the painted room is very different from Castagno—whose side walls meet the frame in a neat kind of carpentry—and does push things forward. Castagno's figures provide a classic illustration of a Renaissance procedure by being balanced with their spatial envelope. Mass and void are in equipoise, as space fits around mass at just enough distance to produce this comfortable equality. This is true although Castagno is untypical in placing his whole scene rather far back in his space, as we learn by examining the perspective of his floor. Usually, in such a tiled floor, when seen in a painting, the second row of tiles has only about half the depth of the first, the third decreases half again, and so on, but in Castagno there is hardly any decrease at all. This is not an error, though sometimes so described, but records the situation in remoter rows of tiles where the

247

diminution has become imperceptible. The rapid diminution happens in our nearer field of vision before we meet the plane of the painting. In extreme contrast, Leonardo's closing down of the frame brings the figures exceptionally near us, making them close-ups, with no floor at all. This aggressive approach to us is "one of the causes underlying the picture's monumental effect," again in Heydenreich's terms.

In relation to the present topic, what is of concern is that Leonardo indeed makes a colossal effect without real colossal measurements. It thus shares a concern with the colossal as an expressive tool with his other major works, the monuments with horses and the *Battle of Anghiari.* These, along with the ones by Michelangelo already listed, appear to support the impression that such an interest is newly typical of the innovative artists of this moment. In a following generation, the colossal became absorbed as one option among many for works of art, as well discussed in the case of sculpture by Bush.

Such an observation might lead to further explorations in many directions. It is possible that this special interest helped in the fortune of the artists. A simpleminded fascination with big things, suggested in the case of Donatello's doctor, could have been an effective aid in the artists' extreme degree of success and fame. A sculpture can—sometimes—become famous merely by being colossal, as one sees from the seven wonders of the ancient world to Gutzon Borglum's Mount Rushmore, a mediocre production in every other respect. When the colossal works are invented by great artists, the effect can then be extreme. The status of Leonardo and Michelangelo as supermen, as famous beyond the famous artists of other eras, may have this as one of its bases. One might speculate in this connection about Titian's *Assunta,* a single colossal work by another great master of the same era not otherwise involved with this tendency. It too was surely affected by its integration in a vast Gothic space. Did Titian's capacity to respond to that demand help in his becoming very famous, as he did about that time?

Another direction to explore might involve the suitability of the colossal to the messages that patrons were sending through these works. Those of Leonardo and Michelangelo were all commissioned by states, either monarchs or city governments. The *Last Supper* is a partial case,

248

commissioned by the duke but for his favored friars, not to be seen by the public and thus not directly addressing the ruled about the status of ruling, as all the other works do. The *Last Supper*'s other exceptional status, as not a real colossus, might be linked to this circumstance. In all times, governments have more means to produce colossal projects than other patrons. Yet that points up that this connection would fail to explain the emergence of a taste for these forms at this date when it had not been present before; one cannot suppose a lesser interest or capacity in *quattrocento* rulers. Our two main ruler patrons are also very unlike each other, a dynasty of military tyrants in Milan, in a somewhat illegitimate continuity from late medieval *signori*, and a self-consciously free city in Florence, which had lately inaugurated mass meetings as a super-democratic device. If the Milanese message seems obvious, one could think that the forcefulness of the Florentine colossal message was perhaps meant to blot out the memory of the Medici, the preceding regime, or perhaps to address the masses assembled, like colossal heads of Lenin in a Soviet parade. Such speculations, evoking the complexity of these matters, may, I hope, demonstrate their fascination and their potential for further thinking.

1. J. Pope-Hennessy, *Italian High Renaissance and Baroque Sculpture*, London, 1963, text volume, 45–47.

2. Hence in writing a textbok, *History of Renaissance Art throughout Europe*, and deciding for the sake of students to report the measurements of every work reproduced, I found that in some cases it was very difficult to do. The matter is discussed in the foreword to that book.

3. In his *Mornings in Florence*; see J. Ruskin, *Works,* London, 1906, XXIII, 366.

4. For the following discussion materials are conveniently available partly in H. W. Janson, "Giovanni Cellini's *Libro* and Donatello," originally issued 1964, reprinted in the author's *16 Studies*, New York, n. d., and more generally in C. Seymour, *Michelangelo's David*, New York, 1974.

5. The report of the statue being brought back down to the ground may, instead, refer to another statue, the second in the projected series. In that case the *David*, profiting by the experience, was never sent up to the top of the building at all. Otherwise the circumstances were the other way around.

6. There is nothing to explain why these various locations, other than near the cathedral, were all somewhere near the city hall. The cathedral authorities owned the work and presumably always continued to do so, and they called the meeting. There may have been a recollection of the earlier *David* of Donatello for the cathedral having been expropriated by the city government, as noted above, or an awareness of their authority to do the same again. The symbolic political appropriateness of *David* to the city is often assumed in modern study as a factor, but this may be too much influenced by a style of art history that consistently finds political messages. It may have been in the minds of the speakers, but it is not among the many arguments they offer. Odder is the fact that the message would have to have been an accidental benefit *ex post facto,* quite uninvolved in the forces producing the work in this case. That is untrue (and thus the work could better match the art-historical style mentioned) to the extent that *David* could perform his political role anywhere in the city, including the cathedral for which he was made, but in that case the original question reemerges why he should go only to the piazza. It will be suggested below that factors of good visibility were of concern, and it may be that the piazza provided the only site with good visibility which was also central. The meeting seems to assume that the work was important for the citizens to see, and that probably excluded such a "suburban" park site as the nineteenth-century copy of the *David* now has, or as Piazza S. Croce would then have furnished. There was really no other central-city open space.

Seymour, op. cit., 135, translates a document of 1501 to say that the authorities wanted to have the figure finished and put "in its proper place," but this is an error; no such point was made in the text.

7. C. Pedretti, *Leonardo da Vinci: Drawings of Horses . . . at Windsor Castle*, New York, 1984, 43. Cf. also p. 17 of this catalogue, in the introduction by Jane Roberts.

8. V. Bush, *The Colossal Sculpture of the Cinquecento,* New York, 1976. This book has been of much value in the present essay; however, it does not address the matter of the generation of interest in colossi.

9. L. Heydenreich, *Leonardo: The Last Supper*, New York, 1974, 64–65.

"UN VISO QUASICHE DI FURIA"

In the literature on Michelangelo the term *teste divine* refers to a specific small group of his drawings. Most of them are highly finished, the remainder being closely linked in other ways to the finished ones. Their finish connects them with just one other small group of drawings, the "presentation" sheets with mythological or allegorical themes done in most cases for Tommaso Cavalieri. Both groups, like all the rest of the drawings associated with the master, have been the subjects of vehement debate as to whether they are by his hand. However, the *teste divine* differ from nearly all the rest in having a special claim to belong to the canon: through their history. Today they are rarely removed from the canon further than being called exact copies of lost originals with the same imagery. Despite this, the *teste divine* have received markedly minor emphasis relative to most drawings catalogued as by Michelangelo. This essay will deal chiefly with one of them, but in the context of the group.

The phrase *teste divine*, in this application, originates in two separate passages in Vasari's *Life* of Michelangelo, both reporting gifts of his drawings to friends. The first and less often cited sentence immediately precedes the better known report of the allegories given to Cavalieri; it tells us that he made for him "molte carte stupendissime, disegnate di lapis rosso e nero, di teste divine." The allegorical drawings came later, "poi."[1]

One of the heads in question is usually and reasonably identified as the sheet commonly called *Cleopatra*, in the Casa Buonarroti, Florence (2F recto; fig. 1). Its history makes it virtually certain that Cavalieri owned it, as implied by two interconnected statements. The first is a line in another of Vasari's biographies, reporting a gift from Cavalieri to the Grand Duke Cosimo of two drawings, one by Sofonisba Anguisciola and one a *Cleopatra* by Michelangelo.[2] The second is a letter of 20 January 1562 from Cavalieri to the grand duke, to accompany a gift of two drawings, one by

253

Figure 1: Michelangelo, *Cleopatra,* black chalk, Casa Buonarroti, Florence (2F recto).

Figure 2: Michelangelo, *Three Heads,* black chalk, Uffizi, Gabinetto Disegni e Stampe, Florence (599E recto).

Anguisciola, the other mentioned simply as one he greatly prized.[3] Both texts manifestly refer to the same event. This record of transfer to the grand duke from Cavalieri can evidently be associated with that of the earlier one to Cavalieri from Michelangelo, in that the *Cleopatra*, named in the latter case, visibly belongs to the category of *teste divine* named in the earlier one, and also in that Cavalieri could not have acquired a Michelangelo drawing through any other means.

The next record is in an inventory, usually described as datable between 1560 and 1567, which will be cited again in this paper.[4] It is a list of six drawings by Michelangelo owned by Prince Francesco de' Medici, the grand duke's heir, presumably all he had. The third of these is "a Cleopatra, walnut frame." Its inclusion tells us that the dating of the inventory can be narrowed to no earlier than 1562, when the Medici acquired this sheet. Hermann Frey published the inventory in 1930, but it remained a sterile text for thirty years until Luitpold Dussler made this and the other linkages to be cited. The inventory seems to have still more to tell us, for it has never been viewed as a whole, only for its help in identifying each item when catalogued. All six drawings match comments by Vasari about Medici acquisitions of Michelangelo drawings, on three distinct occasions: one involving the first two drawings on the list, a second this *Cleopatra*, and a third the last three drawings.

It is usually said, even in the most recent literature, that the Medici then gave the *Cleopatra* to the younger Michelangelo Buonarroti, in 1617, on the occasion of his setting up a Michelangelo museum in his house.[5] There seems indeed to be no evidence that this was the case, though it is reasonable. The *Cleopatra* does appear in a Buonarroti inventory of the late seventeenth century, and remains in the same collection today.[6]

This drawing is unanimously regarded as the best of the known versions, but the attribution has been much disputed. As is also observable in approximately the same way with the other drawings to be considered, it was rejected by most of the early-twentieth-century specialists, notably Henry Thode, Bernard Berenson, Ernst Steinmann, Charles de Tolnay, and Dussler,[7] but has recently tended toward acceptance, as seen in the approving comments of Johannes Wilde, Paola Barocchi, Anna Forlani Tempesti, and Michael Hirst.[8] Berenson detached it furthest from the canon, making it a major example of the corpus of his "Andrea di Michelangelo." Today the choice would seem to lie only between acceptance and calling it a copy of a lost original. This essay will not offer to add to the distinguished existing arguments pro or con on this subtle issue, but instead will consider the work and the other *teste divine* as Michelangelo inventions.

Vasari reverts, some pages after the passage quoted above, to Michelangelo's gifts of his drawings, this time citing three given to Gherardo Perini.[9] These were "in tre carte alcune teste di matita nera divine"; Vasari then adds that they came to Prince Francesco de' Medici after Perini's death, which was in 1564. This reference has long been associated with three drawings that stand out in the surprisingly minor collection of Michelangelo drawings in the Uffizi, Florence, the natural location for Medici-owned works. Two of the three, besides, have inscriptions naming Gherardo in terms suggesting that he owned them, as no other drawings do. The view that Gherardo owned them has been fully confirmed by the fact that they correspond to the fourth, fifth, and sixth drawings in the inventory of Prince Francesco's six Michelangelos.

The fifth item in the inventory, "uno dove sono tre teste," fits the drawing of *Three Heads* in the Uffizi (599E recto; fig. 2), which is inscribed, "Gherardo, io non ho potuto oggi ve" or, in an alternate reading, "... oggi disegnare." In either case, the writer cannot today be where Gherardo is and instead sends this message and the drawing; hence we have the particular piece of paper that was put in the hands of Perini. Thus the provenance seems fully established. There are, besides, no other versions of this sheet, the nearest being a copy of two of the heads only. The attribution history is similar to that of the *Cleopatra*, but even less favorable.[10]

Before completing this survey with the two other drawings given to Perini, it may be helpful to consider the term and the category *teste divine*. It has naturally been extended to other sheets besides the ones Vasari names, generally to other highly finished heads, even though the one with three heads just mentioned is not very finished. A notable instance is the *Profile of a Woman* in the British Museum (1895-9-15-493 recto; Wilde 1953, no. 42). The strong trend to reject their attribution to the master seems to depend on a general negative view of such finished drawings, at least with respect to the extant versions available to inspection. There has been a marked tendency to accept rapid sketches more readily, partly, it appears, because of a sense that spontaneity ought to be integral to the personal works of great artists. They also are more readily readable, as handwriting is, in their individual ways of using the pen, while the unavailability of such a test for finished drawings has seemed to lead, not to the conclusion that no decision is possible as to the authorship, but to a decision against the master. These drawings do not correspond to the image of Michelangelo as *terribile*. The factitious Andrea, whom Berenson evoked as the artist of several of these sheets, had, according to his creator, "a singular preference for female loveliness."[11] It is as if Andrea had been invoked to absorb that aspect of the universal master which today still many observers believe was not present in him. One can well apply to the *Cleopatra* Berenson's further valid observation that the "Andrea" heads have "an intentness of look, as if charged with an unfathomable meaning."[12] Even if today that sounds to us too much like Walter Pater's reading of the *Mona Lisa* or a Giorgionesque protagonist, Cleopatra's eyes really have swiveled to the side just now to follow the smoothly curving turn of her head, evading eye contact with a viewer, to concentrate on whatever it is that interests her more. She is not alone in Michelangelo's repertory in doing this. The *Delphic Sibyl*'s similar turn of eyes and facial contour impose a similar distance from us. To see an analogue for Cleopatra's snake in Delphica's curving and projecting horizontal arm and dangling scroll seems not implausible; and the headbands and the parted lips, with their sensuous evocation, are related in the two. These last motifs also recur in the *Aurora* of the Medici Chapel, as does the sudden juxtaposition, seen in *Cleopatra*, between the inventive ornamental headdress and the simple facial forms with their emotional pull.

The *teste divine* in general have, in fact, always been connected with the Medici years; when it was a matter of a serious problem such as dating, the older connoisseurs did not omit to correlate these drawings with the master's major evolution. Those who have accepted the *Cleopatra* as autograph recently have dated it about 1532–1534, the last possible time in which it could be bracketed with the Medici tombs. Yet the best comparison offered by Barocchi is with the British Museum *Profile of a*

258

Figure 3: Rosso Fiorentino, *Head of a Woman,* black chalk, Fogg Art Museum, Harvard University Art Museums, Cambridge, Bequest of Frances L. Hofer.

Figure 4: Michelangelo, *Head of a Woman,* black chalk, Uffizi, Gabinetto Disegni e Stampe, Florence (598E recto)

Woman, for which she accepted the earlier dating 1525–1528, while the other *teste divine* given to Perini also tend to be placed in the 1520s. One may suspect that the exceptional late dating for the *Cleopatra* is influenced by the nonstylistic factor of the allusion to its being done for Cavalieri, whose association with Michelangelo is of those later years. (Similarly, the records of his acquaintance with Perini are of 1522.) If we hypothesize that the artist's initial gifts to Cavalieri—prior, as Vasari said, to the allegories—might have come from a stock of drawings he already had, then one might consider a coherent dating for all these sheets in the 1520s.[13]

In contrast to their small role in modern views of the master, the *teste divine* seem to have had marked influence at the time on younger artists. The most superficial case is Bacchiacca; the presence in his *Moses Striking the Rock* (National Gallery of Scotland, Edinburgh) of a whole series of similar heads led Giovanni Morelli to attribute the drawings to him; the notion was vigorously contested by Berenson, a fact the more striking in the light of his admiration for Morelli. He reasonably argued that Bacchiacca simply used the drawings as models, just as he "introduced into most of his petty pictures" figures from other sources.[14] The Bacchiacca attribution has recently been revived after long dormancy,[15] this time without the excuse of not knowing the drawings' provenance from Michelangelo's gift, which at least should be addressed. Much more interesting is their influence on Rosso Fiorentino, noted briefly by John Shearman in one case and recently endorsed, with the addition of a second, by Eugene Carroll (fig. 3).[16] The suggestion that the drawings are autonomous works of art also reappears in their two contributions.

It traditionally has been agreed that a second of the three drawings given by Michelangelo to Perini is the *Head of a Woman* in the Uffizi (598E recto; fig. 4), even though it lacks an inscription with his name like the inscription just discussed and a third to be considered next. The agreement was evidently based on its being, like the others, as noted, among the few major figurative drawings connected with Michelangelo in the Uffizi, and also on its clearly fitting the category *teste divine*. Confirmation for this opinion has neatly appeared in Prince Francesco's inventory, where it plainly is found as the fourth item, "una testa di donna e parte di busto, acconciatura antica, con du altri schizi di teste." In the list it is adjacent to

Figure 5: Michelangelo, *Furia,* black chalk, Uffizi, Gabinetto Disegni e Stampe, Florence (601E recto)

Figure 6: Caraglio after Rosso Fiorentino, *Furia,* engraving, British Museum, London

the two drawings with Perini inscriptions, which are the fifth and sixth, while the other three items are accounted for with different origins. Its identification is further supported by the existence, so far as is known, of only one other version of the composition: a copy at Windsor unanimously held to be inferior.[17]

Among the *teste divine*, even including those on longer lists, only this *Head of a Woman* and the *Cleopatra* extend to bust length. Among possible choices of the way to show part of a figure, this is a sculptural sort of concept. The assignment to the breast or its area of a volumetric emphasis almost equaling the head is rare, even in carved portraits. The drawing has received several iconographic readings, on the view that the three heads have a thematic connection, but the inventory writer's neutral description may show better judgment.

The fourth and last of the drawings identifiable with Vasari's citations of gifts of *teste divine* is our principal concern (Uffizi 601E; fig. 5). It shows a startling contrast, after one has become accustomed to the others, so much so as to call the term into question. Even the description in Prince Francesco's inventory is not the usual kind found in inventories, instead reporting: "uno dov'e un viso quasiche di furia"; yet it unmistakably refers to this sheet. It shows, in the Uffizi version, a neat label in capital letters at the top, GHERARDUS DE PERINIS, the best analogy for which is perhaps in bookplates of proud owners, rather than any other kind of verbal graphic design. Another inscription at the bottom assigns authorship to Michelangelo in a form analogous to brass labels that collectors put on frames. Among the several other versions, none has these inscriptions, thus again providing firm evidence that this is the sheet cited by Vasari.[18] (One of these, at Windsor, competed in the older literature for the status of original, very possibly because it is sketchier.[19]) No other drawing connected with Michelangelo seems to have this kind of lettered inscription;[20] the implication that it was held in special regard is confirmed by its having been engraved—the only one of the *teste divine* so treated—before 1562, thus before it was acquired by the Medici.[21] The engraving dilutes the expressiveness greatly, showing only minor *furia*.

This drawing diverges from the rest in far more fundamental ways. It negates any notion that Vasari's term *teste divine* refers to ideal heads; he probably was simply praising their high quality. Indeed, this one has even received the diametrically opposed romantic label of "damned soul," as recently as by Wilde.[22] Still further, the difficulty of associating the *teste divine* with the main trends of the artist's work—which seemed possible to overcome in the other drawings—here seems genuine. This appears not to have been registered as a problem, perhaps because the other *teste divine* have often been consigned to the same unattached status. The problem emerges when comparisons are made with the *Furia* by cataloguers, always in passing. The most usual comparison is that offered by Tolnay and others[23] with a devil's head overlooking Minos's shoulder in the *Last Judgment,* at the lower right. The head is very similar in position and direction and even in some features, so that one could even think of a tracing. Yet the painted head is masklike, with closed mouth, blank expression, and no fury. The most recent comparison I have noted, by Forlani Tempesti in 1984, is with a Medusa head, specifically the one placed on Athena's shield in a drawing of the figure of Athena by Raphael in preparation for the simulated sculptural figure of Athena in the *School of Athens.*[24] While scholars today would naturally seek comparisons between drawings, it seems unlikely that Michelangelo knew this little sketch of the Medusa. He of course knew the painted version well, but that version is toned down greatly from the vibrant sketch, in the usual way, serving to point up the exceptional quality of Michelangelo's drawing in maintaining its fury along with its polish. Forlani Tempesti found even closer the famous Leonardo drawing of a shouting man for the *Battle of Anghiari.*

All these works do indeed belong to a strong and long-lived classical tradition depicting gorgons, as has been observed by several commentators; Poussin in his *Massacre of the Innocents* is a rare rival of Michelangelo in giving the tradition new and furious life. Michelangelo reflects this classical tradition more literally in a shouting satyr, drawn in profile on the verso of the British Museum sheet already mentioned, whose recto, the *Profile of a Woman,* is on the extended list of *teste divine.*[25] The newly discovered verso of the *Cleopatra* is an "anguished," if not furious, version of the recto.[26] It provides the first demonstration among the *teste divine* for a continuity from the *Furia* to the others. Apart from that, it is conspicuous

263

that the cited analogues for the *Furia* are not near it in date, so that the literature thus seems only to confirm its isolation in the artist's work.

The art-historical sense of what is plausible tends rightly, I would suggest, to doubt that one or a few images in an artist's work should be quite isolated; when it seems so, something is probably wrong with the analysis. Thus it is a relief as well as a pleasure to offer here a much more exact analogue for the *Furia* than any of those that have been cited. This is the magnificent engraving by Caraglio after Rosso (fig. 6), dated 1524 by Carroll, following earlier scholars.[27] The engraving certainly has a neat connection with the "c. 1525" assigned to Michelangelo's Furia by Wilde when calling it autograph, influenced, of course, by the information about the contacts between the artist and Perini in 1522. The small differences between the Michelangelo and Rosso heads can best be left to observation of the reproductions. One must only wonder why this connection has not been observed before.[28] I would think the most probable reason is the lamentable tendency to omit prints from the standard art-historical treatment of this period, to which Carroll's Rosso exhibition is an admirable recent exception.

When two very similar images of about the same date are by different artists, standard method seeks, of course, to determine which was the inventor and which the copyist. Yet in this case it might seem wrong to go through the motions, since no one would be willing to assign Michelangelo the role of imitator, even if he were not the older by a generation. Surely Rosso is the receiver. Yet the issue is a real one, for this decision runs afoul of another standard postulate: that in such comparisons the role of inventor is likely to belong to that artist who does comparable things in other works, while the one who is found performing contrary to his wont is likely to be the copyist, his unusual action being neatly explained by his dependence on an outside source. The preceding survey would then call on us to explain the separateness of the *Furia* in Michelangelo's work by a well-accepted and plausible circumstance, his having imitated Rosso. This scenario is uncomfortable, so we are left seeking one that would let us see (a) Rosso's print imitating Michelangelo's drawing, which nevertheless (b) had been done in Rosso's usual vein.

That Rosso had worked in that vein seems sufficiently indicated by his great earlier design, the *Allegory of Death and Fame* known from the engraving by Agostino Veneziano of 1518, which is regularly bracketed in the literature with this second one. Their likenesses are strong both in the purely technical aspect of the effect of inking and, at the opposite pole, what might be called their message on a cultural level. Both refer to the nightmarish fears of fantasized powers that we know much better in this period in northern art, from Bosch to Baldung. This is most conspicuous in prints, which may make us exclude such concerns all the more from our ideas of Italian culture. Yet Rosso creates an Italian vocabulary for it, with ultimately classical, solid human beings placed in space with properly choreographed gestures. Perhaps Michelangelo had done the same when, as a youth, he copied Schongauer's *Saint Anthony*, one of the classics of this genre. That work, which would have prepared him for more of Rosso's print than just the head, has also remained isolated in his oeuvre.

The scenario suggested may seem less self-contradictory when one cites another case from the preceding decade. At that time Michelangelo made drawings enough unlike his usual ones that they have been strongly denied to him, and attributed to a younger artist to whose vein they are related; moreover, that younger artist, Sebastiano del Piombo, used them to produce a typical work. In that case Michelangelo had internalized the context that affected Sebastiano's project in a way unlike his own usual one. Specifically, he permitted himself to work on an altarpiece with a devotional (if nominally narrative) schema, a type usual for Sebastiano, as it was for Raphael and for everyone except himself. We are able to reconstruct this situation, with its subtle levels, with much aid from verbal sources, notably Sebastiano's letters.

A similar deduction in other cases may have been blocked by the absence of similar evidence. Certainly we have the slightest information on the personal relations of Michelangelo and Rosso. Barocchi, whose studies of both artists would make her well informed, has little to report. Just one letter from Rosso to Michelangelo survives, a strange one appealing to the master to ignore rumors that Rosso had disparaged his work. Perhaps more indicative is a slight allusion by Vasari, a little noted comment made in the course of arguing against the idea, still strong today,

265

that Michelangelo had no disciples. He lists some, calling them "gli artefici suoi."[29] The list ends with Vasari himself, a claim that of course can only be accepted in a figurative sense. Before him comes Daniele da Volterra, a more acceptable name, and before him Pontormo, a surprising one, but in a sense well supported by the *Venus* cartoon and perhaps by copies of the *Cascina* cartoon. The earliest, Jacopo da Sansovino, seems to have slight basis. Between him and Pontormo comes Rosso, and the report may at least stand as a claim of contact with Michelangelo.

My scenario would be, then, that Rosso, whose Florentine career had been unsuccessful to a spectacular degree,[30] determined to try Rome, and to take along a sample of his skills. This would have been in 1523, just when Parmigianino was doing the same. Rosso's best success had been the engraving of the *Allegory of Death and Fame,* and so he would like a sample that was similar, but new. A boost from Michelangelo would make the attempt even more likely to succeed. So it was done, Michelangelo providing a drawing that took Rosso's previous success into account and thereby diverged from Michelangelo's own usual imagery.

It is a neat touch that the title traditionally given to the Rosso-Caraglio engraving is *Furia.* Carroll cautiously notes that this is not recorded prior to Bartsch, but neither is any other name, so it is at least the sole candidate to have been the older traditional one. The *Furia* and the *Allegory of Death* are not isolated among prints of this time and place as to their expressive burden. Also with a bow to Michelangelo, Agostino Veneziano produced near the same date the print known as the *Stregozzo.*[31] It was also the time of the witches' sabbath in Rome described in Benvenuto Cellini's autobiography.[32] This aspect of Roman culture at the time may deserve more attention than, so far as I am aware, it has received.

As a coda to this inquiry about particular works, some implications on art-historical procedures may be addressed. It is striking that the recent increased tendency to call the *teste divine* autograph has gone pari passu with more data on their excellent provenances. Earlier writers who rejected them did not speak much about their early ownership, in part, to be sure, because some of the documents had not been published. At best, as with Dussler and Barocchi, those who have rejected the drawings noted the good provenances and then said that, nevertheless, the works

266

were not by the master, without addressing the apparent conflict.

The most remarkable illustration of the problem is provided by Johannes Wilde—the scholar whose brilliant work has had the greatest effect recently in changing thinking about the attributions—in an instance when he changed his mind. It concerns the two drawings from Prince Francesco's inventory not yet mentioned here. Number one is described as an Annunciate, in a walnut frame, and two as a Christ praying in the garden with the three disciples. These, like the others, are known from still earlier references. A letter of 17 March 1564 from Daniele da Volterra in Rome to Vasari in Florence reports the almost vain search in Michelangelo's house after his death for works that could be acquired.[33] In compensation, he notes two drawings, an *Annunciation* and a *Christ in the Garden,* both given by the master to a friend, which his nephew Leonardo Buonarroti would "take back so as to have something to give the Duke." Then, Vasari tells us in his *Life*, this gift to the duke did take place, and he adds that the *Annunciation* had served already as a model for a painting by Marcello Venusti in the Lateran.[34] The painting survives and matches a drawing in the Uffizi (229F),[35] which exists only in that one version. It is a clear pair with a *Christ in the Garden* in the same collection (Uffizi, 230F). Most scholars have rejected the attribution to Michelangelo, most often assigning them to Venusti.[36] Wilde, in his catalogue of drawings by Michelangelo in the British Museum, of 1953, devoted a footnote—seemingly the longest of the very few footnotes in that book—to justifying this rejection, in the face of their apparent provenance from the master.[37] It is a painful case of cumulated errors in a single argument by a fine scholar. Giving exact page references, he cites Vasari as authority for the gift to the duke, not only of these drawings, but of fortification drawings by Michelangelo; and he then cites Giovanni Bottari as authority for the return gift of Michelangelo's drawings from the Medici to the Buonarroti house in 1617, adding that the fortification drawings are still there. Hence the history Wilde gives of our two drawings would not lead to the Uffizi, and it is "mere coincidence" that the Uffizi has the only pair of drawings with these subjects connected with the Venusti painting. (That they are not now in the Casa Buonarroti could be explained by the sales made by later Buonarroti.)

267

However, Vasari does not say (on the page cited, nor apparently anywhere) that fortification drawings were given to the duke. If this were the case, it would have bolstered the idea of a large, later return of drawings to the Casa Buonarroti, where all drawings of that category now are. Indeed, it would seem odd if the duke had wanted to own drawings that had been made to prevent him from entering the city, and the fortification drawings have probably been in the Casa Buonarroti all the time. Nor does Bottari say the Medici gave any drawings back to the Casa; he says this only of the marble *Madonna of the Stairs*, accurately quoting the inventory discussed earlier. Other scholars reasonably suppose that this gift was accompanied by some drawings like the *Cleopatra*, which then does appear in the Casa Buonarroti, as noted; but none, besides Wilde, suggests this for their holdings of Michelangelo drawings as a whole— clearly wrong in view of the Perini sheets—nor for this pair, never recorded in the Casa.

Then, in an article of 1959, Wilde accepted the pair of drawings as autograph works of Michelangelo, now using their good provenance to support the case and not mentioning his earlier arguments against it.[38] His proposal in this case, however, has convinced few others.[39] What then of their direct documentation back to the master, and what in general of the recent linkage of favorable attributions and the noting of good provenances?

If I may rehearse the obvious, we here meet the problem of the difference between drawings and paintings (or sculptures) with respect to the procedure of establishing an artist's oeuvre. In both cases connoisseurs work with successful analogies from works previously known to be by the artist, and these, in the case of paintings, eventually are those known to be his by nonstylistic criteria such as documents and signatures, or, as a next best, by early literary references accompanied by firm subsequent provenances. But in the case of drawings, signatures and documents of commission (or the like) are so exceptional that practically no oeuvres can be based upon them. The same applies to early references and provenances. Hence we turn to less exact methods such as relationships of preparatory drawings to works in other media, with the big caveat that often (as in Michelangelo's case) the majority of such sheets are copies.

To decide whether they are such calls for very refined, or very confident, connoisseurship, giving much weight to the factor of spontaneity, as noted. Hence, the issue of highly finished original drawings is among the most difficult of all.

In this arduous situation, it would seem heaven-sent to be able to study drawings with provenances the equal of those generally available for but a few paintings. Among the six drawings of the inventory, the two inscribed Perini sheets would seem to be that almost unheard of thing: drawings identifiable beyond a reasonable doubt as the very sheets of paper reported by very early reliable writers as the artist's. The other four have excellent claims, although they might conceivably be faulted on the ground of possibly being other versions of the same image. Logically, it thus would seem that the *Furia* and the drawing with the *Three Heads*, and they alone, should be the basis for all attributions of drawings to Michelangelo whatever, if we apply thc same method everyone accepts for paintings. Yet, of course it is obvious that no one would accept that conclusion.

Such rejection is not, I suggest, a matter of the familiar obstinacy of people confronted with a disliked corollary of their own beliefs. Instead it suggests something perhaps even more unsettling, a fallacy in the system used more generally in the case of paintings—that is, in our supposition that early writers like Vasari meant what we mean in alluding to works as being *by* artists. That they perhaps did not mean what we mean may be illustrated in the case of the author who is agreed to be the earliest reliable reporter of the oeuvres of Italian artists, namely Ghiberti. Ghiberti said, for instance, that Giotto was the artist of the *Crucifix* at Santa Maria Novella, Florence, and therefore, when Richard Offner denied that attribution, he implicitly discarded Ghiberti, as an unreliable source.[40] Recent work by Luciano Bellosi and myself, however, has shown, I hope, that he is reliable once we know the meaning he gave to his words.[41] The distinctions between master and shop, crucial to connoisseurs like Offner, were meaningful to Ghiberti, but did not keep him from calling both kinds of works Giotto's. He called forty works "Giottos" but only six of them "di sua mano" (a selection that does not convince today as well as his list of forty does). The Santa Maria Novella

269

Crucifix was not one of the six; it was for Ghiberti a work by the Giotto firm, as opinion today would generally agree.

Berenson, in fact, when writing of these Michelangelo drawings, clearly understood that good provenance does not give evidence of autograph status at all. Speaking of the drawing with *Three Heads*, sent to Perini, he rightly noted that "even if" the words on it are in Michelangelo's handwriting, they do "not, of course, determine the authorship of the drawings, although they would go far to support my theory that they were done in Michelangelo's studio."[42] Provenance from that studio can genuinely disallow an attribution to Bacchiacca or Venusti, but cannot distinguish the master's specific hand from that of his anonymous assistants at the same place and time. One may then question a commonly held viewpoint, illustrated in the comment that the *Cleopatra* "is one of the most securely documented we possess, *but* [emphasis added] has been repeatedly rejected by scholars . . . even Thode believed it to be no more than a copy."[43] Nor can one show that the *Annunciation* and *Christ in the Garden*, just discussed, are autograph on the ground that, if they were not, Leonardo Buonarroti would have been defrauding the duke in offering them to him as Michelangelo's.[44] What he did, and others said, need not correspond to our concepts of authorship or answer our kind of question. Still, even to establish this negative may be of some assistance in our continuing inquiries.

1. Vasari, *Le vite*, ed. Milanesi-VII 1881, 271.

2. Vasari ed. Milanesi-V 1881, 81.

3. The letter was first published by Ernst Steinmann and Heinrich Pogatscher, "Dokumente und Forschungen zu Michelangelo," *Repertorium für Kunstwissenschaft* 29 (1906), 504. The passage on the *Cleopatra* is frequently quoted: "questo diseggno a me tanto caro ch'io reputo privarmi di uno de' miei figliuli"; Cavalieri continues, saying that he has resisted previous efforts to get it from him.

4. The whole inventory is printed only in Hermann W. Frey, *Der literarische Nachlass Giorgio Vasaris*, 2 vols. (Munich, 1930), 2:57, a rare publication, and in its Italian version, Alessandro del Vita, ed., *Il Carteggio di Giorgio Vasari dal 1563 al 1565* (Arezzo, 1941), 107.

5. Hirst, *Michelangelo Draftsman*, 1988, 116, in his valuable catalogue entry, states that it "was returned to the Buonarroti family by the Medici, along with other sheets, in the early seventeenth century": a more cautious variation.

6. This important inventory has been published only once, by Pietro Fanfani, *Spigolatura michelangiolesca* (Pistoia, 1876), 3–43, a rare book, and is sometimes quoted thirdhand with diminished precision. The text he used was an eighteenth-century copy of an earlier manuscript. Its compiler at one point (35) writes that it was done "by me Michelangelo Buonarroti," that is, the grandnephew who died in 1646, and this has regularly been credited, but elsewhere (18) an event of 1681 is recorded. Evidently there were later interpolations, which in the eighteenth-century version before us are blended in, disallowing assignment of any of it to the grandnephew's original. That, or some earlier draft, may well survive, most plausibly in the Casa Buonarroti, and a search for it would seem warranted. The marble *Madonna of the Stairs* is recorded (33) with the comment "che gia con altre robi donate ai Principi e poi dal Gran Duca Cosimo II ridonata alla casa l'anno 1617." This fairly murky syntax is the sole authority for the frequent inference that the grand duke also returned drawings in 1617. The inventory cites many batches of drawings, but only two individual ones that are recognizable (both on 32), the *Cleopatra* and "la facciata di San Lorenzo"—the latter, the unnoted earliest record of the large-scale drawing also still in the Casa Buonarroti.

7. See Dussler, *Die Zeichnungen des Michelangelo*, 1959, with thorough previous citations.

8. Wilde, *Italian Drawings in the . . . British Museum*, 1953, 125; Barocchi, *Michelangelo e la sua scuola*, 1962, 164–65; Forlani Tempesti, *Raffaello e Michelangelo*, 1984, 87; Hirst 1988, 116. Michael Kimmelman, "Newly Revealed Michelangelo to Be Shown," *New York Times* (5 October 1988), C19, quotes Hirst as also accepting as autograph the newly discovered verso.

9. Vasari ed. Milanesi-VII 1881, 276.

10. See the survey of attributions by Barocchi 1962, 235–36; now to be added is Hirst 1988, 60. Berenson assigned it to his "Andrea," Dussler following Thode called it a copy by Antonio Mini, and Barocchi (along with Marcucci) called it a work of Bacchiacca. Only Wilde and Hirst, besides Goldscheider, have treated it as autograph.

11. Berenson, *Drawings of the Florentine Painters*, 1938, 1:360.

12. Berenson 1938, 1:359.

271

13. It is a legitimate counterargument that Vasari specifically says Michelangelo *made* the *teste* for Tommaso, so that the above suggestion would contravene that good principle that it is shaky to disallow one element of a unified piece of evidence that we are accepting as the basis of our reconstruction. However, one may here apply another principle, calling on us to weigh the concerns that mattered to our informant, which may be different from what in his report matters to us. Both Vasari and his probable source, Cavalieri, were surely much concerned with the point that the drawings were a personal gift to Cavalieri from the artist, but their prior status, as newly made or older, may have been uninteresting even if known, or not well remembered when written down thirty years later, in which case the term used may lack "legal" force.

14. Berenson 1938, 1:251.

15. See note 10 above.

16. Eugene Carroll, *Rosso Fiorentino: Drawings, Prints and Decorative Arts* [exh. cat., National Gallery of Art] (Washington, 1987), 138, 148–51, with reference to John Shearman, "The Dead Christ by Rosso," *Boston Museum Bulletin* 64 (1966), 156. In his note 3 (with a typographical error of "1985" in a British Museum inventory number that should be "1895") Carroll notes as a problem the assignment of *teste divine* to a date c. 1532–1534, since he finds the influence on Rosso as early as 1523. He infers that if the late date should be correct, one must infer a very similar earlier lost version.

17. The Uffizi version is accepted as autograph by Wilde (Popham/Wilde, *Italian Drawings at Windsor Castle*, 1949, 264) and Hirst 1988, 60, reviving an older view of Thode and others. For a full citation of opinions, see Barocchi 1962, 233–35. On the Windsor copy, see Wilde, as above.

18. Wilde, Forlani Tempesti, and Hirst have accepted the drawing as autograph. See the survey of opinions by Dussler 1959, 231–32, and Barocchi 1962, 237–238, to which should now be added Forlani Tempesti 1984, 99, and Hirst 1988, 60.

19. This attribution by Berenson was followed by Thode and others, as noted by Barocchi 1962, 237.

20. Gherardo Perini's name occurs on a third Michelangelo drawing, but in this case not implying his ownership. On a sheet of quick sketches (Uffizi 621E) we read a line from Petrarch and the words: "Io vi priegho che voi non mi facciate disegniare stasera perche e' non c'e el P[er]ino." The informal jotting tells us that "voi" is not a person of higher rank, but addresses more than one friend. The two inscriptions naming Perini, here and on the drawing of *Three Heads* (Uffizi 599E), both are messages concerning a visit not being made, by the writer to Perini or vice versa, contrary to custom or expectation, and both are on drawings. Since in the other case the drawing seems to have been sent to replace the visit, and in the latter the nonvisit induces nondrawing, there is implied a context of a custom of friends getting together with drawing as the activity, whether only on Michelangelo's part or not. The literature does not seem to have treated the two inscriptions in relation to each other.

21. The engraving is signed by Antonio Salamanca, publisher as well as printmaker, who died in 1562. It is sometimes said to be datable in that year (for example, by Forlani Tempesti 1984, 73); but no basis for this view is apparent, and it may well derive from a prior notation that this is the terminus ante quem. The engraving is catalogued and reproduced by Mario Rotili, *Fortuna di Michelangelo nell'incisione*, 1964, 55–56, fig. 9. Pietro

Aretino, in his famous letter of 1547 to Michelangelo, from Venice, mentions "Gherardo" as an owner of Michelangelo drawings along with Cavalieri; his ownership was thus presumably well enough known to make it natural that an engraver would have been led to locating it. For the text of Aretino's letter, see Giovanni Gaye, *Carteggio inedito d'artisti dei secoli XIV–XVI*, 3 vols. (Florence, 1839–1840), 2:334.

22. Wilde in Popham / Wilde 1949, 264.

23. Tolnay *Michelangelo*-V 1960, 169, credits the idea to Berenson, who had cited "the head next to Minos" in relation to the Windsor version of the drawing (Berenson 1938, 2:219).

24. Forlani Tempesti 1984, 99.

25. Wilde 1953, 78-79, pl. LXIX.

26. Reproduced by Kimmelman 1988, as in note 8 above, C19.

27. Washington 1987, as in note 16 above, 72.

28. I am happy to see that, in a book not available at the time when this essay was presented at a talk, Michael Hirst independently made the same connection (Hirst 1988, 109). He limited himself, however, to saying simply that Rosso copied Michelangelo, so that the exploration here of how such an event might have occurred, and the resulting explanation of why Michelangelo produced an exceptional image, may still be warranted.

29. Vasari ed. Milanesi-VII 1881, 273.

30. Creighton Gilbert, "The Rosso Exhibition, or, Difficulty Partly Overcome," *New Criterion* 6 (February 1988), 38–42.

31. Rotili 1964, as in note 21 above, 54, pl. 7, dates the print c. 1520–1525.

32. Benvenuto Cellini, *Vita* (Milan, n.d.), section LXIV, 141–44; the event is assigned to 1532.

33. Del Vita, ed., *Carteggio* 1941, as in note 4 above, 101.

34. Vasari ed. Milanesi-VII 1881, 272.

35. Hirst 1988, no. 54.

36. Barocchi 1962, 245–48.

37. Wilde 1953, 112.

38. Johannes Wilde, "'Cartonetti' by Michelangelo," *Burlington Magazine* 101 (1959), 370–81.

39. See the full catalogue entry by Hirst 1988, 133–34, who accepts it.

40. Richard Offner, "Giotto, Non-Giotto," *Burlington Magazine* 74 (1939), 96.

41. Luciano Bellosi, *Buffalmacco e il trionfo della morte* (Turin, 1974), 113–20; Creighton Gilbert, "The Fresco by Giotto in Milan," *Arte Lombarda* 47–48 (1977), 33–35.

42. Berenson 1938, 2:222.

43. Hirst 1988, 116.

44. Hirst 1988, 133.

A "NEW" WORK BY SEBASTIANO DEL PIOMBO AND AN OFFER BY MICHELANGELO

The portrait of a cardinal by Sebastiano del Piombo in the Ringling Museum[1] is well known, having been discussed in all the monographs, by Bernardini, Dussler, and Pallucchini, in the Berenson lists, and elsewhere (fig. 1).[2] It is here presented in a changed form after restoration, which has revealed the presence of a second figure in the background.[3] As the reproductions in the monographs show, this area was previously a uniform black.

The present condition of the painting must be reported in three sections. The background figure is thin and rather sketchy. This is partly due to the troubles which it has undergone, but partly also to a thinner, looser application of paint by Sebastiano, appropriate to the figure's secondary spatial and social position.

In his fuzzy, dusky surfaces and the soft gray tonality, he, more than the rest of the painting, recalls the early work of the artist and his Giorgionesque tonal training. More serious damage appears in the head of the cardinal. This has unfortunately been mishandled through its history by being repeatedly rubbed. This treatment, so regrettably familiar in figure paintings, was evidently for the usual reason, an effort to make the most interesting, detailed, and light-hued part of the painting more clearly visible. It has instead had the effect of flattening the modeled form and blurring the details of drawing. As is common, this damage is limited to the head. The entire remainder of the figure of the cardinal is in fine preservation, with the surfaces virtually intact, as the photograph in the cleaned state shows. This stony, massive, undetailed section is what must be studied in an analysis of the painting.

The removal of the second figure was no doubt done for purely aesthetic reasons, by an owner who was disturbed by the unclassical and

275

Figure 1: Sebastiano del Piombo, *Portrait of the Cardinal Giovanni Salviati* (after the cleaning), The Ringling Museum, Sarasota

Figure 2: Sebastiano del Piombo, *Portrait of Cardinal Giovanni Salviati*, during the cleaning, The Ringling Museum, Sarasota

Figure 3: *Portrait of Cardinal Giovanni Salviati*

asymmetrical appearance of the painting. It is striking that the design is, indeed, complete and balanced without him, a point which will be explored below; it is true that, when one knows about this additional person, the blank corner leaps to the eye, but nothing was ever suggested along these lines before he emerged.

This portrait design with a main and a secondary figure is a favorite device of the artist. Two other cases are well known, the early Cardinal Ferry Carondolet of the Thyssen collection and the Clement VII with Pietro Carnesecchi, the unfinished picture in Naples. In addition, sources mention a lost portrait of Clement with Cardinal Trivulzio and another of Paul III with Duke Ottavio, which must be associated with them. Of the surviving works, the early Carondolet is not nearly so similar to the Ringling portrait as is the Clement. The former is colorful and *plein airiste,* and the two figures make a relaxed balanced design of the High Renaissance. In both Clement and the Ringling picture the main figure can function alone as a classic portrait design. The second figure in relation to him introduces a new note, which has something of a general unstable or Mannerist element, but also a special tension of its own. It transforms the portrait, a permanent nontemporal image like a Madonna, into an event, with momentary relations between figures like a Sacra Conversazione, while yet not surrendering in the slightest the previously rigid icon-like character of the single portrait.

Sebastiano's double portraits have generally been attributed to the influence of Raphael, in such works as the *Leo X with His Nephews* and the Louvre double portrait. While these played their part, it must be observed that the interplay of frozen and mobile implications does not appear in the Louvre portrait, where the symmetrical background figure has the same status as here, but the main figure does not stand alone without it. In the *Leo X*, the pattern is changed and (from the point of view of this concept) diluted by the reduplication of the background figure, making a new classical symmetry of richer harmony, as is so characteristic of Raphael's inventions.

278   Sebastiano's special procedure, however, has a living background in Venice. It is illustrated precisely, for example, in Lotto's portrait of the Della Torre brothers of 1515, and in the important Giorgionesque portrait

of about the same date (sometimes improperly attributed to Torbido) at Palazzo Venezia. In an earlier generation, Jacopo de' Barbari's portrait of Fra Luca Pacioli in Naples (1495) is perhaps the original example,[4] with a compositional system remarkably close to Sebastiano's *Clemente and Carnesecchi* in the same museum. Before Jacopo, it is to be found not in portraits, but in religious works which build a narrative movement onto an uncompromised icon, and may be an invention of Mantegna in the Louvre *St. Sebastian*. All this would seem to demonstrate its essentially Venetian character. It might then well have been swiftly appreciated by Raphael and brilliantly reorganized by him, two procedures which are fundamental to Raphael's habits. It would then be only natural for Sebastiano, a fundamentally Venetian artist much affected by Raphael, to respond by emphasizing it to the extent of repeating it over and over. A final triumph of the tradition appears in a logical place, Titian's *Paul III*, an original synthesis of Venice, Rome, and Mannerism.

The Ringling portrait is certainly more Mannerist than either of the other two surviving portraits of this sort by Sebastiano. The abrupt, unmodulated turn of the head, its transitions concealed behind beard and cape, is reinforced both by the exceptionally emphatic gesture of the hand and the powerful granitic modeling of the masses. The impact of Michelangelo seems more literal here than in any other portrait by Sebastiano, comparable only to the religious works in which the two men were involved together, such as the *Resurrection of Lazarus* and the *Pietà* of Ubeda. The pose of the cardinal may indeed be thought of as a variation on the theme of Michelangelo's "portrait" figure of Giuliano de Medici.

In general, Sebastiano's Michelangelism grows more slowly in portraits than in subject pieces. The monumentality of the *Columbus* (1519) and the *Anton Francesco degli Albizzi*, now in Houston, is majestic in scale and in the tonality which is soft gray in the one, and iron gray in the other, but the placing is relatively symmetrical and easy. The *Andrea Doria* (1526) is pointed, mobilized, and off balance, and its diagonalism appears also in the Clement VII the same year. The greatest spatial complexity appears in the *Clement with Carnesecchi,* not only in the secondary figure but in Clement's gestures and his relation to the frame. In the late *Cardinal Pole*

279

the centrifugal qualities develop to a different stage, with small-scale units of interest. Thus the Ringling cardinal is closest to the *Clement and Carnesecchi* not only in the motif, but in the general stylistic evolution of Sebastiano. The date 1530–32, usually given for the latter, relates, too, to the prolonged work on Michelangelo's Giuliano; our knowledge that it was nearly finished in 1533 comes, in fact, from a letter from Sebastiano to Michelangelo.

The Ringling portrait has been traditionally dated around 1522, which is clearly too early; however, this has the excuse that the subject has been hypothetically identified as Cardinal Enckenvoort, whose portrait Sebastiano did indeed paint, and who was most active in Rome around the time of Adrian VI. Dussler has already rejected that identification, on the basis of Enckenvoort's tomb image, although he retains the dating around 1522, without discussion and perhaps out of habit. By great good fortune, it is now possible to identify the cardinal securely. A copy of the head in the painting, inscribed IOANNES SALVIATUS CARD, has been found in a private collection in England, and drawn to my attention through the courtesy of the owner and of Mr. Cecil Gould of the National Gallery, London (fig. 3).[5] The simultaneous appearance of the second figure and the name of the main one justifies considering the picture a "new" work of the artist. The copy is also interesting because of its stony, impenetrable modeling of the face, differing from the badly preserved face in the original but matching the well-preserved robe and hands, suggesting that the face in the original perhaps had a surface of this kind also.

Giovanni Salviati, born in 1490,[6] was on his mother's side a Medici, grandson of Lorenzo the Magnificent and nephew of Leo X, who made him a cardinal in 1517 along with several of his cousins. For our purpose the most interesting phase of his career is his diplomatic activity in relation to France, particularly in freeing Francis I from his Spanish imprisonment after the Battle of Pavia. He left Rome October 30, 1524, as legate to Francis in north Italy and was the one who informed the pope of Pavia in a letter of February 26, 1525.[7] While he was still in Parma, the pope decided to send him to Spain to work for peace.

Letters from both him and Castiglione report developments there. But by 1527 he had accompanied Francis to Paris. He remained there for several years, and first reappears in Italy on February 18, 1530, in connection with the coronation of Charles V at Bologna.[8]

Thus our portrait must have been produced before 1524 or after 1530. Although dating of portraits by the age of the sitter is a risky sport, and we always underestimate the earlier maturity of Renaissance men, the luck of an unusually long interval tempts one to try it in this case. The cardinal as we see him must be under thirty-four or over forty. It hardly seems possible that he is under thirty-four, even if he aged with rapidity;[9] therefore our portrait must be of 1530 or later, and thus becomes one of the rare documents for Sebastiano's late phase. We have already seen that both Sebastiano's stylistic development and his relations to Michelangelo suggested a date around 1530–32. Perhaps the new evidence of the identification and the restored appearance of the portrait will also help to convince those who have previously proposed 1522.

The famous friendship of Sebastiano and Michelangelo, after many years, ended abruptly in 1533.[10] While there is no need to suppose that Sebastiano's style would have to become less Michelangelesque thereafter, it certainly does so in the later portrait of Cardinal Pole, and Michelangelo drawings would cease to be provided. This leads to a remarkable point: though there is no record of association between Sebastiano and the cardinal, there is a most fascinating document of such a connection between the cardinal and Michelangelo, and what is more interesting still, it belongs to the year 1531. What happened was that Michelangelo, through a third party, offered to make a painting for the cardinal; the cardinal's letter of thanks is dated July 1, 1531.[11]

It may be worth emphasizing that this is a very unusual offer. Michelangelo constantly turned down or put off requests for his work from great people, even the king of France. In this very year 1531 he turned down the marquis of Mantua. He was so busy and so ill that in November 1531, the pope issued, for the artist's support, a *breve* prohibiting him from taking on new work.[12] The people for whom Michelangelo made works were his personal friends, such as Cavalieri and Vittoria Colonna. He must have had some strong sense of gratitude to the cardinal, of the sort that later moved him to present the two marble *Slaves* to the Strozzi, after he had been a guest in their house when ill. All this suggests that the offer was not an empty one, and that something probably came of it. Yet in view of the *breve,* as well as the silence of all reports, we can be sure that Michelangelo never produced such a painting.[13]

But here we have a portrait of the cardinal, perhaps the only one,[14] painted about 1531, in a strongly Michelangelesque style, by the painter most closely associated with him, and which is even more Michelangelesque than that painter's other works, earlier or later. It would have been natural enough for the cardinal, in response to the offer, to ask for his portrait—not only is this natural in general, but it would be even more so on his return to Rome after long absence abroad. It would be equally natural then for Michelangelo to arrange for Sebastiano to do the work—both because of the *breve,* and because Sebastiano was at this time almost exclusively a portraitist and famous as such.

If this hypothesis is acceptable, it adds to the documentation for the old problem of determining the extent to which Michelangelo is to be found in Sebastiano's paintings. That investigation would require a separate study.

1. Inventory no. 6., 41 3/8 x 35 1/4 inches; 1.05 x .99 meters. Purchased about 1847 in Italy by Thomas Erskine; collection David Erskine, Linlathen, Scotland, sold Sotheby's, London, May 5, 1922; purchased by Ringling from Colnaghi, between 1927 and 1930.

2. For the full bibliography, including also comments by Gronau, Fiocco, and Gombosi, see R. Pallucchini, *Sebastian Viniziano*, 1944, 166. Gombosi in Thieme-Becker, 1933, lists the picture twice, once among the undoubted works, at Linlathen, and once among the works which are doubtful or had not been seen in good reproductions, at Sarasota. Palucchini is therefore incorrect in saying Gombosi considered the painting doubtful. Only R. Longhi, *Viatico per cinque secoli di pittura Veneziana*, 1946, 66, suggested a possible different attribution to Pierino del Vaga. W. Suida, in a manuscript draft of the Ringling Museum catalogue, noted that this attribution was to be considered, but canceled this sentence in the final version (1949, p. 65).

3. This restoration was done in Sarasota in winter 1959–60 by Edward O. Korany.

4. The proposal to restore this painting to the young Jacopo dei Barbari was made by the writer in *Scritti in onore de L. Venturi*, 1956, I, 290, with correction of an erroneous date in *Commentari*, 1957, 255. For the purposes of the present study, the consensus of opinion that it was in any case painted in Venice is the major point. I hope that the split into two personalities may now be abandoned; it harks back to the period when Amico di Sandro and pseudo-Basaiti were in favor. It requires not only this idea that there were two painters in Venice at the same time whose names began Jaco... Bar..., but that both were of major talent, which is far less tenable, and further, that one disappears just before the other appears. The split has been supported by two points: (1) the stylistic difference between the Pacioli portrait and later works. I hope I have been able to show the transitions; besides that, in principle, a rejection of divergent early work is based on the fallacy of generalized image of a painter's style based on the composite of a group of mature works, and has now been disproved by what we know of the early work of Giovanni Bellini and others; and (2) the apparent contradiction between the signature "vigennis" on the Pacioli portrait and the reference to Jacopo's "old age" in 1511. But the notion that Jacopo must have been at least sixty in 1511 is an error; on May 2, 1517, Michelangelo wrote in a letter: "Ancora perche io son vecchio, non mi pare perderci tanto tempo." He was then forty-three; under similar circumstances Jacopo would have been twenty-seven when he signed the Pacioli portrait in 1495 as "vigennis." (*Le lettere di Michelangelo Buonarotti*, ed. Milanesi, 1875, 384).

5. Wood, 30 x 24 inches, purchased about 1890 in Italy by Mr. Fred Lee, afterward mayor of Coventry, died 1949; now belonging to Mr. S. H. Barnett of the same city. It was traditionally attributed to Bronzino.

6. Michaud, *Biographie Universelle*, XXXVII, 571.

7. L. Pastor, *History of the Popes*, 1950, IX, 266, 274.

283

8. Op. cit., 280, 294, 316, 388, 434, 437, 441, 452; X, 9, 10, 22, 57, 61, 93. A reference to "le magnifique Salviati" in Rome in 1526 (IX, p. 500) is to his father, Jacopo, though indexed under the name of the cardinal.

9. This view has been endorsed by the various Renaissance specialists who have seen the painting in Sarasota.

10. C. de Tolnay, *Michelangelo*, III, *The Medici Chapel*, 1948, 17–18.

11. A. Gotti, *Vita di Michelangelo*, 1876, I, 212. Tolnay, by a slip of the pen, writes (p. 15), "On July 1, 1531, Michelangelo offered to give a painting to Cardinal Salviati (Gotti, I, 212)"; Gotti actually reports this as the date of the cardinal's reply; by ill luck we do not have Michelangelo's letter. Tolnay errs more seriously in saying that Cardinal Salviati wrote Michelangelo a letter in 1525 (p. 17). This would be of interest since the cardinal was then in France, but, as Tolnay's source reference shows, the letter writer was actually the cardinal's father, Jacopo Salviati. Jacopo, husband of a Medici, apparently managed Florentine affairs for the family during the period when the Medici popes controlled them and after the death of the young dukes. He appears quite often in connection with Michelangelo. Tolnay again confuses the two men, attributing the father's action in 1524 to his son the cardinal, on p. 170, as his source reference again shows. For the purpose of the present study it is of some importance that Michelangelo and the cardinal appear to have had contact only in 1531.

12. Tolnay, op. cit., 12, 15.

13. The suggestion of Wilde that Michelangelo's offer might be related to his sketches of about 1532 for a *Resurrection* has been rejected by Dussler, on the grounds that there is no information either as to the theme involved or whether the work was executed (*Die Zeichnungen des Michelangelo*, 1959, 107). It can be further added that, in view of the *breve*, execution is most unlikely to have occurred, at least by Michelangelo.

14. Vasari's only report of a portrait of the cardinal is as one of a group in Taddeo Zuccaro's *Julius III Giving Parma to Ottavio Farnese* at Caprarola. It is reproduced by A. Venturi, *Storia dell'arte italiana*, IX - 7, fig. 510. A portrait of the cardinal appears in the 1634 inventory of Cardinal Antonio Maria Salviati. It was an individual portrait, not one of a set, and so may well have been Sebastiano's portrait or a copy of it since no other seems known (P. della Pergola, "Gli Archivi Salviati," *Arte antica e moderna* 10, 1960, 196).

TINTORETTO AND MICHELANGELO'S *ST. DAMIAN*

The drawing here reproduced (fig. 1), a recent purchase of the Ringling Museums in Sarasota,[1] is plainly enough one of the many studies of Tintoretto after sculpture. That it is by Tintoretto's own hand, along with a minority of these drawings, seems indicated after the recent work of Forlani,[2] but will be discussed only briefly since it is not a central point here. It matches the Uffizi study of Michelangelo's *Twilight* seen from above, perhaps the most fully accepted drawing of the group, and is in contrast with the various much discussed heads of Giuliano and Vitellius, in its centripetal solidity, the heightening with spots of white, the exploitation of short scalloped lines, and the absence of the assistant's long, thin strokes of shadow and contour.

The immediate question is to identify the sculpture being copied, a matter which in most of the other cases raises no difficulties. Here, however, the drawing does not clearly correspond to any work on the lists we have of the casts owned by Tintoretto. These included, according to Boschini, Michelangelo's *Night* and *Twilight,* all the famous groups by Giambologna, the *Laocoön,* the Belvedere Torso, busts of emperors, the Farnese *Hercules,* the Medici *Venus.* Ridolfi mentions the figures of the Medici tombs in general. This list does not coincide very well with the preserved drawings, and is evidently not complete.[3] Its most conspicuous omission is the model by Michelangelo for *Samson and the Philistine,* from which some thirty drawings of the Tintoretto shop survive.[4]

The present drawing matches a work closely related to these. The two saints, Cosmas, by Montorsoli, and Damian, by Raffaello da Montelupo, executed under Michelangelo's direction and placed on either side of the Madonna in the Medici Chapel, are often slighted in studies of Michelangelo. The drawing corresponds to the one usually identified as Damian, as he will be named here. (It is a token of the neglect of these

Figure 1: Jacopo Tintoretto, Head of *St. Damian* after Michelangelo, black chalk heightened with white on blue-grey paper, 22 x 16.2 cm, Ringling Museums, Sarasota, Florida

works that there seems to be no solid evidence as to which is which.[5]

The connection of the drawing with the figure of Damian does not seem open to doubt, supported as it is by such details as the bump of the nose (perhaps a correction during the drawing process) and the deep shadowed crease above the moustache. Tolnay's fig. 67 is fairly close to the angle of the drawing.

Yet the relationship is subject to several impediments. (1) While some small details recur exactly, others of the same sort clearly diverge, notably the hairline. (2) The *St. Damian* was never famous and no copies are known, so that its accessibility to Tintoretto, who is not known to have visited Florence, does not appear. (3) It is curious at least that Tintoretto's other similar drawings from sculpture exist in numerous repetitions, while this is at present unique (and would still be atypical if a few others like it should emerge). (4) More important, a drawing after a work of Raffaello da Montelupo would run contrary to Tintoretto's habits, which call for copies from important sculptures, either ancient Roman or the works of the most prominent contemporaries.

The solution of the last difficulty comes spontaneously to mind: Tintoretto drew the *St. Damian* not as a work of Raffaello da Montelupo but as a work of Michelangelo. This in turn suggests a solution to (1): the differences from Raffaello's marble may not be whimsies of Tintoretto's, but a faithful copy of Michelangelo's original form, less faithfully rendered in Raffaello's copy. This hypothesis gains weight when we learn that a small model of the saint by Michelangelo did in fact exist, and becomes hard to escape when we learn that it was taken to Venice. If Tintoretto had both model and marble to copy, he would certainly have used the model; in fact, he had the model only. Thus, the answer to (2) above is provided by the same solution that resolves (1) and (4). And the less important (3) is also made plain in the same way. The repetitious copies are from bronze casts owned by Tintoretto, but the model was owned by another collector in Venice and thus not constantly accessible to him. Since all these separate difficulties are nullified by a single solution, it may be adopted with much confidence.

287

That Michelangelo prepared models for both saints is reported by the sources, and is accepted by modern scholars. Following a pioneer study by Gottschewski in 1908, Popp established the dates involved through letters.[6] Michelangelo executed the models in the last phase of the work on the chapel, specifically in the summer of 1532. Montorsoli began to carve the *Cosmas* in 1533, but with interruptions did not finish it until 1536–37. Raffaello completed his work in September 1534.

On the *Cosmas* Vasari is precise: Montorsoli "made a model which was retouched by Buonaroto in many parts; in fact Michelangelo made with his hand the head and the arms of clay, which today are kept by Vasari in Arezzo among his dearest things."[7] It is missing from the posthumous inventory of Vasari's house, and has not been seen since. It has been suggested that he had taken it to Florence.[8] The same writer is briefer on the *Damian*. Michelangelo let Raffaello carve the *Damian* "according to the model which he had made for him."[9] But here there is more information to be had, provided in the unorganized mine of information accumulated by Karl Frey.[10] This comes in an exchange of letters between Vasari and Pietro Aretino. Their dates, as Frey has pointed out, are inaccurate, but precede the death of Duke Alessandro de' Medici on 5–6 January 1537, since he is mentioned in Aretino's letter as living. Vasari, under the date of 7 September 1536, sends Aretino two works of Michelangelo, a drawing of *St. Catherine* and a "head of wax."[11] Aretino's letter to Vasari is variously dated 15 July 1535 and 15 July 1538. He mentions that he has "seen" the sketch of St. Catherine, and continues: "But in opening the little chest sent by the Giunti, in which was the head of one of the advocates of the glorious Medici house, amazement held me motionless a long time."[12]

Though the snarl of the dates and another about medium remain, there can be no doubt that Aretino had, in Venice, a head of one of the two saints. Gottschewski, in the only special article ever devoted to the two figures, gave reasons to call it the *Damian*.[13]

This hypothesis gains support from the fact that Vasari kept the *Cosmas* model himself, and also from the fact that the marble *Cosmas* was not yet finished at the time. The only possibility of its not being the *Damian* which Aretino received would be in the case of a copy of the *Cosmas* model: Frey indeed suggested that a copy might be involved. But of whichever figure, such a hypothetical copy may certainly be assumed to have been made after the model and not the marble; it would have been required by Vasari's aesthetic preference, by Aretino's, by snobbery, and by the importance of not offending Aretino.

Thus the evidence confirms the general opinion of students, that the sculpture in which we are interested represents *St. Damian,* and that a model of the *Damian* said to be Michelangelo's own reached Venice by 1536. It is now clear that the need to label each statue properly becomes genuine; yet it may be worth observing that if scholarship is wrong on both points—if the marbles are wrongly labeled and Aretino's head was of *Cosmas*—then the result for our investigation is the same. The demonstration of its availability to Tintoretto is gratifying, and yet perhaps not essential: in the case of the *Samson and Philistine* the same thing is adequately shown only by the existence of Tintoretto's drawings.

Aretino's description of the model, while it does not individuate either saint, may be read with much interest in the presence of the drawing.[14]

> Ma come è possibile che l'Eccellenza d'Alessandro per compiacere a un serv° di quella consentisse di privarsene? Io ho paura a guardarla e a lodarla, si è ella venerabile e mirabile. Che berli di barba, che ciocche di capegli, che maniera di fronte, che archi di ciglia, che incassatura d'o cchi, che contorno d'orecchie, che profilo di naso e che sfenditura di bocca! Non si può dire in che modo ella accordi i sentimenti che la fanno viva; non si può imaginare con che atto ella mostri di guardare, di tacere e d'ascoltare. Il decoro de la sacrosanta vecchiezza si scorge nel sembiante suo. Ed è pur creta scolpita con le dita de la pratica in pochi tratti.

As this suggests, the best source of the deductions is in the quality of the drawing itself. It may be permitted to evoke it by suggesting that it belongs to a small category of works of art also including the Rubens *Battle of Anghiari:* copies of lost works of great masters by younger great masters who may never have seen the originals.[15] The only modern scholar to offer a stylistic analysis of the marble *Damian* is Adolfo Venturi. Not taking a model by Michelangelo into account, he contrasts Raffaello's forms with those of Michelangelo (as illustrated in his *St. Matthew*). Unlike Michelangelo, the carver has to "particularize, to mince the planes." The statue lacks the master's quality of effort, and substitutes

289

tearful pathos for the impetus of pain.[16] These missing qualities we can find again in the drawing.

The accessibility to Tintoretto of Aretino's collection, which was seen by his many guests, hardly needs comment. It will be recalled that Aretino commissioned a painting from Tintoretto in 1545, and wrote him a letter of praise in 1548. Later, however, he drew away from him.[17]

Tintoretto's drawings after Michelangelo's other sculptures have generally been associated with 1557, the year when Daniele da Volterra made the casts of which Tintoretto owned a set. But the recent observations of Pallucchini, Coffin, and Forlani have tended to place them earlier.[18] Such a view is supported by the dates above, and fits the comments of Ridolfi preceding his reference to Daniele's casts, that Tintoretto while a *fanciullo* studied from the "reliefs of Michelangelo Buonarroti, reputed master of drawing."[19]

Attempts to find the sculptural drawings literally reused in Tintoretto's paintings have not been very successful. The head closest to this one is the left-hand saint in the Berlin altarpiece c. 1570. It seems worth recollecting the remark of Meyer and van den Bercken that the Virgin of that altarpiece had a source in Michelangelo's Medici *Madonna*.[20]

1. Acquired 1959 from Schaeffer Gallery, New York, ex-coll. Dr. Alfredo Viggiano (1884–1928), Venice (Lugt 191a). Black chalk heightened with white on blue-gray paper, 220 by 162 mm. *Verso:* Male nude, pen.

2. Anna Forlani: *Mostra di disegni di Jacopo Tintoretto e della sua scuola, Catalogo,* Florence [1956].

3. Cf. H. Tietze and E. Tietze-Conrat: *Drawings of the Venetian Painters*, New York [1944], 270, for discussion of these and of the drawings after Sansovino reported by Borghini. Ridolfi: *Maraviglie dell'arte*, Venice [1648], II, "6" (actually p. 8).

4. Tietze, op. cit., Nos. 1811, 1813, 1814, etc.

5. The sources make clear that *Cosmas* is by Montorsoli and *Damian* by Raffaello da Montelupo, but do not provide descriptions or other methods of identifying either with either existing statue. (For these sources, mainly Vasari and the Michelangelo correspondence, see A. Popp: *Die Medici Kapelle Michelangelos* [1933], 140.) Attributes are of no help, since the saints are not distinguished from each other in iconographic tradition. (See G. Kaftal: *Iconography of the Saints in Tuscan Painting*, Florence [1952], cols. 289 ff., and L. Réau: *Iconographie de l'art Chrétien*, III, Paris [1958], Part I, 332 ff.) Adolofo Venturi identified the saint holding a mortar in his lifted hand as Raffaello's *Damian*, and the one with empty lifted hand as Montorsoli's *Cosmas*. The confused situation is suggested by his earlier reference to "Raffaello's Cosmas and Montorsoli's Damian" (the only statement certainly wrong) which is corrected in his index (*Storia dell'arte italiana*, X-2 [1936], xiii, 88, 118, 154–55, fig. 95). Anny Popp in contrast identifies the saint lifting the mortar as *Cosmas*, and makes the matter more complex by suggesting, on the basis of an early copy drawing of the whole group and the wall, that the figures have been given locations opposite to those originally intended. Her discussion of the plan of the group is the fullest, but does not broach the matter of the specific identifications (op. cit., especially 129–31). Tolnay does not discuss the statues at all, but his reproductions and their captions, again reversing the locations, indicate that he is accepting Popp's earlier hypothesis (*The Medici Chapel*, Princeton [1948], figs. 66 and 67). The tradition of the Popp-Tolnay identification appears traceable to Bottari, who in the notes of his edition of Borghini's *Riposo* [1730] says of Raffaello's *St. Damian:* "Questa figure è a mano sinistra della Madonna" (p. 332), and similarly of Montorsoli's *St. Cosmas:* "Questa statua è a man destra della Madonna del Buonarroti" (p. 405). Milanesi repeats the notation in his notes to Vasari, suggesting that clarification was still felt to be needed. The reasonable interpretation that the Madonna's own left and right are meant has evidently been adopted by Popp, and also by the authors of the Thieme-Becker article on Raffaello, who in saying "Damian is on the right" presumably mean the spectator's right. (The terms left and right should evidently be avoided altogether.) Borghini himself comments that the *Damian* "mostra affetto di divozione nel viso" and that many believe its right arm too thin (ed. cit., p. 128). Unfortunately these points do not serve to differentiate the figures. I have not been able to consult Bocchi-Cinelli.

Venturi offers the only stylistic analysis of the two saints, which indicates that in both cases the statues are problematic in relation to the artists' other sculptures, as is natural since they are very early works based on Michelangelo's models. Popp's identifications do seem to be confirmed by a comparison of the mortar-lifting saint with Montorsoli's *Matthew* in S. Matteo, Genoa (Venturi, op. cit., fig. 100) in folds and beard. This is the more true in that, apparently, Michelangelo did not give indications for the drapery of the *Cosmas*, as will be seen below.

The conclusion seems to be that all observers except Venturi make the same choice, which is confirmed by a stylistic parallel, but that secure evidence is lacking.

After all the neglect and ambiguity to which the statues have been subject, it seems unsurprising and pardonable that so careful a scholar as Dussler, in his new book, refers to "the two figures of Cosmas and Damian begun by Montorsoli in 1533" (*Die Zeichnungen des Michelangelo*, Berlin [1959], No. 575).

6. A. Gottschewski: "Zu Michelangelos Schaffensprozess," *Monatshefte für Kunstwissenschaft* I [1908], 853 ff; Popp, op. cit., 157.

7. *Le vite* VI, ed. Milanesi [1878 ff.], VI, 634.

8. L. Berti: *La casa del Vasari in Arezzo* [1955], 6.

9. Op. cit., IV, 544.

10. *Michelagniolo Buonarroti, Quellen und Forschungen*, Berlin [1907], 21.

11. Op. cit., VIII, 266.

12. *Lettere sull'arte di Pietro Aretino*, ed. Pertile, I, Milan [1957], 25.

13. "Der Modellkopf von der Hand Michelangelos im Besitze des Pietro Aretino," *Monatshefte für Kunstwissenschaft* II [1909], 399.

14. *Lettere*, loc. cit.

15. A survey of drawings by and in the orbit of Michelangelo, in the catalogues of Berenson, Tolnay, and Dussler, seems to yield only one other drawing that has ever been associated with *Cosmas* or *Damian,* British Museum 1895-9-15-511 Malcolm 74 *recto*. It is usually related to the *Last Judgment* but Wilde has connected it with the two saints, though not suggesting that the relation is close enough to link it to one or the other. Dussler, summarizing the opinions, observes that its generic relationships are no closer to the latter than to the former. Wilde's view that it is by Michelangelo is also disputed by most other observers (Dussler, op. cit., No. 575). Thus the Sarasota drawing appears to be our only token of Michelangelo's model before its translation by Raffaello.

16. Op. cit., 118.

17. Cf. R. Pallucchini: *La critica d'arte a Venezia nel Cinquecento*, Venice [c. 1944], 10.

18. See the discussion by Forlani, op. cit., 6, 12.

19. Op. cit., II, 5.

20. Quoted with apparent approval by H. Tietze: *Tintoretto* [1948], 347.

BIBLIOGRAPHY

The Life of Michelangelo, by John Addington Symonds, London, 1893, often reprinted. A classic of biography, superseded only in secondary details as to the facts.

Michelangelo, by Charles de Tolnay, five volumes, Princeton, 1938–1960. The most thorough work of reference, indispensable for information on all particulars.

The Architecture of Michelangelo, by James S. Ackerman, New York, 1961. The one best book on this theme.

Michelangelo: The Sistine Ceiling, By Charles Seymour, Jr., New York, 1972. Reliable summary guide.

Michelangelo, by Howard Hibbard, New York, 1974. Compact, reliable modern survey.

The Life of Michelangelo, by Ascanio Condivi, translated by Alice and Hellmut Wohl, Baton Rouge, 1976. First published in 1553, by the artist's assistant.

Michelangelo, Six Lectures, by Johannes Wilde, New York, 1978. Clear analyses by an outstanding scholar.

The Complete Poems and Selected Letters of Michelangelo, translated by Creighton Gilbert, second edition, New York, 1965.

Michelangelo, a Psychoanalytical Study, by Robert Liebert, New Haven, 1983.

The Sistine Chapel: The Art, the History, and the Restoration, New York, 1986. Detailed information on many contexts.

Michelangelo and his Drawings, by Michael Hirst, New Haven, 1988.

Michelangelo's Drawings: The Science of Attribution, by Alexander Perrig, New Haven, 1991. Two very different approaches, implicitly in debate.